Fighting Mad

Reproductive Justice: A New Vision for the Twenty-First Century

EDITED BY RICKIE SOLINGER (SENIOR EDITOR), KHIARA
M. BRIDGES, RUBY TAPIA, LAURA BRIGGS, KRYSTALE
E. LITTLEJOHN, AND CARLY THOMSEN

Fighting Mad

RESISTING THE END OF *ROE V. WADE*

*Edited by Krystale E. Littlejohn
and Rickie Solinger*

 UNIVERSITY OF CALIFORNIA PRESS

University of California Press
Oakland, California

© 2024 by Krystale E. Littlejohn and Rickie Solinger

Library of Congress Cataloging-in-Publication Data

Names: Littlejohn, Krystale E., 1985- editor. | Solinger, Rickie, 1947-
    editor.
Title: Fighting mad : resisting the end of Roe v. Wade / edited by
Krystale E. Littlejohn and Rickie Solinger.
Other titles: Reproductive justice; 8.
Description: Oakland, California: University of California Press,
    [2024] | Series: Reproductive justice: a new vision for the 21st
century; 8 | Includes bibliographical references and index.
Identifiers: LCCN 2023040994 (print) | LCCN 2023040995 (ebook) |
    ISBN 9780520396760 (cloth) | ISBN 9780520396777 (paperback) |
    ISBN 9780520396784 (ebook)
Subjects: LCSH: Abortion—Law and legislation—United States. |
    Reproductive rights—United States. | Pro-choice movement—
    United States.
Classification: LCC KF3771 .F54 2024 (print) | LCC KF3771 (ebook)
LC record available at https://lccn.loc.gov/2023040994
LC ebook record available at https://lccn.loc.gov/2023040995

Manufactured in the United States of America

33 32 31 30 29 28 27 26 25 24
10 9 8 7 6 5 4 3 2 1

Contents

Introduction

RICKIE SOLINGER AND KRYSTALE
E. LITTLEJOHN

In the summer of 2022 the US Supreme Court overturned *Roe v. Wade,* its 1973 decision legalizing abortion nationwide. The new decision, *Dobbs v. Jackson Women's Health Organization,* has had predictably brutal and unequal impacts on the lives of people in the United States. In the first months following *Dobbs,* thirteen states implemented total abortion bans. Several others implemented bans based on the period of gestation, and still others continue to squabble over intended bans in courts. The Supreme Court's ruling was a dramatic shock but not exactly a surprise after fifty years of attacks on legal abortion and after former president Donald J. Trump's appointment of three antiabortion justices, explicitly for this purpose.[1]

Dobbs is a singular Supreme Court decision, but it reflects a long history of politicians and other elites treating reproductive capacity as the key site for addressing a variety of challenges facing the nation. This history makes the *Dobbs* decision a climactic marker in the continuous stream of legal, institutional, and cultural efforts across several centuries to control—or regain control—over people's reproductive bodies. In the early history of the United States (and continuing today), elites defined the nation's primary challenges as producing a labor force and controlling land, wealth, and national order, to sustain the country as a "white nation." This aim, over several centuries—before the invention of dependable, self-administered contraception and national legalization of abortion—required the government at the outset to enact laws and policies, pursue military operations and labor practices, and organize everyday lived experience with the aim of shaping and controlling population growth and marking the destiny of newborns according to racial principles.

We must look first at the institution of slavery, a system that was sustained and enlarged by the reproductive labor of Black people. At the same time, the reproductive labor of white women produced a free white population. Clearly, the system that prohibited enslaved Black women from the rights to choose sexual and reproductive partners, the rights to form and protect their families and to parent their children, fundamentally built and defined the brutal system of enslavement. In marked, deliberate contrast, this system ennobled a narrative of the sexual and reproductive "self-ownership" of white women.

Politicians and elites also aimed to produce a continent where public and private ownership of land and other natural resources was no longer under Native stewardship. To achieve this aim, white settlers and national armies decimated Native reproductive bodies and otherwise brutalized Native communities. Immigration policies, too, centered and justified exclusions and inclusion to meet the goal of privileging white reproduction, to build a "white nation." In an effort to exclude Asian immigrants from the United States, for example, a series of laws in the nineteenth century allowed limited numbers of laboring Chinese men into the country (until the Chinese Exclusion Act of 1882 prohibited all Chinese immigrants for ten years) but excluded the wives of these men, thereby limiting the number of Chinese children—citizens—born in the United States.

Later, in the twentieth century, laws and policies extended earlier population-control strategies that associated whiteness, and only whiteness, with citizenship. New efforts continued to enforce racialized reproduction and introduced pseudo-scientific eugenical standards. For example, politicians and policymakers designed public policies to punish poor women of color who public authorities accused of having sex with a man, who got pregnant, or who had a child while receiving public subsistence allowances. Hospital policies supported the involuntary sterilization of poor white, African American, Native women, and Spanish-speaking women, targeting these groups as producing racially and culturally "inferior" children. The rules of social welfare agencies justified removing children from low-income households of color, especially when the head of the family was a woman who did not live with a man and was therefore defined as an "illegitimate" parent.

Today, obstetric care, environmental policies, educational opportunities, child-transfers, and many other resources and practices that impact pregnancy, parenthood, and bodily autonomy still target people based on their race and class. All of these laws, policies, and practices, together with (pre-*Roe*, post-*Roe*, and post-*Dobbs*) lack of safe, legal, and accessible contraception and abortion, have extended and deepened harms many people have suffered over time, based on their reproductive capacity.

The historical record, as well as the experiences of people today, shows that when the state takes the right to control the bodies of individuals with reproductive capacity, the results severely undermine the dignity, safety, and possibilities for full-citizenship status of their targets. When women did not have the right to abortion or the right to contraception, not coincidentally, they also lacked economic rights and other forms of personal independence. And, always, this "dependency" was harsher and more totalizing for people born poor and for people of color. As many of the essays in *Fighting Mad* point out, this harsher, totalizing lack of support for managing reproduction has persisted across time, before *Roe v. Wade*, after, and now, when the

Court has revoked *Roe*. Again, the *Dobbs* decision is another marker of the breadth and depth of hostility to reproductive outcomes and national social arrangements that challenge both white supremacy and male supremacy. This is the context in which we bring together the diverse voices whose work we share in *Fighting Mad*.

In putting this volume together, we clarify the contours of the fight for Reproductive Justice unfolding across multiple dimensions of the struggle, in the period immediately following the fall of *Roe v. Wade*. At this time of incredible volatility, misinformation, and confusion, we have been invigorated by the opportunity to create a resource making sense of the rapid-fire set of events unfolding in the wake of *Dobbs*. The recriminalization of abortion in many states has ushered in heartache and constraint for those in need of abortion. But this period also shows us people fighting for reproductive freedom, mobilizing new strategies to help individuals live self-determined lives under the new legal regime. This book shows that resistance is alive. The contributions illustrate what it looks like when people are forced to live under unsound policies. And, most important, we show what people are doing to protect abortion access on the ground.

At its core, *Fighting Mad* is about what Reproductive Justice means and what it looks like to fight for it. This concept and political activist framework was developed by a group of Black women in 1994, to define the human rights and material conditions that individuals require to live safe, dignified, fully embodied lives, making decisions about whether to reproduce or not, and about having access to the resources they need to be a parent or not, with dignity and safety. The Reproductive Justice framework was developed with recognition that courts and public policy have long been instruments of oppression weaponized to disproportionately harm people located at the axes of multiple marginalized identities. This has been true even when courts and policies seem to aim for empowerment. *Fighting Mad* begins in the context of this recognition, elucidating the ways that people have been denied Reproductive Justice even when *Roe* was the law of the land.

Because *Dobbs* aims to fundamentally restructure the experience of sex, pregnancy, and parenthood in the United States by allowing states to criminalize reproductive autonomy, *Fighting Mad* focuses more tightly on the impacts of criminalized abortion than on other key facets of Reproductive Justice. In fact, *Dobbs* forces us to focus on the meaning and repercussions of this criminalization—the loss of the human right *not* to have a child—and on the uneven impacts of the Court's ruling across society. Nevertheless, in various ways the essays address the full nexus of core claims that constitute Reproductive Justice. Because *Fighting Mad* is devoted to highlighting on-the-ground work in communities, and to following the Reproductive Justice perspective that acknowledges the law's limits in securing reproductive autonomy, we leave close analysis of the legal landscape in the aftermath of *Dobbs* to others.

We want this book to serve as an artifact of this tumultuous period and as a record of the tremendous work people are doing in the crisis, in part so that this period is remembered and its accomplishments remain inspirational and foundational. Nevertheless, as a snapshot of an important historical moment, *Fighting Mad* is not a comprehensive survey of all forms of post-*Dobbs* activism, either activism in the interest of Reproductive Justice or in the interest of state control of reproduction. For example, as we write this introduction, the legal status of medication abortion is unsettled. In early 2023, after a federal judge in Amarillo, Texas, banned the distribution and use of medication abortion, or mifepristone, across the country, the US Supreme Court blocked that ban, keeping mifepristone available in states where and when abortion is legal as the case proceeds through the courts. We cannot know the contours of resistance to that and other court decisions that will surely follow *Dobbs*. We do not at this point have a comprehensive understanding of how *Dobbs* will justify interference in various states with access to assisted reproductive technology procedures such as in vitro fertilization. Or how many hospitals will curb ob-gyn services in the wake of *Dobbs*. Indeed, the impacts of *Dobbs*, strategic responses to the decision, and ensuing developments will continue to evolve over years.

We have been heartened to bring together a group of change agents representing a remarkable breadth of energy and expertise: activists and artists, academics and abortion storytellers, religious leaders, health-care professionals, legislators, and clinic directors. This volume has collected the voices of people working to facilitate abortion access and travel; fighting in courts to protect access to abortion and to protect people criminalized for having one; providing abortion care and support across the spectrum of client and patient needs; and so much more. Creating a platform to share all this work felt like both a service to readers and therapeutic respite for ourselves. For just as we read story after story about tragedies unfolding in the news, we also read essay after essay about how activists are standing fast, in the face of reproductive tyranny, to create better lives for themselves and others.

As such, our methodology reflects the world that we live in. To find such a diverse range of contributors, we scoured the internet and looked for fresh names in news stories. We thought of people whom we knew were doing the work and built out from our networks to find contributors whom we did not know. We had conversations that sparked new ideas for a domain that we believed needed coverage. And we reached out wherever and whenever we could, recognizing that the people were busy doing the work that we so desperately wanted them to write about. We remain ever grateful that they obliged and that we can now share their voices. The perspectives gathered here reflect the enduring commitment of individuals, communities, and organizations responding to state violence, variously banding together on the ground to fight for one another while eyeing the courts to assess each new decision and to find opportunities to minimize harms and champion Reproductive Justice. *Fighting Mad* honors this work.

The essays in this volume grapple with the urgent challenges we face in reclaiming the fundamental requirements of making and re-making human life, and they offer a promise that has been the hall-mark of organizing for freedom: people facing oppression will always fight for self-determination. As one of our contributors, Coya White Hat-Artichoker, writes, now that *Roe* has fallen, we have an opportu-nity to "be bolder, dream bigger, and push at all points of resistance." This book offers a glimpse of how many people are doing just that. The contributors come from and work within many different traditions and contexts. In writing their pieces, the authors have cho-sen for themselves what words to use to describe history, lived expe-rience, and this present moment. They have written in various voices—personal, scholarly, or hybrid—and document their essays accordingly.

Part I   Roe *Was Never Enough*

KRYSTALE E. LITTLEJOHN

As Rickie Solinger and I put together this edited volume, we collectively mourned the fall of *Roe v. Wade* while recognizing that many marginalized people never enjoyed its protections. Many suffered exclusion. How do we chart a just path forward that frees everyone to realize their human right to abortion if and when they need it? In the pieces in the first part of the book, educators, activists, researchers, and doctors join together to give voice to the experiences of exclusion, subjugation, oppression, and violation that have always existed alongside *Roe*. Their contributions offer powerful visions of reproductively just futures.

Educator, writer, and facilitator Ericka Ayodele Dixon opens with a wrenching account of how the state has long violated the right to self-determination for disabled, poor, queer, trans, immigrant, Black, and Indigenous people of color. Coya White Hat-Artichoker, activist and Sicangu Lakota, follows with her own visionary statement, detailing how community memory and knowledge make visible the brutality of sexist, misogynistic colonial structures while simultaneously providing a framework for a better tomorrow. Following this is the powerful statement written by members of the Advisory Council of the Building the Fire Fund, condemning the *Dobbs* decision. This statement, together with White Hat-Artichoker's and Dixon's contributions, calls on us to ground our work in Indigenous Reproductive Justice and disability justice, to honor our collective survival as tied to all life and to fight for all lives marginalized by eugenic logics.

Work by Nomi Kane and the team at Plan C builds on these frameworks by demonstrating the transformative nature of art to raise awareness about abortion with pills as a crucial resource in the fight to self-manage abortion. As the comic and other essays in this volume highlight, people lacked access to abortion even with *Roe,* but abortion with pills offers a way to achieve reproductive autonomy for all. A heartening piece by doctoral fellow Hayley V. McMahon follows, documenting the barriers that have long faced people seeking abortion access in Appalachia. McMahon showcases the power of community action and grassroots activism to challenge the structural barriers that antiabortion politicians erected in the wake of *Dobbs.* Her essay shows that, come hell or high water, there will always be communities on the front lines fighting to get people the abortions that they need.

Next, a poignant piece by researcher and abortion storyteller Sheila Desai highlights the harms of ignoring the abortion needs of Asian Americans and immigrants based on mythologies of exceptionalism. Desai issues an urgent call for us to eradicate racism and xenophobia to eliminate the hidden harms of exclusion. Researcher and obstetrician-gynecologist Carolyn Sufrin closes this part of the book with testimony that indicts the prison-industrial complex for the many violations that it inflicts on the humanity of incarcerated pregnant and birthing people. Sufrin explores how *Roe* had long failed in breathtaking ways for people facing incarceration and offers concrete strategies to alleviate these barriers in their fight for reproductive autonomy within the context of state-sanctioned subjugation. Together, these contributions offer a powerful call for Reproductive Justice for all to remedy the shortcomings of *Roe* as we fight for a better future.

1 *Disability,* Dobbs, *and a Black Perspective*

ERICKA AYODELE DIXON

The overturning of *Roe v. Wade* was yet another stark reminder for disabled, poor, queer, trans, immigrant, Black, Indigenous, people of color that the state will never protect us. It was yet another reminder that the state has been set up to systematically control people like us, if not eliminate us all together. The state's commitment to deny our dignity, safety, self-determination, and very existence has never been in question by those of us most at the margins, which is why, for so many of us, while heart wrenching and terrifying, the *Dobbs* decision is not a surprise. The Supreme Court decision is but one piece of a project that highlights the eugenic logic of the state, its commitment to work toward controlling the population and eliminating "undesired" (that is, those who are not cisgendered, heterosexual, ablebodied, wealthy male) populations.

There's a complicated history particularly for Black disabled people around abortion, the right to choose, and self-determination. The conversation moving forward about reproductive rights has to be broader than just talking about abortion; indeed, to move forward in a post-*Dobbs* world, we have to dissect what self-determination means now for queer, trans, Black disabled people. The *Dobbs* decision derives from a legacy of eugenic practices in the "United States"—practices that specifically, ongoingly, target Black, Indigenous, people of color, disabled, working class/poor, trans/queer, immigrant, and other multiply marginalized people and that work to eliminate us. We must examine the eugenic piece—that is, the unscientific practice that works to eliminate "undesired" genetic traits from the general population and increase heritable characteristics regarded as "desirable." Without this analysis around the right to choose, the possibilities for self-determination and our understanding of the impact of the *Dobbs* decision are incomplete.

In the United States eugenics became the basis of many state laws in the early twentieth century. At that time, politicians, judges, policymakers, religious leaders, and much of the white public in general regarded eugenic reproduction as a justifiable moral obligation and a national project. The aim was to sterilize those deemed unfit to pass along "good" genes, including the disabled, institutionalized wards of the state, and incarcerated people, most of whom were poor and people of color.[1] It is no secret that the country was founded on principles of population control; that leaders at all levels were devoted to the manipulation of genetics and "breeding" to create the concept of "citizenry" as composed of a white, able-bodied, cisgendered, heterosexual male population, while using the brutalities of chattel slavery and the burgeoning economic system to establish complete control over enslaved Africans from the period of white settlement on.

If we think about the "pro-life" or more aptly the "anti-choice" argument—that life begins at conception—we can clearly see a link between this claim and the reality that governed enslaved people of childbearing age: when they got pregnant, fetuses became the property of the enslaver, not the child of the biological parent, a fact that the eugenically-minded "pro-life" movement has yet to grapple with. Indeed, the pro-life movement simultaneously exploits disabled people for the benefit of their antiabortion movement while advocating for disabled people to be eliminated from the population. For example, the antiabortion movement invokes disabled babies and potentially disabled unborn fetuses as a reason for being against abortion. If "every life is sacred," terminating a fetus because of disability or potential disability is unimaginable. However, they are using disabled people as a political pawn instead of seeing us in our full humanity and dignity. In fact, by actively advocating for the end to legal abortions, the antiabortion movement is actively dehumanizing and endangering disabled peoples' lives, safety, and dignity. No individuals are more impacted by decreased self-determination than members of groups pushed to the margins of society.

The state continued to intervene in the reproductive lives of the most marginalized people in the early 1900s. In fact, sterilization and elimination practices in the United States, particularly those enacted on the bodies of disabled people and people of color, influenced the German dictator Hitler. Drawing on US practices, he instructed physicians to sterilize hospitalized disabled people against their will. Subsequently, hospital personnel followed orders to murder disabled people. When we focus solely on the criminalization of abortion and ignore the ways that "reproductive health" has been used as a platform to define "purity" or a "healthy baby" and to codify and categorize disabled people as expendable and removable objects before birth, we do a disservice to the disabled, trans, queer, poor Black, Indigenous, people of color who have suffered centuries of reproductive violation.

Carrie Buck, an institutionalized seventeen-year-old girl in Virginia (wrongly designated as intellectually "subnormal") was grotesquely sterilized in the 1920s. In *Buck v. Bell* (274 U.S. 200, 1927), the US Supreme Court upheld the constitutionality of Buck's sterilization and the Virginia Sterilization Act of 1924. The decision validated the state's right to coercively sterilize people for "the protection and health of the state," thereby officially legalizing eugenic sterilization in the United States. Sterilizations continue deep into the twenty-first century. Ashley X, a young disabled girl born in 1997, is a contemporary case in which Reproductive Justice activists and pro-choice activists alike missed an opportunity to support a young girl in a Reproductive Justice fight. Ashley X's parents decided when she was ten years old, with the support of her physician, that they would give her hormone blockers to stop her from undergoing puberty, to keep her small-statured and "immature," an act that would make her "easier to manage" as she got older. Ashley X had no advocates and did not understand what was happening to her body. Her case helps us understand that when we replace the consumerist slogan "the right to choose" with the concept of self-determination, we can see that Reproductive Justice for disabled people demands we develop both clarity and certainty about the meanings of reproductive freedom and bodily autonomy. This involves fighting for disabled people to receive dignified health care disassociated from the ableist idea of "cure," or based on the stigma that disabled people are asexual or can't understand their own sexuality.

Disabled people—particularly disabled queer, trans, poor Black people—have long faced obstacles to choosing whether or not to have an abortion. They've also been disqualified from parenting their own children. In the 1950s and 1960s birth control was being hailed as a miracle for the white middle-class women who stood to gain educational, workforce, and family-planning benefits. But Black and women of color families, especially those of childbearing age, bore the brunt of the enabling experimentation; at the same time, many were subjected by science and public policy to temporary and long-term sterilization. Poor Black families were also stripped of their ability to raise their children due to strictly imposed, harsh welfare policies that threatened to split up and incarcerate Black families over minor infractions.

The eugenic history of the United States provides the foundation for understanding what we are fighting both for and against. This understanding is crucial for unifying our movements and achieving lasting self-determination, dignity, and affirmative reproductive health for everyone. As Angela Davis says, "radical simply means grasping at the root." To radically transform society and move toward greater liberation, we must understand how we got here. Our disabled, trans, Black, queer, Indigenous ancestors have been fighting for centuries, and it is high time that we listen to them and their lessons. The question—not just for disabled, Black, queer and trans, Indigenous, poor, immigrant people of color, but for all of us—is how do we build mechanisms for self-determination in a world that remains tethered to eugenic ideas, a world in which people with power continue to pursue elimination and control?

First and foremost, we must listen to and follow the lead of our BIPOC disabled community, the members of which have been pushing back against eugenic policies for centuries. We must actively call out ableism when we experience it in our movement toward holistic Reproductive Justice. We must state out loud that people of childbearing age are not all cisgender, heterosexual women. We must recognize that this conversation is larger than the right to an abortion; rather, it is about the right to self-determination in all aspects of our reproductive lives. We must move away from all ideas that prevent us from being able to define for ourselves how we express our sexuality and gender. Reproductive Justice activists must broaden their support for the rights of queer and trans people to bodily autonomy. For a long time, and with particular escalation since 2016, trans people have been under eugenically-based attacks by the government. These attacks have taken many forms, including sports bans and dismantling the right to lifesaving health care. If disability justice, Reproductive Justice, and trans justice movements miss the opportunity to individually and jointly use an anti-eugenic lens to understand and address our current sociopolitical situation, we will all fail. We can only win if we stop leaving disability out of the conversation, specifically disability at the intersections of misogyny, anti-Black racism, and capitalism.

The impact of the *Dobbs* decision on disabled communities is immense and far reaching. Thus, if we are truly going to dismantle ableism within our liberation movements and form communities and a world that demands self-determination, reproductive freedom, and dignity for all, we have to act from a place of disability justice. This framework and practice understands all bodies as unique and essential, each bearing strengths and needs that must be met. It is not enough for the Reproductive Justice movement to be accessible to disabled communities. Disability justice demands not just cross-movement solidarity. It demands that movements utilize the strategic brilliance, knowledge, and history that disabled communities have been deploying for centuries to fight back against eugenic policies, including building robust mutual aid and community strategies to meet our needs outside of the apparatus of the state.

2 Colonization, Resistance, and Indigenous Reproductive Justice

COYA WHITE HAT-ARTICHOKER, SICANGU LAKOTA

To understand the worldviews of Indigenous women as distinct from contemporary feminism, we have to understand history, and to hold our memory as critical to understanding patriarchy, misogyny, and colonization.

There are more than 570 federally recognized tribal nations on Turtle Island, and many more unrecognized or lost. Within my traditional Lakota community, women were considered sacred. It was often said that the men would meet to discuss the community and come up with a plan for what to do next. But a circle of women sat around them. The women had to agree to any decision that was made, or that decision was not carried out. In addition, women owned all the assets of a married couple. If a woman wanted to divorce her husband, all she had to do was to put his moccasins outside the door of the tipi and the marriage was over. The man left with what he was wearing. There was no domestic violence within our communities. Such behavior was unheard of until the colonizers came, imposing their white Western heteropatriarchy via the brutal means of the Christian church in all its denominations throughout Turtle Island.

It's important to tell this historical context from community memory. A lot of what I know or have learned has come from my aunties and activists within my community and allied communities. Much of what

I have come to understand is deeply rooted in communal knowledge. I was born to a feminist mother in rural South Dakota, I was raised to be a feminist. My aunt started the first domestic violence shelter on a reservation in Mission, South Dakota. I was born surrounded by feminist aunties and others fighting colonization since 1492.

Many Indigenous women experienced a higher degree of body sovereignty and freedom than the white women colonizers they encountered. It's important to note this because one of the projects of colonization was to intentionally and brutally subjugate Indigenous women, a project that remains critical to this day: the imposition of sexist and misogynistic structures upon our communities. Under colonization women had to be taught their place, a goal accomplished by forcing women into marriage and monogamy, and making them live under rules that stressed male ownership of women's bodies and their children. In our culture we did not have last names like Europeans. Everyone was given a name at puberty that stayed with them throughout their life. People were identified by who they were related to or through their family units or tiospayes, not by who their father was or by carrying his last name.

When colonizers encountered these traditions and practices, they defined them as wrong. They sought to disrupt our traditional systems and values, as they stole our lands and decimated our food sources, broke down our cultures and familial systems to accomplish the American project. The goal wasn't just to subjugate Native women but also to shift the belief systems of Native men toward Native women. This was the job of Christian missionaries and boarding schools. It was a brutal and murderous process that disrupted generations of Native families and care systems, destruction that we still have not fully recovered from. But we are building new pathways as we do our cultural reclamation work.

The federal government withheld Indigenous people's right to vote until 1924. The Declaration of Independence names us "merciless Indian savages." This country was founded on a need to destroy our cultures, our ways, and our beliefs. Federal policy has impacted Native people's lives since this country came into existence. The US government wrote treaties with our people to ensure our sovereignty over our lands, our people, and our borders. However, colonizers disregarded and brutally violated the treaties, with the intent to make the Native/Indigenous people disappear, so as to fulfill the Christian idea of Manifest Destiny, a cornerstone of the American project.

One of the treaty obligations was and remains health care. And as long as there are enrolled members of our tribes, there are treaty obligations. The government promised Indigenous people food, shelter, and health care. Health care is mostly provided by Indian Health Service, a division of the US Department of Health and Human Services. This means that health care is federally funded and subject to restrictions on federal funding. Over centuries, Indigenous people created traditional systems of care and traditional medicines. But once the US government placed us on reservations, we were restricted to certain tracts of land and became dependent on Indian Health Service for our health care. Very few Native folks at that time or since had access to or could afford private health care. US law deemed our traditional spiritual and cultural practices illegal. As a result, our people took many of the ways we cared for ourselves or healed ourselves or birthed our children underground. Medicines were hidden, including plants that we knew, if used the right way, could induce an abortion. We had traditional ways of family planning. Forcing us into a Western system of medicine was another expression of colonization and an attempt to erase traditional knowledge.

The colonizers' attacks on Indigenous women and our reproductive choices started early and were followed by the introduction of boarding schools and the theft of our children, the imposition of heteronormativity, and the use of sexual violence through Christian missionaries and schools. The forced subjugation of Native women meant that despite the Supreme Court's legalization of abortion with their *Roe v. Wade* decision in 1973, the ruling had little effect on the lives of Indigenous women in real or economic terms. When I was growing up in the 1980s in South Dakota, there was one clinic that performed abortions, one day a month, on one side of the state. Since most Native folks at that time lived on tribal lands and received their health care through Indian Health Service, this was one of the only ways Native women could access reproductive health care.

Federally recognized tribes are considered sovereign nations, nations within a nation, by treaty rights. This means that most of our issues are dealt with at the federal level. We have internal systems of governance that can mirror the United States model of governance, which is not in alignment with our traditional forms of government. Nevertheless, the US government carries its tradition of bias and corruption wherever it goes, including into our sovereign nations. The introduction of the Hyde Amendment in 1977, just four years after the *Roe* decision, with its prohibition of the use of federal funding for abortion services, ensured that for most Native and Indigenous birthing folks, access to abortion care or full reproductive health care would be severely limited. This means that for most Native and Indigenous birthing people, *Roe* did not provide access to abortion rights. Most Native and Indigenous birthing folks living on reservations, with Indian Health Service, never lived in a *Roe* world, so a post-*Roe* world feels economically more difficult than normal but not unusual.

The reality is that passage of the Hyde Amendment impacted low-income birthing folks who depended on federal funding for access to full reproductive health care, especially on reservations and the territories of Puerto Rico and Guam. *Roe* was the law of the land for almost fifty years and for forty-six of those years, it was as if *Roe* didn't exist in the poorest and most rural places, where Indigenous and Native birthing people live. Native and Indigenous birthing people have always understood that their ability to bring forth healthy children is essentially about their whole environment. This is clear in the way we talk to and discipline our children, in the way that we teach them their responsibilities to our people, in the way we love and hold them as a whole community, invested in their growth. This is why Native and Indigenous birthing folks are often considered sacred while they're pregnant. This is why we believe that the environment is so critical: a birthing person is holding sacred water. There is a word in Lakota that translates to "their water" as the first environment.

These are reasons why Native and Indigenous feminism is different from the feminism that infuses a lot of other interpretations of Reproductive Justice. Our view is way more expansive. We see Reproductive Justice as tied to all life. This is why you saw the resistance at Standing Rock. Because we understand that what you do to the land, you will do to yourself. We cannot live on land that has been decimated, we cannot breathe air that is poisoned, and we cannot drink water that is poisoned. Our collective survival means we care for far more beyond our individual needs. We care for those who cannot yet speak for themselves, our children. Indigenous Reproductive Justice is about understanding our connection to all life, not just those closest to us but those who have not yet arrived. We hold nations and care for the future seven generations.

In addition, today we see the agenda of the political Right, influenced by Evangelicals, attacking Indigenous rights and sovereignty. They actively sought to reverse the Indian Child Welfare Act, which would have chipped away at tribal sovereignty and eroded the ability of tribes to care for their children thereby ensuring that the next generation can be raised within their culture. Another way that Indigenous Reproductive Justice is different from contemporary forms of feminism is that we have a distinct government-to-government relationship that honors our inherent right to our bodies and ties to our inherent legal rights as nations. I often talk about Indigenous Reproductive Justice as an issue of *sovereignty*. While a lot of folks talk about body autonomy, we talk about body sovereignty. We tie it to our history and our legal rights. Sovereignty is a stronger stance than autonomy. We assert it is an inherent and guaranteed treaty obligation.

Roe was never enough. For five decades abortion was never codified. White feminists willingly sacrificed the poorest, Black, Brown, and colonized among us for their sense of safety. Since the fall of *Roe,* there is this outrage. But for some of us, it's more like, "So now they're coming for you, too. Scary isn't it?" What gives me hope is that now, when that safety net is gone, we have a real opportunity to build anew, to build a coalition that truly embraces all of us and sacrifices none of us. However, it means that we might have to explicitly acknowledge race, history, power, and justice. If we can't do that, we won't win. Only when we are willing to turn and face our fears and still get up after the fight can we truly say we tried and we lost or we tried and we didn't dream big enough but we changed the game.

That is the challenge post-*Dobbs.* We have to be bolder, dream bigger, and push at all points of resistance. There is no right way or best way, we are fighting centuries of misogyny and sexism, brutality, and subjugation. I hope we can approach this next phase with less fear and more willingness to dream bigger than we knew we could and to win bigger than we ever have before.

3 *Statement from Advisory Council of the Building the Fire Fund regarding* Dobbs v. Jackson Women's Health Organization

AMANDA SINGER, EILEEN BRIGGS, NONA MAIN, CARLY HARE, EILEEN HUDON, DR. PEGGY BIRD, CHARON ASETOYER, KATRINA CANTRELL, RACHAEL LORENZO, DR. CHRISTINA CASTRO, MALIA LUARKIE, STEPHANIE LOZANO, DR. CORRINE SANCHEZ, MORGAN HAWES, COYA WHITE HAT-ARTICHOKER, DANIELLE BREWSTER, AND MORNING STAR GALI

It is dangerous and irresponsible for the U.S. Supreme Court to pick and choose when patients are allowed access to health care. This decision is about domination and control.

—DR. CORRINE SANCHEZ

As women and nonbinary caregivers of the First Nations and ancestral to this land, who are the original and rightful stewards of this land, we have watched the systems of white supremacy grow and expand, while we have always held tightly to our traditional knowledges and lifeways. We know prior to contact in 1492, Indigenous women and LGBTQIA2S+ people had more autonomy, freedom, and body sovereignty than colonizers could grasp or fully understand. Since then, we have lived under the colonizer's cruel and dehumanizing ways and adapted to other Western systems of care for one another. Now we see that they are willing to inflict harm upon their own women, and all women, in addition to what they've done to Brown and Black bodies. This legacy of trauma and systemic oppression greatly affects us, physically and spiritually. Our bodies and spirits continue to carry all the scars and remembrances of brutal systems and strategic policies that have continually asserted domination over those of us they see as a threat.

As the keepers and stewards of this land, and as citizens and descendants of our tribal nations, we state very clearly, *these systems were never built to protect our peoples.* From forced sterilization of our women and relatives capable of becoming pregnant to the implementation of the Hyde Amendment, this is yet another attack on the sovereignty of Indigenous people. What we are witnessing now and what we know will continue to happen to all women and birthing peoples in this country, is that striking down *Roe* is dangerous and will cost countless lives. There is no scenario where women and birthing people will not be put at further risk. It creates a stark choice about how to care for women during this time. Our inherent sovereignty as Indigenous women and people determines that we must decide our own fate, and not allow the state to define these outcomes on our behalf. Upholding *Roe v. Wade* is the very least this country can do, after centuries of the systemic oppression of anyone not white, male, and Christian.

We are not afraid of this fight to come—in fact, we were inherently built for this. We will continue to act for the collective good to bring forth collective liberation.

4 *Plan C*

NOMI KANE AND THE PLAN C TEAM,
ARTWORK BY NOMI KANE

NOTE: Originally published in 2017. Please visit plancpills.org for up-to-date information about how to access pills and support resources.

This "Plan C" is a combination of medications called mifepristone and misoprostol. When taken as directed up to 12 weeks after a missed period, the pills are safe and 95% effective.

 MIFEPRISTONE   MISOPROSTOL

In the US, the most common way to get mifepristone and misoprostol is from health care providers who offer abortion services...

But there are many barriers to access in the US. Because mifepristone and misoprostol enable people to safely and effectively manage early abortion on their own, some are obtaining and taking these pills independently.

In countries like Ghana and Mexico, abortion pills can be purchased easily and inexpensively at pharmacies.

And people in more than 100 countries have access to mail-order services such as womenweb.org, womenhelp.org, and safe2choose.org.

But because of political controversy over abortion in our country, abortion clinics are closing, leaving people in some states with few options.

So, folks in the US are finding ways to buy pills covertly online. . .

Or across the border in Mexico.

Some people are using misoprostol alone, which is roughly 85% effective. Misoprostol can be easier to find because it's prescribed for arthritis, peptic ulcers, and even for pets.

5   *Come Hell or High Water*

A Patchwork of Community Care in Appalachia

HAYLEY V. MCMAHON

In the dust that began to settle after the devastating blow of the *Dobbs* decision and the triggered wave of abortion bans that followed, fear rippled through southern and central Appalachia. In Alabama, Kentucky, Mississippi, Tennessee, and West Virginia, total bans quickly took effect.[1] With varying degrees of success, antiabortion politicians in Georgia, North Carolina, South Carolina, and Virginia began scheming on how they might enact bans that previously had been struck down or pass new bans as soon as possible. In the days and weeks that followed the ruling, no one knew what was actually legal in a post-*Dobbs* world. Could people share information about abortion? Could they travel to other states for legal care? Could they end their pregnancies at home with pills? Could they help pay for others' abortions? Would miscarriage care still be accessible? Would people who self-managed their abortions at home be prosecuted? No one, not even lawyers with decades of experience litigating reproductive rights cases, could be sure. None of it had been tested in court, and the Supreme Court had just made it crystal clear that it would not concern itself with pesky precedents. No one knew how far antiabortion prosecutors and judges would be willing to go.

Appalachians had good reason to be afraid—poor, rural women have long been targeted for investigation and arrest related to their pregnancy outcomes.[2] Pregnant and recently pregnant people have been prosecuted and imprisoned for everything from inducing an abortion at home or experiencing a spontaneous stillbirth to refusing medical treatment or getting pregnant while struggling with substance use.[3] But Appalachia also has a rich tradition of turning fear into collective power. We have never gone quietly. Many people unfortunately see the region as it has been portrayed by a non-Appalachian-millionaire-venture-capitalist.[4] They forget that these mountains have birthed many of the most radical resistance movements in this country's history—the Battle of Blair Mountain, John Brown's Raid on Harper's Ferry, the Elizabethton Rayon Strikes, the Appalachian Volunteers, and the Yellow Finch Tree-Sits, just to name a few.[5] It should be no surprise then that our hollers are home to a number of folks working toward abortion justice.

The truth is that abortion access was hanging by a thread in Appalachia long before the post-*Dobbs* bans. *Roe* was never enough to protect us. For years, politicians in the region have been strategically stacking medically unnecessary restrictions that quickly snowball into de facto bans if you don't have the financial resources to overcome them. That's not to say that *Dobbs* has not been disastrous in Appalachia. It surely has. But this struggle is not new to us. Even with *Roe v. Wade* standing, clinics were already few and far between in most areas. Clinic numbers have dwindled over the years as the constant onslaught of antiabortion regulations forced more and more providers to close their doors. Related laws required patients to attend two separate appointments to fulfill state-mandated waiting periods or have a state-mandated ultrasound before they could have an abortion. This meant patients had to find a way to travel often hundreds of miles roundtrip to the nearest clinic, and then do it again. Then there's the Hyde Amendment, which already denied Medicaid coverage for abortion and left some of the most vulnerable in our communities to try to come up with the $500 or more to afford care. The list of seemingly insurmountable barriers goes on.[6]

The hypothetical post-*Roe* scenarios in every newspaper were already our reality. So, when the outright abortion bans finally came for southern and central Appalachia, we were expecting them. Appalachians shrouded ourselves in a protective quilt of community care that we had been stitching together for years, determined to make do like we always have. Sometimes it is seemingly small acts of love, like the stickers with plancpills.org and ineedana.com resources that began popping up on street signs and in gas station bathrooms. Sometimes it's love that drastically alters the access landscape, like opening a new clinic right next to states that would soon have zero. When it became clear that Tennessee's looming ban would soon end legal abortion care at one of the very few independent abortion clinics actually located in Appalachia, the clinics' management team knew they would need to open a new facility just a few miles over the Virginia border. They also knew they would need a lot of money to make it happen. Within three weeks of creating a crowd-funding page and just days after the *Dobbs* ruling came down, they were open and seeing patients in their new space. More than fifteen hundred people came together to keep a clinic in central Appalachia.

There are also collectives of folks doing the work day in and day out to love and care for our communities. When someone in Tennessee is already struggling to make ends meet and doesn't know how they will afford the cost of their care, local abortion funds step in to get them the money they need. When someone in Kentucky needs to get to a clinic in South Carolina but doesn't have anyone to watch their kids or access to a reliable car, practical support volunteers coordinate a vetted driver, a safe and private hotel room, and trusted childcare. When someone in Virginia needs support because their loved ones couldn't take off work to be at the clinic with them or they chose to self-manage their abortion at home without a clinician, abortion doulas are there to hold their hands and provide emotional support. When someone in Georgia who is already nervous about their procedure is met by hordes of screaming protesters, clinic escorts make sure they get through the door safely. Our patchwork of community care—the collective work we do to meet people's physical, emotional, and financial needs—makes abortion access a possibility for thousands of Appalachians.

Doing this work is often heartbreaking and never easy. On the particularly bad days, I tend to reach for my favorite shirt. It's a faded black one with just the right amount of worn, bought several years ago from a fundraiser for one of my favorite Reproductive Justice organizations in West Virginia. The perfectly defiant gold lettering on the front says, "Come hell or high water, we're funding abortion in our hills and hollers." I love how true it is. Hell and high water showed up, and we're still here.

6 "We Too Have Abortions"

Centering the Abortion Experiences and Needs of Asian Communities

SHEILA DESAI

I found out I was pregnant in my early twenties. I wasn't ready to become a parent and knew that I needed an abortion. Ironically, as a young public health student working at a local health clinic, I had no idea how *I* could navigate the health system or where *I* could safely seek an abortion. I was unfamiliar with abortion funds, had no health insurance, and almost no money. But I was too afraid to ask for help because of the stigma, judgment, and isolation that I feared would follow. Frankly, I also didn't know who to ask.

When I needed an abortion, I felt trapped, confused, and alone. Today, as it was for me growing up, it is rare to see South Asians represented among those who have abortions. I didn't see myself or my community represented in any of the stories I read. I didn't even see them in the pages of research that I studied for school. How was I supposed to get the abortion that I needed? As the days ticked by, seven weeks pregnant turned into nine weeks, and nine weeks turned into eleven weeks. I grew more and more scared. I can say from firsthand experience that not obtaining an abortion that you want, when you want, is terrifying.

Finally, in secret and on my own, I safely self-managed my abortion with misoprostol from the clinic where I worked. Having an abortion was the best decision for me; yet for years I shrouded my story in silence. I didn't speak of the stigma that I felt or the barriers that I faced when seeking my abortion. But through conversations and in my work as a researcher, I continued to notice the lack of my group and other Asian groups in the data, discussions, and stories on abortion. It was as though the financial and logistical barriers to abortion that were so well-documented for other groups simply did not exist for Asian Americans.[1] I knew this wasn't true. Inequities in access to care were only deepening in these communities.[2] Asian Americans continue to be erroneously characterized as a group that lacks health challenges in large part because of a public discourse that stereotypes Asians as a "model minority." This framing implies that Asians are a uniformly successful and healthy monolith. Yet this myth, rooted in US histories of racism and xenophobia, has long obfuscated the heterogeneity of this population and the obstacles many Asian Americans face when seeking abortion and other health care.

While treated as a monolith in mainstream discourse, Asians are the most diverse racial group in the United States, comprising more than fifty ethnicities from more than twenty countries of origin. Each group has vastly different migration histories, cultures, languages, and health systems that inform their health-care behaviors, access, and outcomes.[3] Nearly 60 percent of the population is foreign-born, and many contend with anti-Asian xenophobia and a patchwork of US policies and practices that condition (and limit) health-care access on factors like immigration status, English proficiency, and income.[4] Racial stereotypes, cultural stereotypes, and discrimination also make some Asian groups the target of state-level "sex-selective" abortion bans, which invoke harmful tropes of Asian families' preference for sons and impose undue scrutiny on their reasons for obtaining abortions. Furthermore, language barriers, cultural stigma, and low rates of health insurance coverage exacerbate access challenges to abortion care for many Asian American groups.

This broader context existed well before the *Dobbs* decision; Asian American women and people have long known the consequences of abortion restrictions and other barriers to health care.

Now, with abortion in the hands of state legislators across the country, nearly one-third of low-income Asian American women live in states that enacted abortion restrictions after the *Dobbs* ruling.[5] Combined with existing systemic barriers to care, including cultural stigma and stereotypes, mounting xenophobia, and exclusionary migration policies, the current restrictive environment will only further jeopardize timely abortion care, rights, and justice for many Asian American groups. We should have never ignored or undermined the health and abortion care needs of Asian communities, and we can no longer do so now. The consequences in a post-*Roe* environment—both persistent and new obstacles that delay or altogether prohibit access to abortion—are more dangerous than ever.

Moving forward in the fight to keep abortion accessible to all, we must commit to centering and making visible the abortion needs and rights of Asian communities. We must ensure that the intersection between immigration policy, health care, and abortion rights is addressed in the pursuit of preserving access for all, including Asian immigrants. Reproductive health research must consistently include and disaggregate Asian populations in the study of abortion. They are not an optional subgroup that can be ignored or tacked on by request. My story and those of others show the harms of ignoring barriers to access that people from communities like mine and many others face. Thoughtful work exploring the needs of Asian Americans and immigrants can bring to bear the range of abortion experiences in these groups, dismantle harmful racial and cultural myths, and shape equitable abortion policies and programs.

We must also work to elevate the stories and collective expertise of Asian Americans, especially those who have had abortions and those most impacted by a post-*Roe* climate. Many have long paved paths of resistance, fighting to dispel the injurious model minority myth, challenge anti-immigration policies and xenophobia, and destigmatize abortion in their communities and beyond. Centering such efforts helps ensure that the needs, priorities, and experiences of those traditionally isolated and systematically excluded from the abortion discourse inform and anchor any vision for change moving forward, whether that's advanced by communities, activists, or researchers.

In recent years, as I've started sharing my abortion story, I've learned the stories of others. Stories shared quietly and across generations. Stories shared in my community, in my family, and even among my ancestors. As young women, mothers, and elders, many navigated their abortions as I did: silently and on their own. I often wonder if I would have felt so alone in my own story had I known that others, around me and before me, had navigated similar paths. These days I share my abortion story, in part to interrupt the cultural stigma and stereotypes that shaped my experience, but also to dispel the myth that Asian Americans and immigrants don't have or need abortions. We do.

I share my story so that people in my community, my loved ones, the generations that follow, and all others know that we too have abortions. We too need support as we navigate access barriers and deserve not to feel alone as we do so. Above all, we must see ourselves and be seen in the fight for abortion rights and Reproductive Justice. Our lives and communities depend on it.

7 *How* Dobbs *Will Deepen the Traumas of Incarcerated Pregnant People*

CAROLYN SUFRIN

We're not looked at as people; we're looked at as inmates, so all of our decisions are taken from us, even with our pregnancies.

Deija was ten weeks pregnant when she was arrested and booked into county jail.[1] She shared with me and my research team her decision-making around and attempts at accessing abortion in custody. A mother of four other children, Deija was initially excited about having a fifth child when she learned that she was pregnant. But with the prospect of an undetermined length of jail time looming, she changed her mind and wanted an abortion. She didn't know if it was even an option in jail because, as I quoted her above, she knew that being incarcerated meant that all of her decisions were taken from her—when and what to eat, when to sleep, when she could see a doctor. None of those choices were hers. This extended into choices about her pregnancy.

When Deija finally did see a doctor two weeks into her jail stay, she asked about getting an abortion. The response she received was both judgmental and procedural—the doctor said: "We don't do that here. We used to, but we don't anymore." As Deija told us, "None of the medical professionals here believe in abortion. So, when I brought it up, I was instantly shot down. Two different doctors. They both were like, 'Well, I've had three kids,' or, 'I've had this many kids and I would never get an abortion. Children are blessings. You shouldn't get an abortion.' They wouldn't even discuss it with me. Telling me all the different ways I was wrong and why I shouldn't get an abortion."

This happened to Deija in 2018, in a state with some of the most liberal abortion laws and access in the country. For Deija and other pregnant people needing abortion while incarcerated, June 24, 2022, was not a moment of rupture in their abilities to access abortion. Incarcerated individuals were already living in a post-*Roe* reality without out protected abortion access. Deija's overt denial of an abortion while incarcerated was flagrantly in violation of constitutional standards that had for decades clearly affirmed that incarcerated people retain their right to abortion.[2] But because prisons and jails are out of view of public and legal scrutiny, they institute their own, sometimes unconstitutional, health-care policies.

Two linguistic issues in particular have subtly enabled the stealth preclusion of abortion for incarcerated people: (1) labeling some abortions as "elective" and (2) requiring that institutions of incarceration provide access to health care for "serious medical needs." The Supreme Court mandated the latter in the 1976 *Estelle v. Gamble* case.[3] All abortions are indicated, but medicalizing some abortions as indicated and diminishing others as more "elective" lifestyle choices has misappropriated the classifications of "elective procedures" in health care. "Elective procedures" are those that can be delayed indefinitely without significant impact on a person's life or well-being. Since pregnancy is time-limited, and since procreating or not, parenting or not, certainly impacts a person's life course, abortion cannot be classified as "elective." Yet the widespread use of "elective abortion" in common parlance and even medical circles has allowed prison and jail administrators to claim that this "elective" procedure is not a "serious medical need." As such, they argue, prisons and jails do not need to facilitate access under the requirements of *Estelle*. Although the courts have consistently disagreed with this logic, lack of oversight, lack of required standards of health care, and systemic disregard for reproductive autonomy in custody makes it possible for institutions of incarceration to apply their own rules and policies regarding abortion access (as in cases like Deija's).

Variability in prison and jail abortion policies can make access options for incarcerated people even cloudier. In my team's survey of twenty-two state prison and six jail (including the nation's five largest) abortion policies, we found that some facilities' policies did allow abortion, and some officially did *not* allow it—again, in violation of the law.[4] Some facilities only allowed abortion in the first trimester, even when state law had no such gestational limits. Many of the facilities that allowed abortion put up additional barriers, like requirements that the pregnant person pay for the abortion or even transportation themselves. Regardless of the state, Medicaid is categorically not an option to pay for any health care for an incarcerated person. Restrictions like these, and others, meant that de facto many people likely could not obtain abortion. In the federal prison system the Bureau of Prisons (BOP) does allow abortion—although subject to the financial restrictions of the Hyde Amendment.[5]

At the jail Deija was at, abortion was officially allowed in the first trimester, which meant that at ten weeks she was eligible by the jail's policy. Nonetheless, the jail's doctors told Deija "we don't do that here" and imposed their own moral abortion beliefs to preclude Deija's abortion access. I spoke with other pregnant people at jails and prisons in this liberal state and in an abortion-hostile state. Many of them assumed that because they were in a rights-revoking space of a prison or jail, abortion was categorically not an option. One woman said,

"I mean, I didn't really have a choice of anything, so they didn't really ask." And another said, "I was told that . . . if you wanted an abortion when you're here . . ., you can't because you were the state's property."

If the foreclosure of abortion access for incarcerated people predates the *Dobbs* decision, what might change for the estimated tens of thousands of pregnant people who enter jails and prisons each year?[6] Well, for one, people who need abortion and are incarcerated in a state where it is banned do not even have the option to travel to another state for an abortion. This is also true for the hundreds of thousands of women who are not behind bars but are on probation or parole.[7] For these individuals, their forced pregnancies literally become part of their state-sanctioned punishment. The state's claim to their reproductive bodies becomes extreme in this setting, where carceral control definitionally revokes bodily autonomy. They are conscripted into gestating pregnancies in the harsh conditions of incarceration, with questionable nutrition, disrupted sleep, variable access to prenatal care, and isolation from social supports. This cruelty is not lost on incarcerated pregnant people, of course.

Deija talked about wanting to spare her baby from the harms of incarceration, describing her desire for an abortion in protectionist terms: "Being here is stressful . . . because you don't eat properly; you're hungry. You're stressed out. You're alone. It's not fair to the baby, either. . . . Well, the baby didn't do anything wrong; yet, the baby gets treated like an inmate. So all the stress that I feel, the baby feels. It's just not something I want to put my kid through." If an incarcerated person like Deija gives birth in custody, they do so alone, they may be shackled, and they will likely be separated from their newborns soon after birth. As Deija heartbreakingly said, "You don't know what they're going to do with your baby after you have it. Are they going to let you hold your baby?" The anticipated trauma at the core of her question was one of the reasons she decided to seek an abortion in jail.

Deija's reality, pre-*Dobbs,* will be replicated and expanded now that the previous constitutional protections that at least in theory were in place for incarcerated pregnant people are now gone in more than two dozen states.[8] But recall that Deija was incarcerated in an abortion-supportive state. How might abortion access change for incarcerated people in these states? It is conceivable that at jails and prisons that allow abortion, the increased volume at abortion clinics in supportive states, from out-of-state abortion patients, could trickle down and limit appointment availability for incarcerated people in that state. Incarcerated individuals may continue to think that they do not have a right to abortion, or may be misinformed and think that abortion is now illegal in their state, and thus would not even ask jail or prison medical staff about abortion. People in federal custody are subject to Bureau of Prisons (BOP) policies, which still allow abortion; but if they are in a federal prison in an abortion-restrictive state, BOP would need to transfer them to a facility in another state.

There are also concerns about how carceral health-care systems will fare in addressing pregnancy care needs in the post-*Dobbs* context.[9] It is possible that we will see more pregnant individuals entering jail and prison—because we are likely to see more pregnant individuals in the United States in general, people who would otherwise have terminated pregnancies. While some prisons and jails have been able to provide access to a reasonable quality of prenatal care, many others already do not.[10] So a potential influx of more pregnant people into carceral institutions may strain already constrained systems. Furthermore, if a pregnant, incarcerated person has a medical emergency, like vaginal bleeding, and the carceral facility staff appropriately take them to a hospital for emergent evaluation, the hospital may not provide comprehensive care—for instance, if there is an impending miscarriage, but the embryo still has a heartbeat. The pregnant person would be sent back to prison or jail, where they and carceral staff are ill-equipped to address a life-threatening emergency like hemorrhage.

All of these ripple effects—and the pre-*Dobbs* reality—have profoundly racialized histories and implications. Mass incarceration is a phenomenon grounded in white supremacy, settler colonialism, and structural racism, represented in part by the statistical reality that Black women are incarcerated at twice the rate and Native American women at four times the rate of white women.[11] These disproportionalities also parallel those in maternal mortality rates in the United States. The forced separation from one's newborn after an incarcerated person gives birth and returns from the hospital to prison or jail has harrowing historical resonances with child removals from enslaved and Indigenous families, and even with contemporary practices of the foster care system.[12]

The reality of life for incarcerated pregnant people before and after *Dobbs* builds the case for abolishing our carceral system in order to realize the human rights of Reproductive Justice. The state precludes incarcerated people from having abortions, from bodily autonomy, from having safe pregnancies, and from parenting their children. This violates all of the core tenets of Reproductive Justice—all in one pregnancy.[13] Abolition as a means to Reproductive Justice would include policy changes that invest in alternatives to incarceration, especially for pregnant and parenting people, with concomitant investment in safety-net services. We must be particularly attentive to laws that criminalize pregnant people given what life behind bars means for their liberty and reproductive restrictions. We also must reimagine the so-called child welfare system, or as scholar and activist Dorothy Roberts has called it, "the family policing system."[14] Until such reimaginings become reality, we must have standardization and oversight of health care, including pregnancy care, behind bars. To elide the amplified inability to travel to another state for abortion for incarcerated people in states that ban abortion, for example, judges and prison and jail wardens could creatively deploy furloughs to allow pregnant people to travel out of state—though this seems unlikely.

The nexus of state-sanctioned criminalization and reproductive governance shows up in its harshest, most extreme form in US institutions of incarceration. While abortion access for incarcerated individuals in the United States was already limited before the *Dobbs* decision, the explicitly punitive and intentionally restrictive conditions of confinement underscore the interconnected ways pregnancy in the United States can be experienced as punishment. It shows us the extremes of reproductive suffering and is a microcosm for the punitive regulation of reproduction throughout US society.

Part II   *Never-Ending Emergency and Never-Ending Fight*

Reproductive health-care emergencies in the wake of *Dobbs* are in many cases actually long-standing emergencies that the 2022 Supreme Court decision has brutally intensified. Dr. Warren Hern has been an abortion provider for fifty years, most of those years under externally created emergency conditions that have caused him to fortify his clinic and his own person against violence. Dr. Hern identifies the moment in 1980 when the Republican Party "found its issue," and he traces violent abortion politics since then: constant murder threats—some realized—against him and his colleagues, and the resulting delays and danger to the health of countless people trying to manage their private, reproductive health and their lives.

Another practitioner, Robin Wallace, writes about her reproductive health work in a state university health-care center and also in an abortion clinic in another city, working to empower her patients in the midst of the public health crisis *Dobbs* is creating. She finds herself making promises to patients that are hard but absolutely necessary to keep in this environment, in a southern state with tenuously legal abortion. Rebecca Louve Yao and Alexis Obinna expose the mythic romance of Justice Amy Coney Barrett's formulation: put your newborn in a basket, drop the package at a firehouse, and all will be well—abortion is obsolete. As two veterans of the foster care system, the authors tell us that 114,000 children in the United States are waiting to be adopted. Many will never find the family Coney Barrett promises is out there. As they age, many young people grow more vulnerable, sexually and economically, and are more likely to need services and care, including reproductive health care. These vulnerabilities are compounded for people of color. The authors make the case that for people in or coming out of foster care, *Dobbs* is "another way of oppressing us."

Laury Oaks also tackles Coney Barrett's misguided, or false, argument about safe haven laws as a noble remedy, showing how this "alternative" not only degrades and endangers birthing people but also the children they are urged to leave at firehouses. Oaks argues that these laws, rarely used in any case, rely on racist and classist convictions about who is an illegitimate parent—and who deserves a child. The real remedy, Oaks insists, is the adoption of standards of care for all people, especially those without adequate resources. Journalist Tina Vasquez considers how few mainstream media outlets adequately cover the abortion issue, including the impacts of *Dobbs,* leaving most of the population in the country dangerously underinformed. Vasquez contrasts this situation with the vibrant, engaged, and in-the-struggle SisterSong gathering in the summer of 2022, just after the *Dobbs* decision was handed down.

Francine Thompson, the longtime director of the historic Emma Goldman Clinic in Iowa City, is dedicated to facilitating that vision, providing comprehensive and feminist reproductive health care to marginalized people, many of whom have to travel significant distances to the clinic under the *Dobbs* emergency. Can Thompson's vision be realized under *Dobbs,* in Iowa, with all its new deterrents? She asks, "How do you value the authority of an individual to determine their destiny," while complying with draconian laws designed to rob individuals of just that authority and control? This is the essence of the emergency. The team at CHOICES, the venerable clinic in Memphis, Tennessee, writes about the facility's commitment in the 2010s to provide a full spectrum of sexual and reproductive health-care services, using Reproductive Justice principles. As recriminalization of abortion loomed, CHOICES acted strategically, moving its abortion practice across the state line to Illinois, while leaving the rest of its practice intact and flourishing in Memphis. This story models a crucial commitment to expansive definitions of sexual and reproductive health as well as to coalition-building, under crisis and beyond.

Meg Sasse Stern, at Just the Pill, shows us what a deep, long commitment to bodily autonomy looks like, over a quarter century. In her piece Stern defines Reproductive Justice (RJ) as an activist creed, in addition to a human rights claim. She illustrates what it has meant to infuse her work—building bridges to support communities and foster coalitions—with the precepts of RJ, to nourish clarity, persistence, and creativity in the face of ever-mutating challenges in Kentucky, where she is based, and beyond.

8 *Performing Abortions after* Roe

WARREN M. HERN

Sitting in the Supreme Court chambers on December 13, 1971, and listening to Sarah Weddington make her first arguments in the *Roe v. Wade* case, I did not realize the historical significance of the moment. Nor did I imagine that I would be performing abortions at the first private, nonprofit abortion clinic in Colorado two years later. It was beyond my imagination that I would still be specializing in outpatient abortion services as a physician over fifty years later. I have watched with horror the national convulsion over the right of women to have safe abortions being taken away forty-nine years after it was granted.

In this time I have performed or supervised the performance of safe abortions for more than forty thousand women from throughout the United States, Canada, Europe, and other parts of the world. Safe abortion is a fundamental component of women's health care in the twenty-first century. Taking away the constitutional right of women to have access to this critical medical care is cruel, stupid, punitive, and indefensible public policy. There is no justification for any laws restricting access to this vital health care for women. No woman's life, health, and safety should be at the mercy of the next election, her zip code, her skin color, language, ethnic group, or her income. It certainly should not be at the mercy of Republican politicians who have stepped on the bodies of women for almost fifty years to gain power. Pregnancy is not a benign condition. Women die from being pregnant.

After the *Dobbs* decision, women across the country struggle to find the medical assistance they need to end pregnancies and to have the emergency medical care they need. Stories abound of women who experience ruptured membranes at the eighteenth or twentieth week of pregnancy and for whom there is no hope of having a living, much less healthy, baby as the result of that pregnancy. That pregnancy is now a grave danger to the woman's life. It is an emergency. The uterus must be emptied immediately by a physician who is experienced and skilled at this operation. Otherwise, the woman is at immediate risk of a life-threatening infection, septic shock, and other complications that could end her life within hours. There is no justification for withholding this lifesaving medical care. But those are exactly the consequences of the *Dobbs* decision and the Republican-sponsored state laws that prevent doctors from helping that woman.

It is barbaric and incredible that we have reached this point in the United States in the twenty-first century, but the Republicans and the white Christian antiabortion fanatics who control the Republican Party have brought us quite deliberately to this point. It is not an accident or a coincidence. It has been the plan since 1973. Why? Power.

In his 1990 book *The Politics of the Rich and Poor: Wealth and the American Electorate in the Reagan Aftermath,* Kevin Phillips lists the hot-button issues that the Republican Party was using very effectively to win elections. These issues included abortion, which since 1980 has become the Republican Party's hammer and tongs to power. Why else could white Evangelical Christians give over 80 percent of their votes in 2016 and 2020 to their ostentatiously depraved Orange Messiah, Donald Trump, who represents in every respect the antithesis of the ostentatiously and righteously announced values of Christians of all kinds? Because they are fanatically opposed to abortion, which to them represents an insurrection against the repressive, authoritarian, patriarchal ideology of Christians and upends their intention to out-breed their ethnic competitors—that is, anyone in America with a darker skin or who follows the "wrong" part of the Bible.

Republican politicians have known this since Bob Dole cynically used the abortion issue to come from ten points behind in 1974 to beat his Democratic opponent, Dr. Bill Roy, by 1.8 percent. Dole accused Dr. Roy, who had delivered thousands of babies and had performed a few abortions for medical reasons, of being in favor of "abortion on demand," a concept and expression unknown to Dr. Roy. The flood of antiabortion propaganda in the last few days of the Iowa senatorial campaign in 1978 sunk a highly favored US senator, the liberal pro-choice Democrat Dick Clark. Clark was defeated by a notoriously mediocre Republican candidate who fervently declared his total opposition to abortion. Iowa antiabortion fanatics targeted Clark for defeat, and they succeeded.

The Republican Party had found its issue. By 1980 antiabortion senator Jesse Helms controlled the Republican National Convention, which threw the Republican Women for Choice out of the convention and nominated Ronald Reagan. The Republican platform declared the party's official opposition to safe, legal abortion. The first thing that Ronald Reagan said to the press on Wednesday, November 4, 1980, was that he was going to "make abortion illegal." Two days later, on the *Today Show,* Republican senator Strom Thurmond stated that he planned to ask for the death penalty for doctors who perform abortions. I watched both of these statements from my mountain wilderness home in Colorado, and Thurmond's statement in particular sent chills up my spine. I was already living under constant death threats and had begun sleeping with a rifle by my bed.

On Inaugural Day, January 20, 1981, Reagan welcomed all the major national antiabortion leaders into the Oval Office. Reagan's newly appointed secretary of health, education and welfare, former senator Richard Schweiker, declared at an antiabortion rally that day that the new administration would be "pro-life." The only qualification many Reagan appointees had was fanatic opposition to abortion. Every single Republican president since Reagan has used the abortion issue to win election, and all of the US Supreme Court justices appointed by Republican presidents since Reagan and remaining on the Court are Catholic (Gorsuch was raised Catholic but may now identify as Protestant), antiabortion Republicans who have lied about upholding *Roe*.

The 2016 election of Donald Trump, who stated in an interview with Chris Matthews that "women should be punished" for having an abortion, was the death knell for *Roe*. The Christians got the message, voted for him, and got what they wanted. Now we have a national catastrophe for women who need abortions. Women who have acute medical needs having nothing to do with abortion cannot get the care they need because doctors, nurses, and other health personnel are terrified of state laws that would make them criminals for helping women or subject them to devastating legal actions. Women who have money can travel to get abortions, but women with no money must suffer without help.

A woman in Texas makes an appointment at a clinic in Oklahoma to get an early abortion since the clinic in her town is now closed. By the time she gets to her appointment in Oklahoma, she is too far along to have the abortion there. By the time she gets the next appointment in another state, she is confronted with the same problem. Finally, many weeks later after she discovers she is pregnant, she arrives at my office at a much later stage in pregnancy when the procedure costs more, has higher risks, requires more specialized care, is more stressful, and takes several days instead of a short visit. And she has had to wait several weeks to have her appointment at my office.

A physician in Texas who specializes in high-risk pregnancy care and maternal-fetal medicine and who has referred patients to me for years for those who have pregnancies complicated by catastrophic fetal abnormalities will no longer give his patients specific information about my office because he is afraid of being sued out of existence by the antiabortion fanatics under Texas law. He will tell the patient in cryptic terms that she can find my office if she studies and interprets his instructions. But he can't see the patient for a follow-up exam later for the same reasons. It's incredible. I got the same message from another medical colleague in a neighboring state whose nurse told me that she just shredded my latest letter of referral to him because he can no longer see our mutual patients for follow-up care and must destroy our written communications so there is no evidence he has been in touch with me.

It's a police-state mentality.

A woman with three kids whose husband is unemployed and who is supporting the family on a minimum-wage job finds herself pregnant in a small Texas town where the family-planning clinic has been closed, ending her access to contraception. She doesn't have the bus fare to get to the next town much less pay for childcare while she travels by bus to a neighboring state to get an abortion since the family can't afford another child. What's going to happen to her and to her family? If she loses her job because she's having another baby, how will the family have enough to eat and pay the rent? The Republicans have no solution for this woman or any of the others except punishment and more laws restricting their lives—and votes.

9 *From College Campus to Community*

A Physician's Perspective on Abortion and Contraception Access in Restrictive States

ROBIN WALLACE

College campuses have a different kind of hum in the days between final exams and commencement. Anticipation and nostalgic trepidation hang heavy in the air, mixed with a healthy dose of celebration and well-earned revelry. Students bring that vibe into the medical exam room, smiles of relief that another semester is over and an urgency to take care of all the neglected ailments and routine health-care needs before their on-campus coverage expires. The early days of May 2022 brought yet another element—the *Dobbs* draft opinion had just been leaked and speculative concern became a real and present fear for students capable of pregnancy.

I provide full-spectrum primary care for undergraduates, graduate students, and postdoctoral researchers at a large university in a blue bubble town in a (mostly) red Southern state. I spend a lot of my days offering sexually transmitted infection (STI) screening, destigmatizing abnormal Pap smears, discussing birth control options, placing long-acting contraceptive devices like implants and IUDs, and supporting patients with depression and anxiety. I also provide abortions in my off-campus job and have done so for over fifteen years.

That first week of May 2022, a confident but concerned graduating medical student sat across from me in the exam room. Kendra and I shared excitement for her upcoming placement at the residency training program of her choosing, but it was dampened by the recent SCOTUS leak.[1] She was moving to Texas. Abortion was already banned at six weeks there, and now any remaining hope for that to be lifted was lost. With only two years of clinical training under her belt, Kendra knew enough to be worried about her own access to reproductive health services once she arrived in Texas, never mind the devastation for the millions of Texans who already were living under this tyranny. Having also lived and provided abortions in Texas for eight years, I saw firsthand the tragic consequences of senseless abortion restrictions. The public health crisis that had been unfolding for years had now reached a new flashpoint.

An unplanned pregnancy did not fit into Kendra's rigorous training plan, and while I wanted to reassure her that effective contraception would always be legal and available across the country, in that moment I just couldn't. So that day in May we talked about IUDs and implants and options for accessing abortion out-of-state should she need it while living in Texas. She chose to schedule an insertion appointment for the IUD that would be effective for at least the number of years she anticipated living in Texas. I also gave Kendra contact information for a trusted clinic and the name of my friend and colleague in the city where she would be located, where they would provide abortions when legal, or support for reproductive health care when they couldn't.

As a family physician, my job has always been to meet patients where they are, care for their medical needs, and provide support, education, and advocacy for how to live their healthiest lives. In my practice the education and advocacy pieces have always included comprehensive reproductive care options, both contraception and abortion, but in the months since the SCOTUS leak and the final

Dobbs decision, it is a new priority for me to empower my patients and their reproductive autonomy. I take every opportunity to share knowledge about clinical options and resources and to disclose that I am also an abortion provider and available to them or their friends at any time in need. Students ask me regularly whether abortion is already illegal in our state (it's not, yet), whether Plan B is illegal (it's not, and by the way it does not cause an abortion), and whether their access to birth control is in danger (I don't know, maybe, but I really hope not).

When I am off campus and providing abortion care, I bring that same primary care perspective to my work. Becky came for an abortion early in pregnancy to one of the clinics where I work in North Carolina, because she was too late to access services in Georgia. Instead, she was forced to make the five-hour drive alone and in the middle of the night to avoid the added cost of a hotel room and still arrive for her 8 a.m. appointment. Becky commented on the "messed-up situation" for accessing abortion services in her home state. I tried to engage her by remarking on the promise of the upcoming election and the opportunity to vote for change, but she was resigned that there were no good options on the ballot. Now that November 8, 2022, has come and gone, her response is clearer to me. Abortion itself was not on the ballot in Georgia, politicians were. But in states where the electorate were asked directly, abortion access won nearly universally. Advocating for patients and their access to health care does shape my personal politics. However, when I'm with a patient, I never tell them who or what to vote for, but I often do remind them to vote and make their voice heard.

Here in North Carolina, abortion access is not a sure thing, protected only by our current governor's veto, and at risk with each election. Access for our state is also access for a large swath of the southeastern United States. We have become a safe haven for folks living under abortion bans in nearly all the states beyond our southern and western borders. And we are not without barriers! Before *Dobbs*,

North Carolina already had a slew of TRAP (targeted restrictions of abortion providers) laws on the books. We require a seventy-two-hour wait after securing an appointment and receiving scripted information designed to discourage abortion. Only physicians (and not highly qualified advanced practice clinicians) can provide abortion—including the pills that safely induce abortion early in pregnancy, and these same pills *must* be handed to patients and ingested in front of the prescribing physician, as telemedicine care for abortion is illegal. So while we are opening doors to thousands of folks in need, it's not without significant hardship for them.

I recently cared for a patient who had driven up from Florida, as her pregnancy was beyond the fifteen-week limit recently enacted there. Christina has three children at home and had pregnancies complicated by high blood pressure in the past. She made the long journey with her brothers but forgot her critical blood pressure–lowering medication at home. I was meeting her after this overnight drive, and her blood pressure was through the roof. She was exhausted and had a headache, yes, but it was clear that her body was accustomed to this physical stress. Christina's life was not imminently in danger, so would not qualify for the narrow exceptions in place in most states with abortion bans. But continuing this pregnancy would certainly be life-threatening for her. The counselor who first met her and took her blood pressure came to me for a consult earlier than I would see most patients, as there was a question of whether we could continue to care for her safely in our clinic. I saw worry fall like a shadow across her face, and I said, "You will get the abortion you came for. We just have to figure out the safest way to do it." I prescribed her new blood pressure medication to pick up from the local pharmacy's four-dollar medication list, since her Medicaid wouldn't work outside of Florida, and made sure she had a thirty-day supply to last her until she was back home and able to see her primary care provider again. She completed her abortion the next day, as scheduled.

When I reflect on the promise I made Christina, to provide the abortion she wanted and needed so she could return home to her children and keep promises to them to be a healthy and present mother, I am flooded with recollections of similar moments with patients I cared for in Texas. In the mid-2010s the abortion access landscape was already dire. Pregnant folks often drove hundreds of miles to reach us in Dallas, as services were primarily available only in the largest metropolitan areas, leaving massive abortion deserts in the rural communities. We know from this politically motivated public health experiment that the most marginalized communities suffer greatest from abortion restrictions. Abortion care was delayed or denied more often to people of color, those with fewer resources, and those living in remote areas. So while mostly white, mostly male politicians in Austin were scoring political points by refusing to expand Medicaid and by defunding Planned Parenthood and Title X clinics (which decimated birth control access and likely increased unplanned pregnancy), the maternal mortality rate for Black Texans rose to unfathomable highs. And because this year's reports were conveniently delayed leading up to the 2022 Texas gubernatorial election, we are still waiting for updated data to reflect the impact of the six-week abortion ban, enacted in September 2021, and the complete ban triggered by *Dobbs*. Thus the straight line from abortion bans and resulting forced birth to poor health outcomes for all our communities is well-concealed by those who orchestrate and perpetuate systems of oppression.

My mentors in Texas have been fighting for Reproductive Justice since before the *Roe* decision—disheartening doesn't begin to encapsulate what it must feel like to land full circle fifty years later. But I'm an eternal optimist and search for hope wherever it can be found.

These days I find it at our campus health center—the university students who are demanding reproductive health education, organizing public health campaigns, and mobilizing for reproductive rights; and in our clinics off campus—pregnant people who tell me they need an abortion now so they can be the best parent they can be (again, or for the first time) when it is right. And sometimes, I find the same patient in both places.

10 *What We Inherit*

Foster Youth and the Ongoing Eradication of Our Autonomy

REBECCA LOUVE YAO AND
ALEXIS OBINNA

As policy professionals who also happen to have lived expertise in the foster care system, we bring a multilens perspective to the conversation on reproductive rights and its impact on the child welfare system. This perspective recognizes that the *Dobbs v. Jackson* decision is more than the revocation of a right. For many of us, it is another devastating blow to personal autonomy facing foster youth. To enter the foster care system often means losing what little voice a young person in our society is afforded. Decisions are made for us—by professionals; by strangers; by the court; by a faceless bureaucrat. Revoking our reproductive rights and forcing us down life paths that are not of our own choosing are just more ways that foster youth, transition-age youth, and families are at the mercy of systems that refuse to prioritize our best interests.

At the National Foster Youth Institute we represent the concerns of current and former foster youth around the country. Some of our fellow advocates and organizers who are in care or who have recently aged out of foster care live in locations where access to abortion has been and continues to be relatively uncomplicated—as long as they have the funds, transportation, and, in some cases, permission to obtain it. Other current and former foster youth live in communities where the laws change regularly and access has shifted day-to-day and even hour-by-hour. And some of us have lived in states that made it virtually impossible to get an abortion long before the *Dobbs* decision, through crafty state legislation, deceptive practices by charities, and the intentional dissemination of false information.

There is no national standard of care for foster youth. The county you live in when you go into foster care has an outsized impact on how you're treated and the resources you have access to. But as a group we have always been committed to securing rights for all children and young adults because we understand that taking away another human being's power and autonomy anywhere is a danger to people everywhere. The *Dobbs* decision reinforces that. Our initial *systemic* concern after the *Dobbs* decision was that the already overloaded child welfare system will see an influx of children that it is not prepared to handle. On any given day there are nearly four hundred thousand children in foster care, and states like Florida, Georgia, Texas, and Washington reported not having enough beds or appropriate housing for foster youth in the months leading up to *Dobbs*.

Six-months post-*Dobbs,* it is still too early to tell how the decision will impact the number of foster youth in the system—both the children who have yet to be born and those who are already here and whose parents may have sought an abortion for a subsequent pregnancy. But what we do know is that the majority of children who are in foster care are there because of poverty-related issues, and we know that abortion restrictions exacerbate financial strains. Time and again, our country has shown us that wealthy people get to make decisions about their lives. Poor people do not. And what drastically impacts poor people drastically impacts foster care. Research has found that women who are denied abortions have children with a greater chance of living below the poverty line and who face inadequate food, housing, and transportation resources. Significant policy efforts have been made to reduce child poverty in the United States, with monthly Child Tax Credit payments during the pandemic making a marked impact. Six months before *Dobbs,* 12.5 million children in the United States were living in poverty.[1]

For policymakers and legislators who had a goal of reducing abortion, a compassionate, caring, and child-centered approach to addressing poverty and addiction would have had a less jarring and harmful effect than overturning *Roe v. Wade.* Such an approach would have been better for the overall well-being of our nation's children. In addition to being concerned about systemic strains, we are especially worried about the vulnerable *individuals* impacted by this law—specifically foster youth with the ability to get pregnant. Teen foster youth are twice as likely as their peers to become pregnant. Almost half of females in foster care will experience a pregnancy by the age of nineteen. And a recent study found that, of the surveyed teens who got pregnant while in foster care, 32 percent "definitely" did not want to get pregnant and 12 percent "probably" did not want to get pregnant at that point in time.

According to Casey Family Programs, "[m]any teen parents in foster care have experienced maltreatment, endured multiple placements, and been separated from parents and other important people. These experiences result in significant trauma that, if left untreated, can impact their mental health and ability to form lasting relationships with a trusted and caring adult, and even their own child."[2] About twenty thousand young adults age out of foster care every year, according to the US Department of Health and Human Services. Those who leave care on their own without a dependent relying on them face daunting obstacles. They are significantly and statistically more likely to experience homelessness, poverty, incarceration, and educational and career challenges. A transition-age youth who enters into this already challenging world *with* a child in tow may feel overwhelmed without a strong support system and resources.

The reasons why a teen in foster care who does not want to get pregnant may become pregnant are varied and complex. Sex education and access to birth control may depend on foster parents, social workers, or medical professionals whose goals and beliefs differ from the child for which they are responsible. Girls in foster care also have a higher likelihood of experiencing sexual abuse. One study of girls in foster care who were exhibiting behavioral issues found that 81 percent of them reported being sexually abused; 68 percent were abused by more than one individual. And in 2013, when the FBI conducted one of the largest national raids in history to recover child sex trafficking victims, 60 percent of those victims were from foster care or group homes, a ratio repeated in state and municipal reports from Connecticut to California. The majority of children who have been commercially sexually exploited have had contact with the child welfare system. We have essentially allowed a foster care-to-human-trafficking pipeline to be built in cities across this country without adequately addressing how children are fed into it.

The horrifying truth that antiabortion zealots are able to ignore or simply don't care about is this: abortion laws that do not provide exceptions for rape and incest disproportionately impact vulnerable children—the very children that we as a country agree to care for when they enter the child welfare system.

In the days after the *Dobbs* decision we scrolled social media and saw the photos of the grinning couple standing outside the Supreme Court with the sign "We will adopt your baby." We saw the memes that followed—some well-meaning, some offensive, some genuinely funny. And in the jokes and pithy comments and arguments among strangers, we saw ourselves. We are the children who were not adopted. Alexis watched as her younger siblings were adopted and wondered why she wasn't. Was it that she was mixed race? Presented as Black? Too old? Too quirky? The answers will always be elusive, but what we do know is that we are not alone. Approximately 114,000 children in the United States are waiting to be adopted at this very moment.

At the National Foster Youth Institute we also work with young people whose adoptions failed. A 2016 study of 51,576 children in Illinois who exited foster care through adoption or guardianship found that about 13 percent experienced failed adoptions. African American children and children who had multiple foster placements prior to adoption were particularly likely to experience discontinuity in their adoptions.[3] Often these children are returned to foster care. But in some alarming cases, they may experience something called "rehoming," an unregulated transfer of custody that results in a child being placed with another family without the involvement of an official child welfare system, court, or adoption agency. Adoptive parents who are unsatisfied or overwhelmed with caring for their adopted child may use internet message boards and social media groups to find another individual or family willing to take custody. In some states a basic power of attorney document between strangers may change the course of a child's life, put their safety at risk, and further traumatize them. The National Foster Youth Institute has worked with young adults impacted by rehoming to share their testimonies with members of Congress in an attempt to raise awareness and strengthen the enforcement of laws that require agency involvement in adoptions.

Adoption is not the answer that some of the Supreme Court justices seem to think it is. And while memes may create powerful or memorable messaging, they cannot replace the more challenging, complex work this moment calls for: poverty alleviation, affordable childcare, and access to health care that empowers a caretaker to make the best possible decisions for her family. As foster youth, what we inherit from the bureaucracy that becomes our de facto parent is a set of intractable issues: poverty, systemic racism, and sexism. Oftentimes, these issues take us away from our family of origin and prevent us from living the lives this country prides itself on promising children. What the *Dobbs* decision takes from us is not only a right that we once thought secure. It has become another tool for oppressing us. Another decision out of our control made with no regard for the hopes, dreams, and plans of our nation's most vulnerable children and young adults.

As an organization and a network of advocates, it will be challenging for us to strategize on how we'll mobilize to improve the effectiveness of the child welfare system until we have more data. We will continue to advocate for increases in federal funding for child welfare like the Supporting Foster Youth and Families through the Pandemic Act, the John H. Chafee Foster Care Independence Program, and expanding the Child Tax Credit for at least another couple of years. These bills focus on addressing the root causes that lead to children being placed in foster care and ensure that our systems are better equipped to provide for those who do end up needing care.

In this new post-*Dobbs* world we have to continue the fight for true Reproductive Justice in ways that arm young people with inclusive, accurate information and services about sexual health and family planning. Too often we hear our members say they simply didn't know what was available to them when they were in foster care. The failure to share resources is another way the system takes power and self-sufficiency away from foster youth. We may not know what future data and numbers look like at this point in time, but we can tell you without a doubt what this moment *feels* like. It feels lonely. Callous. Like a punishment for the circumstances of our births. We worry about the message that sends to children and young adults who are currently in foster care—the literal daughters and sons of this country.

11 *The Multiple Dangers of Baby Safe Haven Laws*

LAURY OAKS

During Supreme Court arguments in *Dobbs v. Jackson Women's Health Organization,* Justice Amy Coney Barrett suggested that safe haven laws reasonably lift the burden of parenting and forced motherhood under abortion bans. In response to the justice's claim, national and global journalists as well as Reproductive Justice scholars and advocates contacted me because of my 2015 book, *Giving Up Baby: Safe Haven Laws, Motherhood, and Reproductive Justice* (NYU Press). Some had never heard of such laws, which legislatures in every state passed between 1999 and 2009, allowing people to anonymously relinquish infants at locations such as hospitals, fire stations, and police stations. Others expressed concern about abortion bans creating a "need" for safe havens that they worried could prove harmful.

In the post-*Roe* context, in which many states have banned or restricted abortion access, we need to pay close attention to the ways that support for so-called baby boxes or safe havens fit in with support for faith-based crisis pregnancy organizations. These laws purport to focus on the well-being of babies, but they utterly ignore the people who gave birth and relinquished them. This is a dangerous position—that accessible, safe, legal abortion care is unnecessary because we have safe haven laws to deliver unwanted newborns to deserving foster-adopt families. It diminishes abortion as a health care issue and denies the physical and mental health toll of pregnancy and childbirth in unsupported circumstances. We know that social and economic inequalities affect access to affordable and high-quality care, sustaining disparities by age, race, class, disability, sexuality, immigration status, rural/urban residence, and other lived categories. These inequalities create pressure to relinquish, not to parent, for many people who give birth.

We need to ask, do safe haven laws clearly promote a social good? Who benefits in the process of constructing anonymous newborn relinquishment as socially acceptable, even desirable? If the main feature of safe haven laws is legal anonymity, what does that say about attention to pregnancy and postpartum physical and mental health needs? Why would our society condone anonymous infant relinquishment while failing to provide adequate pregnancy and parenting resources? Critical analysis is particularly important now, when abortion bans and even likely restrictions on contraception are the unjust reality in much of the United States.

To comply with safe haven laws, parents can only relinquish unharmed infants within certain age limits, stipulations that define the rare value of the perfect "safe haven baby" in the adoption system. States specify wildly different age limits, from seventy-two hours old to seven days to one or more months, up to one year in North Dakota. State timelines, policies, and procedures for regaining custody also differ. Crossing state borders to surrender a newborn or changing one's mind after doing so might contradict local laws and not be protected. Clearly, promotion of safe haven laws depends on the characterization of adoption as a rescue mission, swiftly transferring babies away from "illegitimate" parents, not as a failure of the state to support parents and children. An Illinois safe haven leader imagines her target-parent-relinquishers as "unselfish" and making a "sacrifice . . . to give that child a bright future, isn't that just awesome? Just beautiful, to be able to do that for your child when you can."

Surely many parents who face hardship and grapple with the question of relinquishment could benefit profoundly if they received desperately needed parenting supports instead of encouragement to give up their children. However, predicated on the idea that parents lacking adequate resources are unfit, safe haven laws emphasize the message that when safe havens are available, only irresponsible people will fail to use them because it is the unquestionably right thing to do. Safe haven advocates argue that the central attractive feature of safe havens is anonymous relinquishment. In this, they overlook current realities, including the feasibility of successfully (and anonymously) using a safe haven site. The Safe Haven Baby Boxes website states "Anonymity Matters" but has also released information about safe haven babies, including in one case a handwritten note reportedly left with the baby, compromising the anonymity of the relinquishing person.

Today the ubiquitous use of phones with cameras and surveillance cameras in homes, businesses, and streets, not as common the 1999–2009 decade when original laws were passed, also undermines the real possibility of anonymity—as do genetic testing, social media, and other strategies that relinquished children can mobilize to contact their biological family. The goal of anonymity can also endanger postpartum support. People considering using a safe haven solution may be fearful about being identified, leading them to avoid seeking adequate medical assistance even though medical providers are policy-bound to protect the security of health information.

Safe haven advocates argue that "saving" even one baby justifies these laws and efforts to bolster and expand their use. In fact, far more than one baby has been "rescued," although the overall number is extremely low compared to all newborns. Although there is no national, centralized statistical tracking of the numbers of safe haven relinquishments, some advocacy organizations, states, and counties do compile data. A 2022 investigation by CNN journalists concluded that at least 3,251 babies nationwide were surrendered since 1999 and that some states had no safe haven use for a span of years. *Texas Tribune* reporter Jaden Edison found that Texas had 172 safe haven relinquishments between 2009 and 2019, 21 in 2020, and 7 from January to June 2022. There's evidence that some hospital births ending in adoption are being called safe haven relinquishments, in part because some safe haven advocacy groups facilitate hospital births through their efforts as crisis pregnancy centers and/or as adoption agencies. Crisis pregnancy centers, which may receive state and federal funding, seek to prevent abortion by counseling against it, distributing parenting resources, and promoting adoption. In short, safe haven laws have not provided alternatives to legal abortion.

Safe haven advocacy messages elide the social injustices that make motherhood more challenging for some while promoting negative stereotypes of some groups as undesirable mothers, including young people, BIPOC (Black, Indigenous, people of color), people living with disabilities or in precarious financial situations, and people in various kinds of relationships and/or having immigration status. As feminist historian Rickie Solinger has argued succinctly, "motherhood is a class privilege in America." The anonymity of safe haven and baby box relinquishment means that we have a dearth of information about the range of backgrounds and factors leading to that step. But even in difficult circumstances and when denied access to abortion, most pregnant women will opt to raise their child. The five-year Turnaway study published by Diana Greene Foster following one thousand US women found that only 9 percent of women unable to get a wanted abortion placed their baby for adoption. This suggests that social services designed to support parenting in difficult situations, not increased safe haven use, meets the reproductive needs of those living in states with abortion bans or onerous limitations and who are unable to travel for abortion care.

Clinical studies at Children's Hospital in Los Angeles by a researcher who works with safe haven babies and their adoptive families demonstrate the importance of specialized care for pregnancy and newborn health in the context of chronic stress, inadequate prenatal care, and in some cases drug exposure. The results of this research can be mobilized to argue for standards of care to meet the needs of all structurally marginalized pregnant people. Indeed, a Reproductive Justice analysis forces criticism of the safe haven assumption that newborn surrender is a social good and necessary option in states that ban or severely restrict abortion. Scholars and advocates have the responsibility to reveal, alleviate and even eliminate the racist, classist, ageist injustices that urge some people to surrender their newborns at safe havens, relinquishing the right to raise or to have future contact with them.

It is imperative to make visible the injustices of safe haven laws and lift up the voices of those calling to end them. By strategically working within and beyond safe haven antiabortion, pro-adoption discourses, it is possible to expand pregnancy and parenting resources to meet the diverse needs of individuals and communities.

12 Reproductive Justice Has the Blueprint for Post-Roe America, but Are We Ready for It?

TINA VASQUEZ

SisterSong is perhaps the single most formative Reproductive Justice organization in the United States, and its Let's Talk About Sex (LTAS) conference provides a powerful opportunity to connect with and learn from organizers, activists, advocates, health-care providers, and attorneys who create much of the scaffolding the movement relies on. The conference returned in August 2022 for the first time since the pandemic began, and much had changed since the last gathering in Atlanta in 2019. Notably, we no longer have a constitutional right to abortion, according to the Supreme Court's June decision in the *Dobbs* case.

It was an interesting time to gather in Texas for LTAS. Just as attendees poured into Dallas on August 25 ahead of the opening plenary, the state's trigger law went into effect, making it a felony punishable by up to life in prison to provide abortion care outside of very narrow exceptions. Admittedly, I attended the conference for selfish reasons. I was desperate to spend time with people who cared deeply about Reproductive Justice and were actively fighting for abortion rights. I wanted to learn from grassroots organizers and activists and map out future reporting about their work. But I also just wanted to know how it would feel to attend the nation's largest Reproductive

Justice conference at a time when—to use a phrase I repeatedly heard at LTAS—"everything is on fucking fire."

According to the conference app, more than eight hundred people attended LTAS. Outside of one editor, I wasn't able to identify a single other media person attending in-person sessions. Journalism is one of our most powerful tools for culture and narrative shift, and as the media organizer Alicia Bell says, "If we shift culture and narrative, we can shift our material conditions across all the issues we care about." The Supreme Court's decision to overturn *Roe v. Wade* is one of the most important news stories of the year—and certainly an event that will affect the fabric of our country for decades. Each morning as I waited for the hotel elevator to head down to conference sessions, I would stare at the *Dallas Morning News* building from the window, wondering why the mainstream media—and by extension, the larger public—continues to ignore Reproductive Justice. This is true even now that it's abundantly clear that the national pro-choice groups that received millions of dollars in donations and foundation support to defend access through federal courts never seemed fully prepared to actually accomplish this goal.

I think a lot about where we would be if leaders in the Reproductive Justice movement were given the same access and resources. What kind of culture change would be possible if we shifted out of the pro-abortion and antiabortion binary and instead embraced the human rights framework that is the crux of Reproductive Justice, one that accounts for all of the contradictions and nuances of being a person in the world? LTAS provides a space to imagine that world. If you follow the work of SisterSong you know that the organization prioritizes narrative shift work and that you should expect the unexpected. While the conference came with a number of surprises—a panel discussion with actors from "P-Valley" and a very intimate performance from singer and activist Mýa, to name a few—what was perhaps most surprising was LTAS's focus on movement wins.

The conference theme was "Our Blueprint for a Body Revolution," and when SisterSong executive director Monica Simpson greeted the crowd during the kick-off plenary to Beyoncé's "Break My Soul," the message was clear. Any attendees who came to Texas looking to dissect the fall of *Roe* would quickly learn they were at the wrong conference. During one morning plenary, Oriaku Njoku, the new executive director of the National Network of Abortion Funds, shared what was essentially a love letter to abortion funds, describing them as a series of autonomous organizations that provide mutual aid. In other words, they simply provide what communities need. "*Roe* was the floor," Njoku said. "And when the floor is rooted in heteropatriarchy and white supremacy, you have to tear the whole damn house down and build again on land fortified by the reproductive justice framework."

There are plenty of examples from the Reproductive Justice movement of what this can look like in practice. During morning plenaries, Marsha Jones, the executive director of the Black-led Texas Reproductive Justice organization The Afiya Center, which cohosted the conference, broke down how Black Texans have pushed back on reproductive injustice for decades. Rockie Gonzalez, the deputy director of the Austin Justice Coalition, described how the abortion fund movement in Texas went from being predominantly white-led to predominantly BIPOC-led in just a few years. Kimberly Inez McGuire, the executive director of Unite for Reproductive and Gender Equity (URGE), discussed how relentless grassroots organizing led voters in Kansas to reject a constitutional amendment that would have banned abortion—a striking and unexpected win in one of the most conservative states in the country. Kwajelyn Jackson, the first Black executive director of Atlanta's Feminist Women's Health Center, discussed dismantling the white feminism that imbued the nonprofit and working to make Reproductive Justice "tangibly experienced in clinic care."

One of the most moving things at LTAS was one of its most quiet offerings: a conference room transformed into the home of a person who self-managed their abortion. Created by Kimberly Inez McGuire for Abortion On Our Own Terms, the "Stigma Free Zone" was an exhibit that guided attendees through what a self-managed abortion can really be like in a safe, supported, and private space. Children's items littered the entry point to remind us that most people who have abortions are already parents. Strewn about the cozy and welcoming apartment were comfortable clothes, a teapot, a heating pad, and snacks, illustrating all of the things a person would need to feel nourished.

I walked through the space with a small group of women, growing emotional as I took in the details. It would take me a few days to figure out why I was so moved by the display: it was the opposite of the cold and clinical surgical abortion I had at nineteen. I remember feeling herded through the process, just another patient to get through that day. It never occurred to me that I could feel truly cared for while terminating a pregnancy. Natasha Chabria, an attorney with the organization All* Above All, described the space perfectly: "A physical manifestation of reproductive justice."

Even a few minutes at LTAS makes one thing abundantly clear: young women of color—and young Black women *specifically*—fuel the Reproductive Justice movement. Young people from across the country flocked to the conference, excited to learn strategies for talking to their families about sexual and reproductive health and for organizing their communities and college campuses. West Texas's abortion fund, the West Fund, traveled to Dallas with a group of teenagers. One of them told me it was her first time leaving El Paso and that the conference opened up her world. I've attended LTAS three times, long enough to watch young attendees, interns, law students, organizers, and volunteers transform into leaders in the Reproductive Justice movement. In other words, young people are the experts, and we have a lot to learn from them about demanding more and better.

If I learned anything from attending LTAS, it's this: post-*Roe* America is not a lost cause. This is a moment of opportunity. Reproductive Justice has the blueprint for the future we all deserve, but are we finally ready to let this movement lead the way?

13 *Krystale E. Littlejohn Interviews Francine Thompson, the Emma Goldman Clinic, Iowa City*

Krystale E. Littlejohn: *The Emma Goldman Clinic has been central in the fight against assaults on abortion care and Reproductive Justice in Iowa. Can you talk about the clinic's legacy of activism that has shaped how you continue the fight for feminist health care in the wake of* Dobbs?

Francine Thompson: The clinic is no stranger to adversity. The inception of the clinic was around adversity. It started nine months after the *Roe* decision in 1973. The folks that started the clinic were a group of women that attended the university and had been involved in Women's Referral Service at the Women's Resource Center, referring women seeking abortion care to other states. The group that started the clinic wasn't made up of physicians. They weren't business people. They weren't medical people. They weren't lawyers. They were students. And in 1973, they were also women. A woman couldn't even get a bank loan without a signature from her husband at that time. And so that really stalwart group of folks got together, decided they were going to do this, and we have been continuously operating since then.

Krystale: *There have of course been challenges since the inception of the clinic. What are some of the issues that you've been dealing with recently, especially in the wake of* Dobbs?

Francine: A couple things have happened in the state legislature prior to and during the pandemic and prior to *Dobbs* that really impacted the clinic and our staff: the opening up of the six-week ban, the twenty-four-hour certification, and the first passage of the constitutional amendment that proclaimed that abortion was not a guaranteed right in the state of Iowa. All of those things really weighed heavily on staff in the organization and board and on myself as the executive director. I've spent a lot of time trying to assure people that, yeah, some things are going to happen, but here's where we're at. The clinic does more than provide abortions. The clinic is a long-term staple in the community, in the state, and in the nation. We're going to figure out first and foremost how we're going to continue to be here. So we've been having conversations and making preparations for the long-term sustainability of the clinic, whether or not abortion is available in the state of Iowa.

Krystale: *That's a lot of changes. Can you talk about how that's affected things?*

Francine: Now with the twenty-four-hour certification, there are two visits, so everything needs to happen at that first visit. Our time constraints are tighter, whereas before we could allow a lot of slush. Somebody could be two hours late for their surgery and we would still figure out a way to see them, assuming that they really had some challenges and struggles to get there. And we know that they probably did. When our timeframe got a little tighter, we weren't able to accommodate a lot of that. And we tried to be really clear about that upfront, but the result has been that clients are angry. They're angry about all of the restrictions. Why do they have to come back? And so there's a lot of anger that's directed at staff who are really just working hard to comply with the legal requirements, but who also have chosen to do the work because they are compassionate about it and have genuine empathy for the clients that we see. It's challenging and we're working really hard to take care of them.

Krystale: *Absolutely.*

Francine: At the same time that we take care of our clients, we also have some lines that we create for our staff. We're not going to let staff be called names. This isn't about us and we're trying to provide the service. We're really busy, especially with the increase in people coming from out of state, and we're doing the best that we can. And that's a change.

Krystale: *Can you talk about the central goals of the clinic and how the clinic has worked to meet the needs of your clients given restrictions?*

Francine: Our mission's really unchanged from the original mission, which is to provide reproductive health care to marginalized populations. That has always included the LGBTQ population. It's included those who are living on lower incomes, and of course, ethnically marginalized people. So anyone who's experienced challenges to accessing health care. And the challenge for us now is to figure out how we do that amid continuing restrictions. We've just learned and adapted. We're flexible. When any new legislation comes up, we make the changes and we do it. It certainly makes things harder for the people that we see, but we're really nimble.

The advantage to being a small, independent, and only clinic is that we're responsive. We're primarily a service provider and so we have to figure out how we get through this in order to keep delivering services to the folks who need them because the phone doesn't stop ringing because there's twenty-four-hour certification. We think it's a bad law, but we still have to figure out how we're going to see those folks that were scheduled when this new law went into effect. So our primary goal and mission is to continue to provide those reproductive services and to continue to keep as much of our service philosophy and services as we're able to, which gets harder and harder. It's like, how do you value the authority of an individual to determine their destiny, but yet have to comply with the law and notify a parent because of parental notification laws or jump through these other hoops. It's challenging, but our goal is to continue to provide safe, compassionate, reproductive health care for people in the state of Iowa and in addition to those who have been traditionally marginalized.

Krystale: *Absolutely. Related to centering the needs of marginalized people, can you tell us about how the clinic resists coercive practices around birth control that affect marginalized people and others every day?*

Francine: When you start to incorporate a more medical model of care and medical personnel into your delivery of care, the clinical model of care is a bit different and so an abortion procedure might often be viewed as an opportunity for contraception. And it doesn't feel coercive because they're not thinking about power differentials, which is another big thing in feminist health care. When you speak as a physician, you're speaking as an expert and most folks think they should do what the expert says. So we've changed a few things so that we don't allow consenting for contraception on the table. That happens beforehand. It seems like a really simple thing, but it's so important. We're trying to get informed consent, have them have a safe procedure and be compassionate to give them the support that they need during that time. You can't talk to somebody about wanting an IUD and make that decision and have them consent on the table while you're in the course of providing abortion services, because they do see you as an expert and there is a power differential and what does that mean? If they say no, are you going to do the procedure? So that's a key way that we think about meeting patients' needs and resisting coercion in the clinic.

Krystale: *As we're talking, it's making me think about how the clinic's namesake believed in the importance of contextualizing birth control by attending to political, social, and economic forces that contribute to efforts to suppress both information and use. Can you talk about how the larger commitment to political, social, and economic equality shapes the work that you all do at the clinic?*

Francine: The short answer is that we have had to act very fast. We've been very reactive. We're just trying to staff clinics and get people seen. And that's been really challenging and taking up most of our time, energy, and capacity in the last couple years. That's just the lens that we see things through.

Krystale: *Right, and we know that getting care can be difficult for people when they're dealing with others trying to make it harder for them—specifically, people who try to harass or intimidate them. The clinic has a unique approach for using that negative energy to help clients via the Pledge-a-Picketer campaign. Can you talk a little bit about what that is and provide some insight into other ways to be involved for people who are interested in doing more?*

Francine: I wish that I could say that we originated the Pledge-a-Picketer campaign. I think it was originated by either one of the feminist clinics in Washington State or California. But it is really, for 501c organizations that can accept donations, it allows us to get a donation that's related to the number of picketers. So, when people pledge to commit, say a dollar for every picketer, then we send them the total amount of picketers at the end of the month and then they send us a donation for that amount. It's been a program that's been in place for over twenty years and it's been pretty successful because it allows people to feel as though they are involved in fundraising. It also keeps them engaged on a regular basis—they get information each month about what's happening on a regional and national level. It's a real tangible way to feel as though they're helping the clinic and there's other ways to help out as well.

Krystale: *That's great.*

Francine: Most often it is a direct donation to our sustainability fund. We are really trying to look at sustainability in the absence of abortion provision at the clinic. So that means that until the legislature changes in Iowa or on a national level, if *Roe* gets codified perhaps, then we are looking at how are we going to continue to remain open and doing whatever we might be able to do to get us through that two- to four-year period of time where we may not be able to provide abortions. But there are other ways that things like clinic supplies continue to be needed, not in the direct provision of abortion care, but you still need toilet paper and paper towels, and paper. So those are things that folks can do either as a direct donation to the clinic or through Amazon Smile.

We also utilize the energy and capacity of volunteers and we got such an outpouring of volunteers after *Dobbs*. A lot of it was people wanting to give rides and to give practical support. We said, we are not doing that right now because there are a number of organizations that have been doing it and have the capacity. We were able to refer a number of volunteers to those other organizations. But we do have volunteers who come and help us. We do have direct service training opportunities, but it does involve a level of commitment that a lot of folks aren't able to do. So we've got other volunteer opportunities, just about what individuals can do in their own personal lives to speak up and support abortion rights and speak up and acknowledge discrimination and oppression where it occurs with BIPOC and LGBTQ folks. If people do that too, that's also a way of supporting the clinic.

Krystale: *Absolutely. So to wrap up, can you tell us about what you see as the most pressing issue that people should be attuned to moving* *forward to make sure that people have access to the abortion care and birth control that they need and deserve?*

Francine: I think that we have to figure out how to engage the people that we serve and give them information. I've been at the clinic for thirty-five years and we've talked about this at different times. It's important to help people understand that it extends beyond them.

So to give some context, going into midterms, our governor decided that she wanted the Supreme Court to reexamine the six-week ban, which had already been permanently enjoined and had actually passed the time for that reopening. But true to form, because sometimes they have their own rules, they were able to open it back up and the hearing was heard on the six-week ban and a decision will come; they have sixty days. Whichever way the decision goes, it would go back to the Supreme Court, which is now no longer favorable for us. And that could be next year, this time, where we may not have abortion available in the state of Iowa. If the decision is not in our favor at the end of the year and we apply for a temporary injunction until it's heard, and that's denied because of course the same folks that grant the temporary injunction make the decision, then it would be sooner. Whatever amount of grace they would give us after the decision, and they don't have to give us any, we would not be able to provide abortions, or we'd be under the rules of a six-week abortion ban, which we know is pretty close to a total ban.

So I think we need to figure out how to give people a reason to get involved or seek more information. It is helping folks to understand why it's an important issue. We don't want to be coercive, but we have to figure out how to engage folks in their care and act in their own best interests. At some point, it wouldn't even be an issue if everybody who's ever had an abortion had voted to support reproductive freedom in Iowa. I see so many people who just aren't even engaged or don't even know that there's a battle going on. If we had those folks voting, we wouldn't be in the place that we're at. I don't think people know how close they are to not being able to sit in that chair within a couple months in the state of Iowa. So I don't know how to get them engaged, but I think we have to.

Krystale: *Absolutely dire circumstances and it's frightening to see how close people are to losing complete access.*
Francine: Right. And I don't have the answer, but it has global implications so I think it's crucial that we figure it out.

Krystale: *There's no question about it. Thanks so much for all your work and for taking the time to talk with me.*

14 *Sustaining Full-Spectrum Sexual and Reproductive Health Care after* Dobbs

JENNIFER PEPPER, WYNDI ANDERSON, HOLLY CALVASINA, AND MADISON WEBB

[I want to] bring attention to the radical, brilliant, counter-narrative CHOICES represents. And, by that I mean [broadcast this] place and [its] approach that is about bringing things together rather than . . . tearing things apart.[1]

This is what Lynn Paltrow, former executive director of National Advocates for Pregnant Women wrote in an email to CHOICES leadership just a few months before the *Dobbs* decision on June 24, 2022. For almost a decade CHOICES leadership had worked tirelessly to build a full-spectrum sexual and reproductive health-care practice that provided abortion services for those who no longer wanted to be pregnant and provided midwifery-led prenatal and birth services for those who wanted to continue their pregnancies. On August 25, 2022, Tennessee's total abortion ban, with no exceptions for the life of a pregnant person, went into effect, bringing an end to CHOICES' forty-eight-year history of providing abortions in Memphis, Tennessee. It was heartbreaking for patients, staff, and the community.

Nonetheless, CHOICES' commitment to its communities and the full-spectrum model of care remains unwavering.

During the summer of 2021, when the US Supreme Court announced it would hear the *Dobbs* case, CHOICES leadership knew abortion access would be lost in Tennessee within the next year. As in the past, CHOICES consistently responded to increasing attacks on abortion, continuing to care for patients accessing abortion, and *finding a way to continue to serve communities and provide critical health care*. The CHOICES team developed a plan to (1) open a second clinic in Carbondale, Illinois, to continue providing abortion services; and (2) ramp up prenatal care, birth services, and other sexual wellness services in the Memphis clinic.

CHOICES: Center for Reproductive Health is an independent, nonprofit reproductive and sexual health clinic founded in 1974 by Priscilla Chism and fellow feminists in Memphis, in response to the *Roe v. Wade* decision. When other health-care providers in the city chose not to provide abortion, despite *Roe*'s national legalization of the procedure, CHOICES' founders knew pregnant people needed access to abortion and moved boldly forward to provide that care. According to outside experts, "CHOICES' feminist roots and non-profit ethos have fostered a deep commitment to a patient-centered model of care that prioritizes clients and their individual needs."[2] In 2009, CHOICES began to realize its vision of becoming a more comprehensive community health-care provider by expanding the clinic's practice to include HIV testing and prevention, comprehensive family planning, and sexually transmitted infection testing and treatment. A further expansion of services a few years later included an increased focus on LGBTQIA2S + inclusion, including fertility assistance for same-sex couples and gender-affirming care for transgender and nonbinary patients.

Over the years CHOICES' services continued growing and diversifying to meet the needs of its burgeoning patient population. In

2017, CHOICES launched its full-spectrum reproductive and sexual health-care program that includes perinatal care, community birth, abortion services, and a range of inclusive sexual and reproductive health services with an emphasis on serving communities with the least access to care informed by Reproductive Justice and Black feminist thought, and to services led by nurse midwives. In September 2020, CHOICES finished construction on a new facility that included the first freestanding birth center in Memphis.

The *Dobbs* decision underscores the ongoing struggle for Reproductive Justice in the United States. People of color, particularly those in marginalized communities, face disproportionate barriers to accessing comprehensive reproductive health care, including abortion and community birth services. CHOICES envisions a world where sexual and reproductive health care is recognized as an essential human right. All communities deserve access to the full range of reproductive and sexual health-care services, including abortion, midwifery-led prenatal care, community birth, gender-affirming care, and many other critical health-care services. CHOICES' staff centers the most vulnerable and recognizes the community has its own power, promise, and potential to address health concerns. CHOICES' providers work hard to eliminate power hierarchies and understand the importance of acknowledging the patient as the expert of their own life. By taking this approach, CHOICES shifted its paradigm from only abortion rights to all aspects of reproductive freedom, including the right to have children, to not have children, and to have access to all reproductive options.[3] CHOICES understands that the same person needs various sexual and reproductive health-care services at different times in their life. And no one should have to leave their community to meet their basic health needs.

CHOICES' vision for the future uniquely positioned the organization to meet the *Dobbs* decision head on. When the Tennessee state constitution was amended in 2014 to declare that there was no guaranteed right to abortion in the state, CHOICES knew that a future without abortion access was a real threat. Leadership began to prepare for this future. In January 2022, CHOICES moved forward with a bold plan for preserving access to abortion services for patients in hostile states as well as expanding access to other essential reproductive and sexual health services in an area where they are in demand. After careful consideration of geographic location, regional transportation systems and patterns, state laws, and local community dynamics, the decision was made to open a second clinic in Carbondale, Illinois.

Even before *Dobbs,* many people had to leave their communities to access abortion care. *Dobbs* certainly exacerbated this hardship, forcing patients to travel even further to access basic health care. Carbondale is a three- to four-hour drive from Memphis, Nashville, and Louisville, and a stop on the Amtrak railway from New Orleans to Chicago, with stops in Memphis and Jackson, Mississippi. The state of Illinois, in the words of Governor J. B. Pritzker, was set to become a "beacon of hope for [people] who need reproductive health care."[4] According to the *Chicago Tribune,* "nearly 10,000 women traveled from out of state to have an abortion in Illinois in 2020, a roughly 29% increase compared with the previous year, according to the most recent Illinois Department of Public Health data available."[5]

CHOICES leadership made it a priority to involve the local community in the expansion to Carbondale. Working closely with local community leaders, government officials, law enforcement, nonprofits, and community organizers, the clinic's staff sought to understand the needs of the community and how CHOICES could help address them. This approach to community engagement and involvement reflects CHOICES' commitment to respect for the people in the communities they serve. "You come into somebody's house, you need to introduce yourself, break bread with people," Jennifer Pepper, CHOICES' president and CEO, told the *New York Times.*[6] CHOICES' clinic in Carbondale opened in October 2022, becoming the southernmost abortion provider in Illinois.

Although no longer offering abortion services, the CHOICES clinic in Memphis still offers a wide range of critical reproductive and sexual care, including midwifery-led prenatal care and birth in a freestanding birth center and a full range of sexual and reproductive health-care services, including gender-affirming care for transgender and nonbinary individuals. As of the end of 2022, CHOICES' midwifery practice has supported more than 350 births. Despite fitting sociodemographic categories that might define them as "high risk," birthing parents at CHOICES are almost five times *less likely* to have a c-section, and four-and-a-half times less likely to have a preterm birth than other birthing parents in the state of Tennessee.[7] These outcomes reflect the special kind of care CHOICES provides and speak to a future that is possible—a future where sexual and reproductive health care is recognized as an essential human right.

Siloing abortion practices in stand-alone abortion-only clinics outside of the larger health-care system was a bad idea. Abortion is one of many sexual and reproductive health-care services a person will need throughout their lives. CHOICES believes the future of reproductive health care is the full-spectrum sexual and reproductive health center model. This model recognizes the importance of providing a wide range of services, including abortion. In the ongoing struggle for Reproductive Justice in the United States, CHOICES serves as a model for how to work in partnership with communities to provide comprehensive reproductive and sexual health care. The CHOICES model of full-spectrum sexual and reproductive health care represents a hopeful vision for a future where all people have access to the care they need and deserve.

15 A Reproductive Justice Activist in Kentucky

Under Attack, Fighting Back!

MEG SASSE STERN

In 1999, I became a clinic escort. I was eighteen years old, joining a small group of tired volunteers on the sidewalks outside of what would be the only and the last abortion clinic in Kentucky. I was young, but it was clear to me that bodily autonomy was worth protecting. Even though we knew the road ahead was a rocky one, I still could not have imagined that almost twenty-five years later I would be working remotely for Just The Pill, an out-of-state abortion clinic—the only abortion clinics we have now—and applying lessons learned through trial and trauma to new efforts at home in Kentucky, defending trans rights and drag events.

At the same time, if someone had told me then that this is where we would be today, I would have believed them. I am getting ahead of myself, though. As a queer Kentuckian, I know all too well the impacts of stigma and misinformation encircling sexuality in our culture. I know what it's like to need health care and resources that are out of reach. This, even as a person with privilege living in a city with access to a lot of opportunities. I've also stared into the eyes of people who truly believe that queer joy, bodily autonomy, Black and Indigenous power, and sex for pleasure are part of a long list of concepts that deserve to be punished, if not eradicated.

It's not a glamorous role to play. I've been knocked around. I've been called terrible names. I've heard whispers steeped in the most misinformed indoctrination imaginable, which I won't repeat here. It was through interactions like elbows in ribs and trampled feet that I learned the value of *just being with someone* who is enduring the hateful punishment served up on the sidewalk outside of the doctor's office. In those times and spaces I was fully aware that the vitriol swirling around was not about me, or any individuals, *nor* was it rooted in compassion as the perpetrators claimed. This realization laid bare a critical lesson: how to accompany people who wanted nothing to do with a political moment or religious dogma on the way to the doctor. *I could simply walk with them, so they were not alone.*

Prior to the *Dobbs* decision and Kentucky's trigger ban taking effect, I had grown weary from knowing that our "post-*Roe*" reality was quickly becoming more widespread. In 2012, a full decade before the fall of *Roe,* a handful of comrades and I began creating practical support networks to fill the widening gaps in access. We were well aware that *especially* in places where communities are heavily dependent on cars for travel, those who lack resources and support are hit hardest when any health-care need arises. We got to work:

1. We developed systems to screen and train trusted volunteers.
2. We learned how to share up-to-date information such as which hotels near distant clinics were friendly, and which were not.
3. We explored ways to transport people, money, and resources as safely as possible, while powerful forces wanted nothing more than to stop us.

Thanks to practical support and clinic escort communities in pockets all over the United States, we were able to prepare for what many people still believed would never happen.

We have spent years practicing Reproductive Justice values and learning how to practically build community and center the experiences of people most impacted by injustices. This means many abortion providers and access advocates in our networks have become well positioned for this new landscape. It is so much more than driving people to clinics and walking them inside. The larger goal has been to build bridges across communities and coalitions throughout regions. We've organized with labor unions, become legislators, trained in medical schools, marched with movements for social change, and created our own community care and safety infrastructures. Despite the power we embody, we can't prevent the harm that many communities are already facing due to new laws, old laws (sometimes used in new ways), and even the *fear* of laws that may not even be in effect yet.

The ground that we're resisting on has fundamentally changed. While we're adjusting to abortion access without *Roe,* we're also seeing the next steps in the right wing's playbook aimed directly at trans and nonbinary bodies. This pulls back the veil of our descent into fascism even further and demonstrates what James Baldwin named in his 1970 "Open Letter to Angela Davis": they will indeed come for us in the morning, and for you in the night.

The harmful tactics, motivations, and outcomes are the same: public shaming, isolation, gaslighting, medical abuse, criminalization, and death. In many ways our resistance can be the same as well, but here's the catch: we must stop feeding the myth that any attacks on bodily autonomy and the agency to create thriving families in safe communities may not affect us all, because they do. Here are two critical points we must understand:

1. Abortion seekers are not having a political moment; they are accessing pregnancy care.
2. Trans folks are not making a statement when they go to the doctor; they are tending to their needs—which may also be pregnancy care!

I know I don't have all the answers. But two things I know for sure are captured in two of my favorite questions. They help us reassess what we believe about taking care, and I think that work is for everyone:

1. What does it mean to "do no harm" in care provision if providing lifesaving care is outlawed?
2. How can we build our collective "we keep us safe" abilities now that the state is attacking most of us?

Part III   *Strategic Action for Securing Access*

RICKIE SOLINGER

The *Dobbs* decision is the most powerful expression yet of the backlash against reproductive self-determination, and it clarifies how important strategic action will be to the future of Reproductive Justice in the United States. Essays in this part of the book provide a sampling of what strategic action looks like around the country today.

Eesha Pandit, who works with multiple organizations developing activist strategies, emphasizes that one of the truths *Dobbs* clarifies is that "our ability to make choices about our health care, our family formations, our private lives are all one and the same." She points out that when LGBTQIA2S + people live with violence, poverty, various forms of discrimination, lack of health care, and other harsh burdens, they also often face a diminished or lack of abortion access, together with the evisceration of privacy rights. In the time of backlash the slope is slippery, and we stand to lose more than we already have. But we can't be "steered by fear," Pandit argues. Our analysis of what we must accomplish forces us to "move from the periphery" to action.

Virginia Rodino, another strategic activist, uses the refrain "abortion rights is a labor issue," and as such, she urges, we must recognize that an effective response to *Dobbs* relies on the collective activism of workers and other participants in a mass movement for self-determination, expressing "a groundswell of fury" after *Dobbs*. Today, labor leaders and workers are demanding abortion access and full reproductive health care in their contracts and insurance coverage, stronger demands, she argues, than the lukewarm programs of neoliberal politicians more interested in political power than in the fundamental needs of the people.

Keeping in mind Rodino's call, we turn to five mainstream politicians, each of whom has devised strategy to bolster abortion rights and access in the face of *Dobbs*, each occupying political office in a difficult state. Saint Louis mayor Tishaura O. Jones tells a deeply affecting story about her friend and colleague from whom she draws strength and power as she herself develops as a creative, abortion-rights policymaker, in the context of Missouri's increasingly anti-abortion, repressive state government. Assemblywoman Melissa Shusterman of Pennsylvania describes the work she did throughout the state in 2022, in an attempt to fend off the red wave everyone was predicting. She helped find the best Democratic candidates, bolster their campaigns, get out the vote, and assist in registering wins for the party dedicated to protecting abortion rights and access.

Kansas state senator Dinah Sykes writes about her transition from the Republican Party to the Democratic Party soon after she arrived in Kansas, and her participation in the abortion-rights referendum organized not by the Democratic Party but by Kansans for Constitutional Freedom (KCF), a group led by Reproductive Justice advocates and organizations that provide abortions. KCF astounded the country with its overwhelmingly successful campaign affirming abortion rights in that state. Sykes underscores how political consciousness and participation was built by door-knockers and driveway conversations across the state.

Also in Kansas, Suzanne Valdez, Douglas County district attorney, joined the national nonprofit Fair and Just Prosecution, pledging, along with thousands of other prosecutors around the country, not to enforce, in Valdez's case, any Kansas laws enacted to criminalize abortion and reproductive rights. She defines her duty as educating the public about why laws criminalizing abortion providers and their clients will create a public health disaster. Given her position, Valdez explains how she balances her promise to enforce state laws with her right to exercise prosecutorial discretion, prosecuting only in cases that she believes threaten public interests and raise safety concerns.

In Texas, Austin City Council member José "Chito" Vela refused to "abdicate our responsibility"—to address reproductive health-care needs—even in the state that invented laws to punish everyone, including taxi drivers, who facilitates any part of reproductive self-determination. Vela worked with a variety of people in the capital city to craft a resolution, the GRACE Act (Guarding the Right to Abortion Care for Everyone), to protect abortion access in Austin. He ended up getting requests for information from similarly positioned politicians and policymakers around the country who want to replicate this program.

In the struggle to protect abortion access in antiabortion states, prosecutors focus largely on refraining from prosecuting medical providers and their clients. Cynthia Gutierrez, an abortion doula, describes her work in the sector of abortion provision that decenters providers and focuses on individuals pursuing self-managed abortion, using medication. Gutierrez describes the nature of her work as an abortion doula—and a storyteller—helping to create "sacred space" that supports people having abortions to be their "authentic selves" in this setting.

Next, amplifying the domain of medication abortion, the interview with women who run Plan C, an online information hub helping people learn how to end an early pregnancy by accessing abortion pills, focuses on self-help as a key strategic response to *Dobbs*. Elisa Wells and Amy Merrill describe the founding of Plan C; how the founders used the work of feminists in other countries as models; and the group's current plans to make abortion pills as widely available in this country as possible, destigmatizing and normalizing pregnancy termination.

Finally, Carly Thomsen's essay about the pedagogical, political, and community-building virtues of making art and presenting exhibition brings our concept of "strategic action" into new territory. At Middlebury College, Thomsen created a Public Feminism Lab in which students read texts that would help them think about crisis pregnancy centers. Then the group met to discuss those readings and to reimagine the material as art. Thomsen's essay considers the questions and range of resources that animated students' work and the outstanding reception of the exhibition across campus and community. This piece illuminates what Thomsen calls "the galvanizing nature of art" and "its use for reproductive justice activism work."

16 Reproductive Justice and the Fight for Queer Liberation

What the *Dobbs* Ruling Illuminates

EESHA PANDIT

This story is a familiar one: movements rise up in the face of injustice, we organize, we push, we win. Then comes the backlash.

Backlash is not an entirely straightforward phenomenon; it comes from opponents and allies alike. Those who never wanted us to win, or those who wanted us to win a little less. Activists for reproductive rights have seen a nearly five-decade-long bout with backlash, watching the victory of securing legal access to abortion be chipped away minute by minute, year by year. Those of us who live at multiple intersections, and face multiple systems of oppressive force, know exactly how this happens. Our lives are shaped by the smallest textures of the laws that govern them. We know that the backlash is never in only one arena.

We have known, for these same five decades that Reproductive Justice and queer liberation are inextricable. Not merely the way people describe them as sides of a coin, but in fact as the same side of the same coin. Because so many of us, across the spectrum of gender and sexuality, need access to safe abortion care. Because so many of us are parents, or hope to be. Because so many of us live in parts of this country where our families are being separated, where our very humanity is on the ballot.

On June 24, 2022, the United States Supreme Court struck down *Roe v. Wade* and *Planned Parenthood v. Casey* by issuing the *Dobbs v. Jackson Women's Health Organization* decision, which found that there is no right to abortion protected by the federal Constitution. We, who live at some of these intersections, knew that it was not, it was never merely about the right to abortion access. All our rights are linchpins in the fight for bodily autonomy, as the Court made clear in both the opinions and the dissents.

We do not live single-issue lives, a lesson visionary lesbian poet and theorist Audre Lorde taught us. Our wins are aligned, as are our losses. Our fights are connected, and the opposition remains united against us all. The most important lesson that backlash can teach us has very little to do with legislative policy and the courts: it is that we must understand the historical legacies that shape our current institutions, and with that understanding, we can face the fact that the solution to injustice will never be found singularly in our legal system and the courts. Our ability to make choices about our health care, our family formations, our private lives are all one and the same.

Activists for LGBTQIA2S+ rights knew that the *Dobbs* ruling held implications that we had been tracking and fighting for decades, for all our rights, collectively. Lack of abortion access impacts LGBTQIA2S+ people directly. Many LGBTQIA2S+ people—specifically queer cisgender women, nonbinary people, and transgender men—have had abortions. And lesbian, bisexual, and queer cisgender women are statistically more likely to have had them than cisgender heterosexual women. That is because people in these groups are more likely to suffer systemic harm and neglect like discrimination, poverty, lack of health care, limited counseling on contraception, and incomplete or inadequate sex education.[1]

Many of us live with violence or its constant threat. LGBTQIA2S+ people often experience domestic violence and become pregnant after being raped. For every one survivor in this situation who is a cisgender heterosexual woman, there are ten LGBTQIA2S+ survivors.[2] Notably, 36 percent of transgender people who have been pregnant considered trying to end pregnancy by themselves "without clinical supervision," and almost one-fifth of them went through with an attempt. Not feeling safe in their homes or relationships while also fearing discrimination at the hands of medical providers can lead pregnant trans people to consider self-managing their abortions.[3] While self-managing an abortion can be an effective and safe option for many, it should be a choice that is made intentionally and with support, not because clinical care is unavailable or unsafe. Clearly, even with *Roe* in place, safe, comprehensive, reproductive health care was not available to everyone. Now that the protections of *Roe* are wiped away, these same communities will face even more difficulty in getting the reproductive health care they need.

The *Dobbs* ruling threatens to eviscerate the legal right to privacy, upon which so many of our liberties are based. The right to privacy serves as the bedrock for abortion rights, same-sex sexual intimacy, and same-sex marriage. For nearly fifty years the right to privacy has been our safeguard, allowing many of us autonomy over the most personal life choices. However, the Supreme Court ruled in *Dobbs* that the Fourteenth Amendment's substantive due process protection of liberty does not include a federal right to abortion. The Fourteenth Amendment was always a precarious place to locate all these fundamental rights, as many LGBTQIA2S+ activists have argued. We find ourselves in the position of being far too reliant on state-sanctioned rights at a time when all our social institutions are under attack from extremist forces both inside and outside the government. In addition to abortion rights, marriage rights, and the right to have consensual sex, there are other vital parts of the human experience that are at stake. In his concurring opinion on *Dobbs,* Justice Clarence Thomas wrote that the court should reconsider precedents set in cases that established access to contraception and same-sex marriage as federally protected rights.

As the precarity of our right to privacy has shown us, the slope was always slippery. As the conservative justices on the Supreme Court have indicated, and as the politicians who put them there have said outright: overturning *Roe* was always the goal. *Dobbs,* then, is not a dramatic outlier. Instead, it is a mirror of where we are now. Where many communities have been for decades, at the mercy of historically racist, sexist, xenophobic, and homophobic institutions to secure our personal and collective freedoms. The foundation upon which our rights were granted was never as strong as some thought it was. Now we see the fault lines—the weaknesses—clearly. And it is time to shore them up. We must build out our toolkit for justice. The law alone cannot get us where we seek to go. Although Congress recently passed the Respect for Marriage Act, that bill does not ensure that all people in the United States can be married to whomever they chose. It merely ensures that if you can be legally married in a state, or if you are already married, that your marriage is protected, for now.

The decades-long targeted attack on transgender children should have told us all everything we needed to know about what was coming, and what is at stake. Anyone who cares about bodily autonomy must move from the periphery, unequivocally joining the fight to protect and defend trans kids and adults from criminalization and harm. Transgender young people, parents, and communities represent possibility, power, and beauty. They have always borne the brunt because the right has made them a key target for control. In our feminist communities, and in many mainstream LGBTQIA2S+ spaces, we have turned away from the right to gender expansiveness as self-determination, and trans liberation, thinking that this was not our fight, or that even if it was, it would inspire too much backlash.

The backlash is never about us, as we are learning, it is inevitable. Our movements cannot be steered by fear of the inevitable but by a clear-eyed confrontation and acknowledgment that our freedoms are not merely interconnected—they are inextricable.

17 Workers' Role in Defending Abortion Rights

VIRGINIA RODINO

Abortion rights are a labor issue. Abortion is not a Republican versus Democrat issue. It is not something that is going to be solved through elections of political candidates.

Access to safe abortions allows girls and women to stay in school or university, remain or enter the workforce, and have choice in their career paths. Participation in the workforce and economic security is inextricably linked to greater access to reproductive health care, which includes the right to abortion. Without that right, girls, women, and people who can become pregnant may no longer have bodily autonomy. The right to control our bodies is tied to the right to control our labor. As Teamsters Local 117 vice president and legislative director Brenda Wiest commented: "Every woman in our country will be impacted in some way with low-paid working women bearing the brunt of it . . . the impacts of the decision will be felt in almost every worksite across the country. . . . Earnings, retirement, promotions, healthcare, vacation, sick leave—these all are covered by our Union contracts. The decision whether and when to have a child has a tremendous impact on a working family's earnings, retirement, healthcare, and leave."[1]

More than 60 percent of people in the United States support abortion rights. But the ineffectualness of the people's political representatives, Democrats and politicians in general, in protecting our basic rights signals how we need to build mass movements to maintain, protect, and struggle for our rights and freedoms. Workers and their institutions and organizations are needed to overcome the inability of electoral politics to protect their health and well-being. In fact, it is the neoliberal politics of the Democrats that allows for women to be pushed into poverty without an ability to access abortion and reproductive care. The corporate party absorbs, neuters, and deradicalizes movements in an effort to build a larger voting base, not to create the change we need to see.

It is important to recall how abortion rights were won in the first place, emerging from a broader political movement for women's rights. Safe and legal access to abortion rights was one of the central demands of the women's liberation movements in the United States and other countries in the 1960s and 1970s. Activists prioritized both practical support—for example, providing people places to stay during their abortions and money for travel and medical care—and demands for legislative change. Three years before *Roe v. Wade,* the National Organization for Women organized fifty thousand people in the streets of New York in a Women's Strike for Equality. The marchers' demands combined labor issues and reproductive autonomy: equal work opportunities, childcare, and free abortion upon demand.

Today women's marches can still mobilize large numbers of people to demonstrate against sexism and misogyny. Five million people marched against Trump's inauguration in January 2017; defending reproductive rights was a central theme. Our reproductive rights were created from a groundswell of fury, and that is what we must build upon today to beat back these attacks. In fact, we can see this groundswell on the rise. About four hundred workers at twenty-eight reproductive health clinics in five states in the Midwest—Iowa, Minnesota, Nebraska, North Dakota, and South Dakota—announced in late May 2022 their intent to unionize with SEIU Healthcare Minnesota and Iowa. About two hundred workers at Planned Parenthood in Massachusetts are also seeking to unionize with 1199 SEIU. Labor unions representing more than 220,000 Massachusetts workers joined a statewide effort to support abortion rights in the state. The News-Guild-CWA is preparing for collective action to strengthen their bargaining agreements, and Vox Media Union announced that its collective bargaining agreement includes a commitment from management to create a policy that guarantees abortion access, including a $1,500 stipend to travel if care is not available within one hundred miles.

Other uses of worker power to strengthen access to abortion include such ideas as negotiating a travel stipend plus additional time off to allow workers to use the stipend. Union members covered by multistate health-care plans can push for "reciprocal abortion coverage" that allows members in states where abortions are illegal to receive covered care where the procedure is allowed, with the home plan footing the cost. Union release time can help members access abortion care, including transportation or childcare services. And health-care trusts can be written to guarantee abortion coverage. Abortion rights are workers' rights. The right to control our bodies is part of an ancient battle to control workers' labor. This attack on reproductive freedom is part of an ongoing class war. The Coalition of Labor Union Women of the AFL-CIO and the country's four largest unions as well as other unions joined friend-of-the-court briefs on the side of the Jackson, Mississippi Women's Health Organization, favoring freedom of reproductive choice and in opposition to Mississippi's fifteen-week abortion ban.

When the ban was upheld by the Supreme Court, unions spoke out, and workers began to take action. International president of the Association of Flight Attendants-CWA, AFL-CIO, Sara Nelson said,

Choice and self-determination are at the foundation of why we formed our union seventy-five years ago. In the earliest days of commercial aviation, we were allowed few choices in the workplace. Every part of our bodies and our lives were dictated by management. Airlines only hired white, single, childless women under age thirty-two who met specific height, weight, and male defined appearance standards. Even if you met those "standards," getting pregnant, having a baby, choosing to marry or gaining a few pounds meant giving up your job and handing in your wings. Our first demands as a union were seniority-based scheduling, to stop managers from using schedules to coerce us to choose between sexual exploitation and earning a living.[2]

National Nurses Union copresident Jean Ross noted that the takedown of *Roe v. Wade* "should be viewed as part of the broader far-right assault on gender-affirming health rights in this country, including the laws targeting trans youth and their families, attacks on LBGTQ individuals, and homophobic bans on the word 'gay' in education."[3] AFL-CIO president Liz Shuler wrote that "access to health care without fear and intimidation is every person's right. We must be able to control our own bodies—which has a direct impact on economic justice and the ability of working people to make a better life for themselves and their families."[4]

Service Employees International Union president Mary Kay Henry said, "Ultimately, protecting Roe is about protecting women's fundamental right to control our bodies and our destinies."

Workers are bargaining for abortion access in their contracts and demanding health-care coverage by their insurance carriers. Unions can use their legal resources to defend members who are sued or prosecuted for performing or assisting someone in getting an abortion. Health-care workers can demand to bargain a wider scope to protect their medical judgment.

Union members have been joining protests and rallies across the country since May 2022, showing up in opposition to the attacks against reproductive justice.

This fight is about workers' rights, including our right to make decisions about our health, body and sexual life. The way workers can win the fight is to join together to resist and wrest control of our lives out of the hands of corporations, right-wing judges and politicians. We can only do this as a mass movement. Building this movement is the task before us. The only way to win true liberation for women, with free access to abortion and other reproductive rights, is to fight back against a system built on exploitation and oppression. And to win this fight we must join together. A successful movement for change cannot be built in isolation.

There is much opportunity to build national and international alliances over this issue, and to build alliances with other movements, such as the gay liberation and LGBTQIA2S+ rights movements. We saw these coalitions naturally forming in Pride and other demonstrations in the United States and elsewhere.

It is up to us, as workers, to use our political arguments to get union members mobilized and branches involved in the struggle, passing resolutions that commit resources. We cannot let our anger be dissolved into arguments about which politicians to vote for. We can only win back our rights and freedoms as a mass movement. Building that movement is the task before us as organized labor in the United States.

18 *Keeping the Faith in Missouri*

MAYOR TISHAURA O. JONES

In the City of Saint Louis, decades of disinvestment, white flight, and discriminatory government policies left an entire half of the city to fend for itself. In turn, we experience ever-growing disparities in generational wealth, job access, income, and health care—all of which hit Black and Brown women hardest. As a blue city in a red state, Saint Louis's problems are perpetuated by an overwhelmingly white, male, and Republican legislature in the State of Missouri. Our region is often at the mercy of state leadership chomping at the bit for any opportunity to stall attempts at progress, whether it's to preempt our own gun safety measures, reverse our city's minimum wage increase, or shut down what was the only remaining abortion clinic in the entire state for many years.

I was born and raised in North Saint Louis. Growing up, I witnessed the effects of failed policies from city and state leaders. Accessible transportation, affordable childcare, and even healthy food options increasingly became scarce. Although *Roe v. Wade* was in effect and abortion the law of the land, the ability to make our own health-care and family-planning decisions remained a struggle for women of color. I'll admit, I was lucky. I had a family and community that refused to let me fail, which was evident when I decided to run for office just months after becoming a new single mother to my son,

Aden. They pulled out all the stops to ensure that I had the childcare I needed to be successful as I launched my career in politics as a state representative. It was because of them, and Aden, that I wanted everyone to have the same level of support that I did.

Fast forward to October of 2015. Aden had just turned seven years old, I decided not to run for another term in the legislature and was continuing my career in public service, serving my first term as the first Black woman elected as treasurer for the City of Saint Louis. That was when I met Cora Faith Walker. We were invited to participate in a bipartisan women's group, and as usual, we were the only Black women in the room. I remember thinking, "Who is this sharp young lady?" I was immediately drawn to her like a moth to a flame. I was impressed by her class, her quick wit, and her beautiful smile that seemed to light up the room. She had a fire in her, ignited by a lifetime of loved ones whose distrust and inadequate access to health care had left them behind and struggling. Through her upbringing, she witnessed many of the same struggles among Black women as I did, channeling her frustrations into a master's in public health and a law degree, a career as a health-care advocate to combat these disparities, and eventually a successful run for the Missouri House in 2016.

Cora's election came only two years after the murder of Michael Brown, and the subsequent uprisings in Ferguson, in what was now her district. By year's end, both Donald Trump and now-former Missouri governor Eric Greitens would be elected to office, and Cora would be fighting against the backlash for credibly accusing one of her colleagues (who shall remain unnamed) of sexual assault. Despite the legislature becoming increasingly more radicalized against protecting women's bodies, Cora stood her ground even when nobody believed her. She made it clear at every opportunity that reproductive health care neither started nor ended with abortion, and she never backed down from her advocacy for a full spectrum of reproductive health care that spanned the lifetime of women and their families. She and I remained united by our mutual familiarity with the lengths our Republican colleagues in the Missouri legislature were willing to go as they halted any reasonable effort to protect sexual assault survivors, implement tax credits for contraception and donations to diaper banks, or to fund the Children's Health Insurance Plan.

It was during this time that we started our "Woo-sah Wednesdays." We would call each other early in the morning, gossip, laugh, and motivate each other to push through another week as Black women in public service. We'd end each call with a meditation: "Woo-sah." In 2019, Cora's passion carried her into the position of policy director for neighboring Saint Louis County, where she found better opportunities to fight to protect our right to bodily autonomy as the legislature stripped it away. Even when COVID-19 hit the Saint Louis region and vaccines hadn't even become available, Cora championed and won a statewide ballot initiative to expand Medicaid in Missouri, centering the needs of Black, Brown, and poor mothers and families whose health outcomes would be most impacted by the expansion. And almost immediately Cora pivoted to helping me secure my election as the first Black woman elected mayor of the City of Saint Louis in April of 2021.

Now both government executives and recovering legislators, our Wednesday check-ins continued. My first year went by so quickly, but she and I always made time for one another. We even traveled to Jamaica with a small group of friends to celebrate my fiftieth birthday. Then suddenly on March 11, the morning after celebrating my birthday, Cora lost her life to heart failure. The response that followed was all too familiar. Speculation swirled. Rumors, false information, and speculation dominated the local media. It made her transition so much more difficult to accept, knowing she was getting the same treatment as she did when she called out her abuser just five years before, or when any woman dares to report her abuse and seek support. All the vitriol was exactly what she had fought against throughout her short but highly accomplished career.

The day the *Dobbs* decision dropped, I wished she was there with us at that moment. She would have been mad as hell, just like I was. Missouri was the first state in the country whose trigger laws went into effect, immediately banning abortion procedures statewide, and the first to openly and brazenly celebrate it. At that moment I channeled Cora as if she was on the other end of the phone . . .

Woo-sah

Saint Louis also had a plan that day though. Alderwoman Annie Rice introduced a bill to leverage funds from President Biden's American Rescue Plan Act for a $1.5 million Reproductive Equity Fund, offering support for postpartum recovery, lactation help, doula access, and providing abortion access through logistical support. It was a culmination of the work of the community Cora worked so hard to build—a coalition of advocates, medical experts, and many others who knew we needed to be prepared for the inevitable. Within a few weeks I signed this historic legislation. The ink from my signature was barely dry on the legislation before our attorney general filed suit to stop this bill. This felt like the same pattern all over again—all the work and fight that went into addressing the broad spectrum of health care that disproportionately impacts Black women was reduced to another political "gotcha" while our families continue to do more with less.

Woo-sah

As of this writing, we remain in litigation over these funds, but our efforts to fight for Saint Louis families have not stopped. In Saint Louis we continue to rally the unprecedented federal resources at our disposal to tackle health disparities and protect our youth. Across the river in Illinois, our partners with Planned Parenthood have taken their first mobile abortion clinic on the road to ease access to their services from neighboring states like Missouri, and despite increased traffic continue to welcome abortion seekers across state lines to get the procedures they need. No matter which side of the river folks live on, Saint Louis will continue to do everything in our power under the law to reverse the health disparities that have plagued our communities for decades.

Some days it feels like the fight will never end. In a deeply anti-choice state like Missouri we celebrate the small victories as a reminder that we can and will do more and keep advocating for the people who need it most. It was fighters like Cora who always carried the torch to the next fight, even after her transition. While some things change and new challenges arise, the more I recognize that many things remain the same. And yet we keep pushing because that's what she would have done. We carry her words with us everywhere we go:

> Is it true?
> Is it good?
> Is it kind?
> Is it useful?
> Is it necessary?
> If not, then feel free to keep it to yourself. We've got work to do.

19 *Organizing in Pennsylvania*

MELISSA SHUSTERMAN, WITH
JENNIFER L. BROWN

I was first elected to the Pennsylvania General Assembly in 2018. That year voters swept many incumbent Republicans out of office and a historic number of women ran for the first time and succeeded. Women's marches spread across the world, and in Pennsylvania women were beginning to see the results of their collective strength at the polls. While, in time, the pink hats may have been relegated to the closet, the shocking Supreme Court decision to overturn *Roe v. Wade* reactivated women and drove them to the polls to protect their reproductive freedoms. As a female, Democratic legislator who was involved in House races across the state, I saw how this denial of women's rights reshaped voter opinion during the 2022 midterms.

In the lead-up to the 2022 midterms, political analysts were certain a "red wave" would wipe out the Democrats' 2020 electoral gains. This was a plausible narrative since midterm elections have historically been unkind to the incumbent party, and President Biden continued to suffer from lackluster polling despite quietly racking up wins for Democratic policies. Ratings leader Fox News set the political discourse, hammering home doomsday talking points about inflation, gas prices, and crime, while most mainstream media relentlessly followed suit, burying policy victories like the American Rescue Plan, the CHIPS and Science Act, and historically low unemployment that would improve the lives of Americans and bolster our economy. However, the biggest issue of 2022—one certain to change the political landscape and fortunes of Democrats—was largely ignored by the media and political pundits.

On May 2, 2022, Supreme Court Justice Samuel Alito's draft opinion for the *Dobbs v. Jackson Women's Health Organization* case was leaked. In late June the Court's 6–3 ruling overturned *Roe v. Wade,* canceling the constitutional right to an abortion and causing a seismic shift in the political landscape.

Conservatives had finally made good on decades of threats to radically restrict abortion, and it was clear they were not going to stop at overturning *Roe.* In many states trigger laws, poised to ban abortion if *Roe* was overturned, immediately went into effect. In other states Republican-controlled legislatures rushed to enact harsh measures denying women the freedom to make their own choices about their bodies. Pennsylvania was no exception. Republicans in the Pennsylvania General Assembly moved forward with SB106, a veto-proof constitutional amendment that would make any activities supporting abortion illegal. Enacting an amendment to the state constitution is intentionally a multilayered process; SB106 would need to pass in two consecutive legislative sessions, then a referendum would be put up to Pennsylvania voters. The resoundingly pro-abortion results of similar referenda in other conservative states like Kansas and Kentucky should have been instructive for Pennsylvania Republicans, but the majority party proceeded with their restrictive plans.

The 2022 Pennsylvania midterm upset was the culmination of several elements carefully falling into place at precisely the right time. The immediate need to protect the reproductive freedoms of pregnant people was the ultimate catalyst, but the impact of the upset was strengthened by years of political groundwork. Following the 2020 Census, the Pennsylvania Reapportionment Commission members, which included Democratic Senate Leader Jay Costa and

Democratic House Leader Joanna McClinton, understood the importance of ungerrymandering our districts to ensure fair elections. For decades Republicans guaranteed easy victories simply by drawing the lines and diminishing the voting power of minority communities. The Census revealed a declining rural population in Pennsylvania, while our urban centers experienced substantial growth. This growth was most notable among our state's population of color in southeastern Pennsylvania, an area and demographic that favored Democratic policies. I did my part by giving a platform to the nonpartisan advocacy group Fair Districts PA and their efforts to enact competitive electoral maps and equal representation in Harrisburg.

Watchdog groups, like the Princeton Gerrymandering Project, gave the new Pennsylvania maps high ratings for fairness. Though the maps continued to give Republican candidates an edge, they also created greater representation for minority communities and shifted voting power from depopulated rural areas. The Democratic House Campaign Committee saw polling in the wake of the *Dobbs* decision and seized the opportunity to expand voter participation. Canvassing efforts started immediately after the May primary when traditionally this level of organizing would not have started until midsummer. Knocking on doors earlier allowed Democrats to register and mobilize more voters who were fiercely motivated to protect abortion rights. County Democratic organizations improved upon their solid 2020 presidential mail campaigns by sending multiple rounds of reminders to apply for mail-in ballot applications and even the ballot applications themselves.

Voters were already fired up about the issues; now the Democratic Party had to deliver candidates worthy of their support. In my role with the Democratic caucus, I traveled the Commonwealth recruiting passionate candidates and advising their campaigns. It was an honor to help mentor candidates, many of whom had never run for office before but were driven to improve their communities. Even though SB421 eliminated straight-party voting in Pennsylvania, Democrats were fortunate to have strong top-of-ticket candidates with name recognition and popular support. Governor-elect Josh Shapiro spent his career building a strong political network throughout Pennsylvania. First, as commissioner in suburban powerhouse Montgomery County and then gaining recognition nationally by winning several high-profile political and consumer-protection lawsuits on behalf of Pennsylvanians. US Senator-elect John Fetterman's everyman appeal resonated with blue-collar workers and white-collar progressives. In addition, both candidates employed Gen Z communications teams that devastated their opponents with a native understanding of social media; their witty snark positioned their candidates as relatable to younger voters burdened by debt and economic uncertainty.

Meanwhile, Republicans chose to ride ex-president Trump's coattails by embracing his endorsed candidates (no matter how unfit for office). Sean Parnell, the original GOP US Senate frontrunner, was forced to drop out amid domestic violence charges and even then, reluctantly. With no other serious contenders left in a rather shallow bullpen, Republicans pinched their noses and shifted support to New Jersey transplant, Dr. Oz. In the race for governor, Republicans doubled down on extremism with Doug Mastriano, who openly embraced Christian nationalism, antisemitism, and a total abortion ban without exceptions.

Overturning *Roe v. Wade* and pushing for abortion bans and greater restrictions at the state level was a major miscalculation for the Republican Party. The writing was on the wall for anyone willing to pay attention. By September, 65 percent of voters felt overturning *Roe* was a "major loss of rights," and more than 50 percent said the Supreme Court's decision strengthened their motivation to vote, a significant increase from the May polls, before *Dobbs*, that showed 37 percent of voters so motivated.[1] Among Black women under age fifty, that number jumps to a whopping 61 percent; likewise, 58 percent of young Hispanic women rushed to the polls to protect their reproductive rights.[2] The GOP clearly opened Pandora's box and unleashed a wave of anger that transcended demographics. Poor neighborhood or wealthy suburb, white or Black, it did not matter. Access to abortion care affects all women—our mothers, our sisters, our daughters, our cousins, and our partners. This election proved that abortion is a deeply personal choice that should be left between a pregnant person and their doctor, and legislators should have no say in these healthcare decisions.

Democrats also deserve credit because they put together a winning strategy. Moving forward, extending our wins, Democrats need to identify universal issues that have broad mainstream support and champion them: health care, parental leave, commonsense gun laws, and marijuana legalization, to name a few. Democrats must also prevent their own ideological creep to the right in vain attempts to appease the radical right. Also, we must seek new, energetic faces to lead our party. Young voters have demonstrated that they are here and they will be heard. Lastly, I am thankful that my constituents continue to put their faith in me as a legislator. They reelected me to safeguard their freedoms, not limit them. They have my promise always to be fighting for them.

20 *Protecting Abortion in the Heartland*

STATE SENATOR DINAH SYKES

Kansas has a particularly violent history when it comes to antiabortion extremism. In 1991 the Summer of Mercy in Wichita radicalized hundreds of antiabortion zealots and fostered a community for them to build long-term political power. Dr. George Tiller, the state's most well-known abortion provider, was shot in both arms by these extremists. He was later assassinated in his church.

I moved to Kansas just as the rhetoric around abortion reached this deadly crescendo. And when I ultimately decided to run for public office in 2016, I knew that the Republican Party to which I belonged would be hostile toward my position on the issue. Like countless Kansans, I understand that abortion is deeply personal, can zigzag the moral spectrum, and must not be politicized. Abortion is health care, it is necessary, and ensuring its availability is critical to fully trusting and caring for our neighbors. Kansans for Life, one of the most powerful special interest groups in Kansas politics, disagrees. Being a moderate Republican in Kansas is not unusual. Being one in the Kansas Legislature is next to impossible. Ultraconservative leadership ensures that your policy priorities are leveraged against votes for deeply regressive and unpopular bills that harm your constituents but benefit campaign benefactors. Special interest groups threaten and bully independent thinkers who won't toe the party line, pledging to primary legislators who prioritize their communities over conservative hegemony. But I wasn't sent to Topeka by ultraconservative leadership, and I certainly was never a favorite of those powerful special interest groups.

Two years into my first term, my friend and colleague from across the aisle, Laura Kelly, decided to run against Kris Kobach—one of our state's most racist, xenophobic, and unabashedly antiabortion sons— for governor. My support for her candidacy finally pushed me to change parties, though I had largely voted with the Democrats since the day I was sworn in. When I joined the Democratic caucus, I finally found my political home—a group of people who approach issues facing our state with different perspectives, but with a foundation of strong values. It is with this group, and the few remaining moderate Republicans, that we defeated the first iteration of the "Value Them Both" constitutional amendment during the 2020 legislative session. This amendment was spearheaded by the Value Them Both coalition, made up of Kansans for Life, the evangelical Family Policy Alliance, and the Archdiocese of Kansas. The amendment was introduced in response to the 2019 Kansas Supreme Court decision in *Hodes and Nauser v. Schmidt*, which found that the Kansas Constitution—*not, notably, the US Constitution*—affirmed a right to personal autonomy. This fundamental right includes the right to abortion.

The Value Them Both coalition responded swiftly the next legislative session, with amendment language at the ready, as well as slick purple branding of a woman holding a child, made in the shape of a heart. Together with legislative leadership, the coalition ensured that any major legislative priorities—including a compromise on Medicaid expansion, which would have provided access to health care to more than 150,000 vulnerable Kansans—remained contingent on the amendment's passage. When it was defeated, the remaining moderate Republicans were eviscerated during the August 2020 primary. That November, Kansans failed to elect enough Democrats to the legislature to break the Republican supermajority. And so in the first month of the 2021 legislative session, the antiabortion constitutional amendment passed both chambers of the legislature with its required two-thirds majorities.

Amendments to the language, either to moderate its impact or to enfranchise Kansas voters, were considered "poison pills" by the antiabortion lobby. The confusing language explicitly provided a path to a total ban on abortion:

> Because Kansans value both women and children, the constitution of the state of Kansas does not require government funding of abortion and does not create or secure a right to abortion. To the extent permitted by the constitution of the United States, the people, through their elected state representatives and state senators, may pass laws regarding abortion, including, but not limited to, laws that account for circumstances of pregnancy resulting from rape or incest, or circumstances of necessity to save the life of the mother.

During the hours of debate in both the Senate and the House, female Republican legislators led the charge, claiming that the legislature would never yield the power to ban abortion they were demanding with this change to our constitution. Their male counterparts more than once stood up to say that they in fact would.

The constitutional amendment was placed on the August 2, 2022, primary ballot. In Kansas primaries are closed elections, meaning voters must vote the ballot for the party with which they are affiliated. When registration books closed in the summer of 2022, the statewide party breakdown was 26 percent Democratic, 44 percent Republican, and 29 percent Unaffiliated/Independent. Kansas does not have ballot measures, Democrats traditionally have uncompetitive primaries, and Unaffiliated voters have very little to vote on, if anything at all. To the Value Them Both coalition, depressed turnout typical of

August elections was the path to victory. This was the challenge facing Kansans for Constitutional Freedom, a 501(c)4 formed by Planned Parenthood Great Plains, the ACLU of Kansas, Trust Women (the Wichita clinic and advocacy group founded by the late Dr. Tiller), Unite for Reproductive and Gender Equity (URGE), and the Kansas Values Institute. These organizations had worked in collaboration for years in the fight against anti-choice efforts in the Legislature. Their mandate was now to develop, fund, and run a campaign that had never been attempted before in our state.

It is notable to me—a leader of a party that claims choice as a signature issue despite perennial tensions around abortion as a litmus test for political candidates—that this campaign was *not* spearheaded by the Democratic Party. This frustrated many Democratic activists in the ramp-up to the election, and party leaders have certainly taken credit for and built on the work Kansans for Constitutional Freedom and other grassroots groups did during the campaign. But that work always should have been led by Reproductive Justice advocates and organizations that provide abortions. And at a time where our country is so polarized and vitriol toward members of the other party is rampant, it was critical that Kansans were approached not from the left or the right, but rather from an organization that would give them permission to vote their conscience.

Kansans for Constitutional Freedom invested heavily in research to guide their campaign strategy and messaging, allowing them to plan for the electorate they expected while building the electorate they wanted. From polls, online journals, and focus groups, three themes emerged: the amendment was another government mandate threatening Kansans' freedom and rights; the true consequence of the amendment was a total ban on abortion, without exceptions; and Kansans support our neighbors' decisions in highly personal situations, regardless of our own beliefs. These messages would shape the nearly $10 million Kansans for Constitutional Freedom spent on television, radio, digital, and direct mail communications in the weeks leading up to August 2.

This research also created a framework for the interactions Kansans for Constitutional Freedom volunteers like myself had with voters at the doors—as well as conversations Kansans had with one another around dinner tables, at book clubs, and in grocery store parking lots. As someone who's knocked thousands of doors in my area, I'm no stranger to hard conversations in driveways and at doorsteps. What shocked me this summer was the level of attention Kansans had to the election, especially after the US Supreme Court's ruling in *Dobbs v. Jackson Women's Health Organization* in June overturning *Roe v. Wade*. Nearly every voter I talked with, regardless of political affiliation or voting history, knew the stakes, knew their position, and had a plan to vote.

It was difficult to square the energy and passion I found at the doors with the apprehension that seeps into my brain every election in Kansas. We are a commonsense state, but we take people at their word and are willing to give our political leaders the benefit of the doubt—to a fault. *The only public poll,* released in late July, showed the amendment passing by a vote of 47 percent in favor to 43 percent opposed. Internal polling conducted by Kansans for Constitutional Freedom showed a similarly tight race; the final tracking poll had the amendment failing by a vote of 47 percent to 50 percent.

In the weeks leading up to the election, I joined similarly anxious volunteers and Democratic leaders in the scorching Kansas heat as often as I could, as much to persuade voters as to calm my own nerves. I texted my family and friends at night to make sure they had plans to vote. I offered to bring campaign staff—including my own communications director, whom I encouraged to take a step back from official duties so she could help run the ground game for the campaign—treats, which they declined on account of their jittery stomachs. We all held our breaths and put our heads down as the world watched whether Kansas, the first state to hold a referendum on abortion in a post-*Roe* America, would strip our neighbors of their rights.

It wasn't even close. Kansans overwhelmingly rejected the constitutional amendment by a margin of 19 points. Factions within the Value Them Both coalition blamed themselves for going both too far by including language without exceptions, and not far enough by refusing to confirm their plans to ban abortion outright. They also blamed Kansans for Constitutional Freedom for confusing voters, despite themselves having stacked every possible deck in favor of the amendment's passage. Kansans reaffirmed their position this November: we reelected our pro-choice governor, Laura Kelly, to a second term; we sent Congresswoman Sharice Davids, who vocally opposed the amendment and rallied volunteers several times in the weeks preceding the vote, back to Washington for her third term with her largest margin of victory ever; and we inched nearer to breaking the Republican supermajority in the Kansas House, which will allow us to block future attempts to subvert and undermine this critical right.

There is much work left to be done, but I know that the political power Kansans have built to defeat this amendment will ensure that we are prepared for the fights ahead.

21 A Kansas Prosecutor's Resistance to the Post-Roe Antiabortion Movement

SUZANNE VALDEZ

In April 2019 the antiabortion showdown in Kansas began when the state Supreme Court decided *Hodes and Nauser v. Schmidt,* a seminal case in which the highest court interpreted the Kansas constitution to guarantee a woman's right to abortion. Soon after *Hodes* was decided, ultraconservative Kansas GOP legislators and evangelical Christians focused their political agenda on banning abortion rights in Kansas. To completely eliminate abortion protection, the state constitution would have to be amended by a simple majority of Kansas voters to overturn the high court's ruling in the *Hodes* case. The ballot question, called "Value Them Both," appeared in the August 2, 2022, primary election, approximately three years after *Hodes* was decided.

Putting this extremely important constitutional question about women's reproductive rights in a midterm August primary election was purposefully contemplated by the Kansas Legislature, which is overwhelmingly Republican and anti-choice. Primary elections in Kansas traditionally have much lower voter turnout because high-stakes voter decisions typically present themselves in the November general election. Not only was the timing of the Value Them Both amendment dubious, the language of the ballot question was designed to be extremely confusing. A "Yes" vote on the question would amend the state constitution and effectively overturn the *Hodes* decision. A "No" vote would keep the status quo, meaning a woman in Kansas would retain her state constitutional right to choose what *Hodes* guaranteed.

With the *Hodes* decision protecting reproductive rights in Kansas, antiabortionists were eager for the outcome of the highly anticipated US Supreme Court decision in *Dobbs v. Jackson Women's Health Organization,* which was the Mississippi case that triggered review of *Roe v. Wade.* But no matter the outcome of *Dobbs,* the Kansas Legislature teed up the constitutional question to further limit and potentially ban existing abortion rights in the state. After *Dobbs* and the reversal of *Roe,* the stakes obviously became much higher when Kansas voters took to the polls in August 2022 to vote on the Value Them Both constitutional amendment.

Once *Dobbs* was decided in June 2022, pro-choice proponents had six short weeks to inform and educate Kansas voters about the implications of the Value Them Both amendment, including the potential extreme harm to women's reproductive rights that would predictably occur if the amendment passed. As Douglas County (Kansas) district attorney, I immediately joined the national nonprofit organization Fair and Just Prosecution in their effort to preserve a woman's right to bodily autonomy. I pledged, as an elected official, not to enforce any Kansas laws enacted to criminalize abortion and reproductive rights. I publicly advocated against the Value Them Both amendment because I anticipated that if the amendment passed, the Kansas Legislature would act immediately to criminalize women's reproductive rights and potentially ban contraception. I feared that criminalizing a woman's decision to have an abortion, which is a personal and often difficult choice a woman may make in consultation with her medical provider, could detrimentally affect the health and safety of many women in my community.

In a landmark defeat, which spoke loudly in support of a woman's right to choose, Kansas voters decisively rejected the amendment by nearly twenty percentage points. But strong antiabortion advocacy did not wane despite the ballot defeat. Antiabortionists vowed to continue the fight to dismantle a woman's right to choose. Thus the Kansas antiabortion movement remains alive, and the battle is far from over.

Kansas bans abortions after twenty-two weeks and has other strict requirements and limitations concerning how and when abortions may occur. Notwithstanding the Value Them Both amendment loss, the Legislature will likely move forward to further limit abortion in meaningful ways. Indeed, Kansas attorney general and antiabortionist Kris Kobach, who took office in January 2023, has already signaled such intentions.

In addition, in recent Kansas election cycles there have been grassroots attempts to remove pro-choice Kansas Supreme Court justices. Justices are appointed by the governor and face a retention vote in staggered slots in general elections. These grassroots efforts have gained momentum. The expectation is that a Republican-elected governor will appoint more conservative jurists to the Kansas Supreme Court if a removal effort is successful. For now, reelected Democratic and pro-choice governor Laura Kelly will have another four-year term in the Kansas Statehouse, and the Supreme Court justices who were on the November 2022 ballot easily surpassed the 50 percent threshold favoring retention. But replacement of jurists on the high court is possible every two years when justices slotted for a retention vote are on the November general election ballot. In the future should a pro-choice justice be removed from office or retire and be replaced with a conservative justice, a reversal of the *Hodes* decision is a valid concern.

So how does all this horrifying and unsettling potential legal up-heaval regarding women's reproductive rights continue to possibly involve the jurisdiction of the district attorney in Kansas? In antici-pating a possible "parade of horrors," now that there is no federal constitutional right for a woman to choose and the issue of abortion is left solely to states to decide, Kansans must not take for granted that the right to abortion recognized in the *Hodes* decision is the final word on this fundamental protection. Furthermore, as district attor-ney, it is my duty to inform and educate the public about why laws that are enacted to criminalize abortion seekers and providers pose a grave public safety concern if they are enforced.

My jurisdiction, Douglas County, is home to university town Lawrence, Kansas, which is overwhelmingly comprised of voters who are highly educated and pro-choice. When I assumed office as district attorney, I took an oath to uphold the federal and state con-stitutions and to enforce the laws of Kansas. Importantly, my obliga-tion as chief prosecutor in my community is to ensure public safety, pursue justice, and to allocate scarce public resources responsibly and transparently. In Douglas County approximately 80 percent of voters rejected the Value Them Both constitutional amendment. Our voters loudly declared that a woman's right to choose is a highly per-sonal medical decision, and certainly not one that the Kansas Legis-lature should abolish or criminalize. Thus in the future should the Legislature criminalize a woman's reproductive rights, I as district attorney would be faced with a difficult decision that involves balanc-ing my sworn oath of office, which is to enforce state law, with the right to exercise prosecutorial discretion that favors other significant and legitimate public interests and safety concerns.

As I analyze and deliberate about this delicate balancing test, my community's interests and safety are overwhelmingly more impor-tant. It is simply impossible to ignore the valid concerns for women who will be forced to seek illegal and unsafe abortions if faced with no other choice. My office cannot justify allocating scarce public resources to prosecute abortion seekers and medical providers who could potentially face serious criminal penalties including incarceration. Lastly, I cannot ignore the clear will of voters in my community. Through the electoral process I am duty bound to honor the trust given to me and my office, and I am responsible for enforcing the laws that represent our local values and safety concerns. After careful and serious reflection, I believe that prosecutorial discretion outweighs and favors nonenforcement of any criminal abortion laws that the Kansas Legislature may enact.

To further emphasize the long-standing importance of prosecutorial discretion in the criminal justice system, adultery remains a crime in Kansas and jaywalking is a criminal offense, too. My office does not allocate scarce public resources to prosecute individuals who allegedly commit either these two offenses. Why? Because enforcement and prosecution of these archaic and paternalistic laws do not reflect our community's values and interests. Certainly if my office prosecuted every individual who committed adultery or jaywalked in my jurisdiction, we would quickly deplete the limited resources that we have to prosecute serious and violent crimes, like sexual and domestic assault, drug distribution, and gun violence.

Finally, and importantly, while the *Dobbs* decision took America back decades to the pre-*Roe* era and has created unimaginable situations where women must travel to an "abortion-friendly" state or potentially undergo secret back-alley procedures due to the unavailability or expense of a medically safe abortion, criminalization of abortion today will be exponentially worse and more dangerous for all women due to technological advancements made over the past fifty years. Digital footprints such as web browsing and search histories and location data found on phones and computers, which create almost irrefutable digital evidence and are used frequently to investigate and prosecute all categories of serious crime, will be used by mostly male law enforcement officers to build cases to charge women seeking abortions as well as abortion medical providers.

Anticipating a "parade of horrors" in Kansas while I am district attorney, I will invoke prosecutorial discretion not to use local tax-payer dollars and resources to prosecute criminal laws that are enacted with the intent to limit a woman's reproductive rights, or to prosecute any health-care provider who provides abortion services. When initiating any criminal prosecution in the district attorney's office, a common mantra is "We can, but should we?" Should the Kansas Legislature ever enact laws that criminalize abortion while I am district attorney, the answer will be: "No, we will not."

22 *Protecting Abortion in Austin*

JOSÉ "CHITO" VELA, WITH JENNA
HANES AND RAMEY KO

I did not run for office because of abortion. I ran because I care about my home—Austin, Texas—and I wanted to work on a local level to make it better. Nobody expected my office's work to feature in the *Washington Post,* the *New York Times,* and *POLITICO*—myself least of all. For well over a decade Austin has been one of the fastest growing cities in America. Like other rapidly expanding cities, Austin's economy and population have grown along with the cost of living and demand for housing and services. Austin is no longer the slow-paced, quirky little town of hippie country musicians and men in neon tutus I experienced thirty years ago as a student at the University of Texas.

Most of my career before taking office dealt with the rights of workers, immigrants, and people below the poverty line. I ran because of the affordability and housing crisis in our city, the effects of which I witnessed daily as an immigration and criminal defense attorney. I ran because the Austin way of life grows increasingly out of reach for many who built their lives here. I ran to tackle the local decisions that impact our daily lives. Controversial national issues such as abortion are beyond the purview of local government, or so I thought. I did not expect our City Council to have to confront the destruction of a cherished and long-established civil right, much less in the first six months of my term.

In a state so openly hostile to reproductive rights, we could not abdicate our responsibility to defend our residents from fear and persecution. Texas's abortion trigger law, which took effect thirty days after the *Dobbs* decision, is one of the most draconian in the nation. The so-called Right to Life Act makes performing or helping someone obtain an abortion a first-degree felony, punishable by up to ninety-nine years in prison. Alongside the criminal statute, Texas implemented a civil law allowing private citizens to sue people for the same conduct. When faced with the prospect of teenagers receiving life sentences and miscarriages becoming evidence of a crime, what else could we do?

Even though many had suspected the Supreme Court would overturn *Roe v. Wade,* my whole team was shocked the night the draft *Dobbs* opinion leaked. It was a bitter and jarring reminder that we cannot take anything for granted in our democracy, especially with an unbalanced Supreme Court and a gridlocked Congress. Devastated and angry, but determined, my staff and I immediately began planning our city's response. Within twenty-four hours of the leak, we developed a working draft of our legislative response. We knew we had to be smart, subtle, and legally sound. Texas tightly constrains the authority of its cities, and they subject us to more state control than in other states. Our legislature's favorite pastime is interfering in Austin's local affairs. Moreover, Austin's charter places operational authority over municipal government in the office of the city manager; the City Council may only provide direction to the manager and pass ordinances. More akin to a Board of Directors, the City Council sets broad policy but exercises no direct control over city staff or the day-to-day functions of government.

As a city, we cannot make legal what the state makes illegal. Attempting to protect abortion and other reproductive rights with an ordinance would have been easily overturned by the courts, while simultaneously provoking a confrontation with the state legislature.

The Council is also prohibited from either issuing direct orders to the police chief or modifying the Austin Police Department's policies and procedures. Working with stakeholders, advocates, the city's Law Department, and other Council offices, we crafted a resolution called the GRACE Act—Guarding the Right to Abortion Care for Everyone—which used all the powers at the City Council's disposal to protect reproductive rights. While Texas law prevents us from truly decriminalizing abortion, as a city, we do have control over our budget and how we choose to prioritize the use of resources. The GRACE Act takes advantage of that broad discretion afforded to cities to limit or eliminate the use of city resources to the greatest extent possible (including by the police department) for the criminal investigation and enforcement of state abortion laws or the storage and distribution of information related to such cases.

By establishing the deprioritization of abortion law enforcement as the general policy of the city and directing the city manager to implement the policy, we avoided running afoul of state abortion bans and laws prohibiting the City Council from directing staff or intervening in investigative decisions. In addition, by predicating the resolution on the city's power to allocate limited resources, we made it difficult for the legislature to intervene without significantly disrupting the entire legal framework for municipal government. Limiting our discretion in the area of abortion would be exceedingly difficult without doing away with city discretion over policy and budget priorities in general. We can never rule out any possibility with our state government and courts, but our approach offered us the best chance of success.

Our nuanced approach was motivated by more than the desire to protect the GRACE Act in Austin; we intended from the beginning to create a model that other cities could adapt and use, especially fellow progressive strongholds in Texas. To my surprise, when we announced that we would be sponsoring a resolution to protect reproductive rights, elected officials and advocates from all around the country began contacting us about passing the GRACE Act in their cities. Surely someone else had already had the same idea, but cities with better political climates, more abortion resources, and fewer legal limitations reached out to us for guidance. We had even planned to consult other cities on their approaches. Many who contacted us not only wanted to use the GRACE Act as a model but actually copied the language word for word. The response was so strong that some cities passed their versions of the GRACE Act before Austin did! In the months since Austin passed the GRACE Act in June 2022, dozens more cities have adopted some version of our legislation; many of the laws mirror our language (particularly in Texas) and bear the name GRACE Act. National and international coverage of the resolution continues as each new version passes, and even today, many sources erroneously cite Austin as the first city to pass abortion rights protections in the wake of *Dobbs*.

When confronting monumental challenges that fundamentally alter our way of life, the feeling of helplessness comes naturally to all of us. As my office began to conceptualize the GRACE Act, experts and activists alike told us at every turn that the city had no power and that there was nothing we could do that would make a real difference. They warned us that the state would target anything we tried. I lost count of the number of warnings that we would likely face an avalanche of lawsuits. Many of our ideas did not hold up in the face of the legal and political realities in Texas, but we kept thinking and considering every approach, no matter how improbable. The *Dobbs* decision itself represents the culmination of decades of anti-choice activists testing and probing every legal theory, every policy approach until they began to see results, discover the right pressure points, and win court cases. Arguments that seemed laughable years ago are now the foundation of new law. Winning the most unwinnable fights demands both creativity and perseverance, which we must exercise to the same or greater degree as our opponents.

I also learned that to provide an example for others, you must accept the reality of your situation. Recognizing your limitations leads to unconventional approaches and better outcomes. Understanding other policy developed in the same conditions provides valuable insights. While developing the GRACE Act, we looked at a previous resolution passed by Council deprioritizing enforcement of cannabis laws to see how the authors worked around the limitations of our city charter and state law. We also examined the arguments made by opponents and supporters regarding the legal effect of Council's action. Many of us know the exhortation to not let the perfect be the enemy of the good; we learned to not let the perfect be the enemy of the possible. Finally, and perhaps most important, we learned that you should never assume that others have had the same idea as you or have acted. We took for granted that many other cities would already have developed ways to mitigate the worst impacts of *Dobbs;* I never expected the GRACE Act to be a prominent example at all, much less one of the first local responses in the nation. If my team had waited for someone else to come up with a better idea, or for another city to take the lead, abortion rights at the local level may not have been protected as widely and as quickly as they were.

While I have been solidly pro-choice my entire life, I never expected to be on the front lines of the fight for reproductive rights or for the GRACE Act to be an inspiration to so many municipalities and local officials around the country. However, I also never expected our own democratic government to aid and abet the violation of personal autonomy and eviscerate an established right. Desperate and unprecedented situations make everyone afraid, but my team and I learned that it is possible to draw strength from action. *Dobbs* was one loss, but as millions of people in cities around the country have proven, we refuse to accept defeat.

23 *My Journey to Becoming an Abortion Doula*

CYNTHIA GUTIERREZ

In January 2023, I celebrated the ten-year anniversary of my self-managed medication abortion. My abortion was one of the first times in my life that I had personal bodily autonomy. My abortion brought me freedom. My abortion empowered me to have the life I have today. I will be forever grateful. While I was releasing my pregnancy, though, I was completely terrified and alone. I didn't know about abortion doulas or abortion funds.

When I got the medication, nobody fully explained to me what the process could entail: vomiting, dizziness, fever, and panic. At one point my symptoms were so severe that an ambulance was called to send me to the local Catholic hospital. As I said, I didn't know about abortion doulas. I had no idea that my experience could have been supportive, tender, and gentle. I thought I had to keep my abortion a secret and lived with internalized stigma. A year later, when I was community building with folks in California, I shared my abortion story for the first time.[1] I felt seen. In that moment I knew that I didn't want other folks to feel alone during their abortion—that was the moment that the idea of being an abortion doula was planted in my spirit.

Abortion doulas offer compassionate emotional support, physical support, and resources to people before, during, and after their abortion. During the COVID-19 pandemic, I noticed an increase in people reaching out and wanting the support of an abortion doula. Their reasons for wanting an abortion varied, but two experiences were common. No one wanted to be pregnant during a time of economic uncertainty brought on by a global pandemic that loomed over everyone. Yet people often faced a persistent wave of misinformation, or they had no information about how to access an abortion.

I vividly remember supporting a person wanting an abortion in the San Francisco Bay Area. She was able to access the medication for her self-managed abortion without my help. She shared that it was harder than she expected to get the mifepristone and misoprostol, especially considering that we were in California. She shared that she had some anxiety about the physical pain that she could experience as she terminated the pregnancy. She shared that she knew this was the right decision for her. Due to the increase in COVID-19 infections, she wanted me to provide remote support. We communicated regularly as we created a plan for her to take time off work and take care of herself at home. Together, we figured out the logistics that she would need to account for as she went through her abortion journey. We discussed all the supplies that could bring her comfort and made sure that she had what she needed. With her consent I created an aftercare package to support her in the days after her abortion. I was there to hold space for all the emotions and sensations that she experienced: the physical cramping, the tears, and the relief.

Supporting this person and others persistently reminds me that my role as an abortion doula is in direct alignment with my Reproductive Justice activism. As abortion became a mainstream media topic, I noticed more folks reaching out to share their abortion stories. By this time I was an active abortion storyteller with We Testify and a board member for ACCESS Reproductive Justice.[2] I had people messaging me and disclosing that they had an abortion, some within the past couple of years, some a decade earlier. The more courageous

I became with sharing my abortion story, the more it created space for other people to boldly share their abortion stories as well. I rediscovered that a part of my work as an abortion doula is to hold space for these experiences. There is not an expiration date on supporting people who have abortions. They need support on day one and they need support hundreds of days later. My role as an abortion doula means that I can create a sacred space for people to show up as their authentic selves as abortion havers.

Today, so many years after my abortion, when people in my community, folks involved in Reproductive Justice, or even strangers reach out asking for support with their abortion, I say, "I'm an abortion doula. How can I help you?" Everyone deserves that support. As an abortion doula, I dream of and organize for a world where everyone who wants an abortion doula will have access to one. People having abortions deserve all the doula love and support that we can give. I imagine that as much as birth doulas are slowly being acknowledged, abortion doulas will not only be embraced as a possibility, but they will be embraced as the norm.

24 *Krystale E. Littlejohn Interviews the Founders of Plan C*

Krystale E. Littlejohn: *Plan C has been such an important resource for people—both before and after the* Dobbs *ruling. Tell us what problems people faced when you first started plancpills.org in 2016.*

Amy Merrill: One of the ways that we like to contribute to the conversation is to remind people that people who want abortions have been up against barriers for a really long time. *Roe,* for all of its intended protections, was not protecting rights and access for half of the country, there were already bans, and so it was already a patchwork quilt of access. So, we really asked, given that millions of people all around the world are safely self-managing their abortions, why don't people in the United States know about these five little pills that could change your life? So that is one of the misconceptions that we work to correct. It's not just "the pills are essential in this moment of crisis management and harm reduction." They also are just essential to our well-being and should be in our hands in a less medicalized way.

Elisa Wells: I would add that even before these pills were approved in the United States, they were politicized. The approval of the pills was delayed by ten years from when other countries had it approved. And then when mifepristone was finally approved in the United States, the FDA attached all of these restrictions to it. So we've known for decades that politics was interfering with access to these pills, and we wanted to show the transformational potential of this technology to really change the narrative about abortion access in the United States. We wanted to share the learnings from other countries where these pills are readily available over the counter, starting with people in Brazil who have used pills off-label to self-manage their own abortions since the 1980s.

Krystale: *Absolutely, and given what has happened with* Dobbs, *we know that this is the time more than ever that people need information and thankfully Plan C is bringing it to them. So let's talk a bit about what Plan C is and how it's meeting the needs of so many people who rely on it.*
Amy: Plan C is an information campaign, but at this point it's so much more. It's really about catalyzing new routes of access and sharing a vision that these pills should be in people's hands. We started with a website because we recognized that this information just needs to get out there. That these pills exist, that they're safe and effective, and that there are ways to access them in every state to safely self-manage abortion. So our website remains our number-one tool. We maintain it as a hub of information and resources, a sort of first stop—here's what you need to know in order to make a decision that's best for you, including detailed information about how to get pills, even in states that restrict access.

We don't give out direct legal advice because we're not a legal entity. We are also not clinicians. So we're always highlighting partner resources that can help people assess their situations and make the decision that's best for them. We see the key resources for people who want to self-manage their care as Plan C for how to find pills, the Repro Legal Helpline for understanding legal risk, the M + A Hotline for medical support, and Repro Care for peer and doula support. And there are a ton of other great resources out there as well. We talk about putting the information in your back pocket. You might not need it now. You might not need it ever, but someone in your life probably will need it at some point.

Elisa: I'll add that from the very beginning, a key goal of Plan C was to demonstrate a new, demedicalized model of abortion access and move agency back to the individual's hands. Our tagline is convenience, confidentiality, and control. So that was part of what was radical about us. We did see this as a very user-centered option, whereas others still clung to the provider-centered model. And that's still the case. We still center the user and their ability to directly access pills. We're not saying that it's the only thing out there, but we are saying that it needs to be part of the spectrum of offerings for abortion access, which in a perfect world would include fully legal access through clinics and telehealth services as well as through alternate routes for self-managed care. Ultimately our vision is that abortion pills will be legally available over the counter in the US.

Krystale: *Definitely. Tell us about what inspired you to start Plan C given how transformative the very idea of putting pills in people's hands was.*

Elisa: Both Francine Coeytaux, our other cofounder, and I, are long-time reproductive health specialists, with a lot of our work in other countries. There were two times when the disparity in access between the United States and other countries was really stunning. In Ghana we visited the DKT International office, who three months before had just launched an MTP (medical termination of pregnancy) product. And in just three months their sales were skyrocketing. People were like, "Wow! There's something I can do." And this was without a doctor's prescription. The second stunning moment was in Ethiopia. We asked our Ethiopian colleague to try and purchase these pills in a pharmacy. And she came out about ten minutes later and for less than seven dollars, she had purchased a good quality product. So we're just standing there in this small town in Ethiopia thinking,

"How is it that here for less than seven dollars, people can have access to an abortion and meanwhile in the United States—this was in 2014—there were all these legislators in Texas who even then were putting restrictions on people's access?"

So it was our work around the world that allowed us to see the transformational power of these pills, and in particular how demedicalizing access could improve health outcomes for women and people who needed them. For me, recognizing that transformational potential was part of the genesis of it. And, also, just being sick and tired of seeing one restriction after another pop up in the United States. At some point, you give up on trusting the systems to help with what should be basic access to medical care.

Amy: For me, I had been doing international work on anti-human trafficking and sex slavery and had been deep into conversations about sexual stigma, about sexual health and clinics in Southeast Asian countries. And then getting a chance to meet Francine and learn about this method and the ways that it had been stymied, misconstrued, and misunderstood, my jaw was on the floor—and I think that that's where I had that "aha" moment that we're describing here. An increasing number of people have internet access in this country. We have mail order. We're super used to ordering things online and just getting what we need right away. And all of that made me think about the revolutionary nature of what happens when you move the locus of control into a person's hands and what that could look like for abortion. So, last year, there were 1.7 million visitors to our website. And how many people clicked off of our website to find resources? That number, something like six hundred thousand people clicked off to find resources out of an estimated nine hundred thousand people in this country who need abortions every year. It's not that we served that percentage, but in terms of numbers, we're really out there reaching people and that's powerful.

Elisa: Yeah, I'd just add that when we first started out, a lot of people assumed that our work researching alternate routes of access and publishing the results on our website was illegal. They said, "You can't do that." The donors told us, "We can't support your work." One even said, "That's untenable," and withdrew funding. That particular comment came after there was an article about us in the *New York Times,* which is exactly what we told the donor we would do: raise awareness of this issue. So it hasn't been easy, but we're glad we have been able to be a voice to put power back in the hands of people who need abortions.

Krystale: *Within the context that we've been talking about, thinking about what's happened in the past, what's happening now, and what might happen in the future, tell us about what you see as the next frontier in your work.*

Amy: We don't see this administration doing something radical to reverse the impact of *Dobbs.* We think that we're going to be here for a while, and so we see the need for alternate routes of access and de-medicalized approaches, like getting pills in advance to keep in your medicine cabinet, as more essential than ever from a harm-reduction and basic human rights perspective. What I hope that we can do at Plan C is just stay the course with sharing what we know to be true about existing routes of access, about safety, about efficacy, and about options where people can get these pills in advance because then you're not even dealing with asking for permission or asking for a prescription and waiting for it for two weeks in the mail. You just have them and you might take them five weeks in, which means that whatever ban exists in your state won't even affect you. So we're going to keep staying attuned to forward-thinking ways to help people.

Elisa: We are also actively working on supply issues and how we might speed up the delivery or reduce the price of various options. We're really grateful to be working in an environment where there are complementary skills and issues being addressed by other organizations. As Amy described, in this post-*Roe* world, alternate routes of access are going to be primary for people. The work that If/When/How is doing to speak out against criminalization and to help people understand potential legal risk is just hugely important, as is the work that the M + A Hotline is doing to help provide medical support to people. So, to the extent that we can help amplify that messaging and help people understand that they have access to these resources, we see that as an important role. And, eventually, we all hope for a world in which these pills are available in multiple ways that best meet the needs of the end-user. So, through clinics, through telehealth, through self-managed options, and even over the counter. And also making sure that aspiration abortion is available to people who want that and that abortion at different gestational ages is available to people who need that. So, though Plan C focuses on pills, and specifically pills by mail, we see ourselves as part of the broader landscape of abortion access in which all of those parts are so important because it has to be a spectrum of offerings to meet the needs of all users.

Krystale: *As we eye the future, what do you think about the FDA's finalization of the rule that would broaden pharmacy availability of abortion pills?*

Elisa: There has been much excitement about the FDA decision to allow pharmacies to stock abortion pills. Yes, this is a much-needed development—abortion pills absolutely should be stocked in regular and mail-order pharmacies. But rather than being excited, we are dismayed that it took so long for the FDA to make this change. Mifepristone is so safe that it never should have been restricted in the first place. And the FDA change has added new requirements that pharmacies must meet to stock mifepristone, making it different from every other medication they stock. Frankly it is ridiculous. Plus it does nothing to address the severe barriers to access that exist in states that have passed bans on abortion altogether. We can't celebrate this as a victory when there is no or very poor access for so many people in the United States. People need to understand that access to abortion in the United States remains a public health emergency.

Krystale: *We've covered so many different aspects of your work, and we were just talking about how it's a team effort to ensure that people have access to abortion. So what are steps that people can take if they want to be involved or do more? What would you all suggest?*

Amy: We have a Plan C community that is a great place to start. It's basically a place for someone who says, "I'm fired up, I really want to help. I go to school or I work in an office, or I have some people in mind who I want to be having this conversation with." We help equip them with the basic facts to have that conversation. Or they want to have community, and we have a Discord board where people are chatting and connecting with each other, and it's a really supportive environment for grassroots activists and volunteers. And it sounds obvious, but it's just still the case that half of the country doesn't know about abortion with pills, let alone doesn't know about the alternate routes of access. So sharing information is just the simplest, cost-effective, free way of taking action on this issue.

Elisa: As Amy said, sharing information is so important. Just talking about abortion helps to destigmatize it, and talking about abortion with pills and self-managed abortion can help people understand that it's not this big scary deal. It is really a very simple medical treatment that you can get when your period is late. And of course, vote, although we feel a little deflated about that call to action these days, but we have to say it. Making our voices heard at the ballot box is so important, even in a broken system.

Krystale: *Thanks so much for talking with us and for all the work that you do.*

25 *Feminist Art as Feminist Activism*

Creating An Anti–Crisis Pregnancy Center Exhibition
in the Post-*Roe* Landscape

CARLY THOMSEN

At exactly the same moment as the Supreme Court's decision to
overturn *Roe v. Wade* was made public, I was facilitating Middlebury
College's first Public Feminism Lab, a feminist-theory-seminar-
meets-art-critique space through which we discussed and made art
related to abortion, crisis pregnancy centers, and Reproductive Justice. Up until the moment the *Roe* decision became breaking news,
we had used our feminist lab to center questions regarding the place
of joy, pleasure, and fun in abortion justice activism and, furthermore, how art can be a vehicle for generating these feelings. But in
this time of anger and mourning, these concerns seemed juvenile,
silly, irrelevant even.

Yet we couldn't walk away from our project—not that we wanted
to—or really even change directions; our art exhibit on crisis pregnancy centers was slated to open a couple of months later, and the
process of creating art and installing the exhibit was being captured
by a film crew making a documentary about crisis pregnancy centers.
We had to keep showing up, talking, and making art. Through
this process we came to believe the new post-*Roe* political landscape

actually requires that we take *more seriously* the political potential of feminist art as well as the joyful affects it can generate. In this essay I share the story of the Public Feminism Lab and use it as a case study to argue for the power of visualizing a reproductively just world devoid of crisis pregnancy centers.

Crisis Pregnancy Centers: A Brief Overview

Crisis pregnancy centers (CPCs) are religiously motivated, antiabortion nonprofit organizations that function as the backbone of the antiabortion movement. Critics describe these unregulated centers as "fake clinics." Their key goal is to prevent what they call "abortion-minded women" from obtaining abortions. Scholars, reporters, and activists have demonstrated the deceptive tactics CPCs use to reach their goals: disguising their political and religious motivations, often through giving themselves neutral-sounding names; implying they offer abortions when they do not; opening near abortion clinics or in former abortion clinics with the intention of confusing, and thus hijacking, those en route to clinics; and peddling false medical information.

Scholars found, for example, that 80 percent of CPC websites listed in state resource directories include false or misleading medical information, such as the erroneous claim that abortion leads to breast cancer, infertility, and mental health issues, among other claims repeatedly proven false (Bryant et al. 2014). Such inaccurate information is given credence by the aesthetic decisions of CPCs, which suggest that they are medical clinics when they are not. For instance, some CPC volunteers wear white lab coats, and some CPC websites and mobile buses are decorated with medical imagery (Chen 2013; Thomsen et al. 2021). Perhaps more worrisome, CPCs also increasingly offer free ultrasounds, although they do not make clear to clients that these ultrasounds are meant to be "nondiagnostic" and therefore are not medical in nature. Importantly, the medical misinformation that CPCs spread through these approaches does not only impact the people who end up in CPCs. It has a broader social function, and that is to spread antiabortion ideologies. CPCs frame abortion as traumatic, damaging, dangerous, and hurtful to women. They include statements on their websites and in their materials about "post-abortion stress syndrome," a condition that is not medically recognized precisely because, as Diana Greene Foster's groundbreaking *The Turnaway Study* demonstrates, 95 percent of people who obtain abortions feel it was the right decision. Put more directly, this "syndrome" was made up by antiabortion activists for political purposes, and CPCs are a key site through which antiabortion activists work to make this fake syndrome seem credible.

Under the guise that they are medical facilities, CPCs collect what clients often think is private medical information—even though CPCs are not required to comply with HIPAA or other patient privacy laws precisely because they are not medical facilities. And CPCs are not shy about their use of these practices. A statement from Next Level, a data management software company developed by Heartbeat International reads: "As big data revolutionizes industries around the globe, now is the time to do the same for life-affirming work of pregnancy help. As we pool together what we've learned separately, we can begin to wield game-changing predictive and prescriptive analytics that lead to stronger outcomes." As worrisome as their collection of private, personal data for movement building purposes, CPCs in states where abortion is illegal are set up to aid in state surveillance and potentially even the prosecution of people who obtain abortions—a concern that advocacy organizations, such as The Alliance, are issuing warnings about.

Today there are more than twenty-six hundred CPCs in the United States and just seven hundred abortion clinics—numbers that were reversed in the 1980s. More volunteers, volunteer hours, and resources go toward CPCs than all other forms of antiabortion activism combined (Munson 2008). In short, CPCs are central to the US abortion story, and yet, as I read the news coverage of *Roe*'s reversal, I was struck by how little even mentioned CPCs.

The Public Feminism Lab and Art Exhibit

The Public Feminism Lab consisted primarily of three things: reading texts helpful for thinking about CPCs, meeting to discuss those texts, and translating these ideas and conversations into art. Each of the fellows were current Middlebury College students who occupy a diverse range of social locations: Black, Brown, and white students; women, transgender, and nonbinary students; students with disabilities and chronic health issues and those without; queer and heterosexual students; and students who grew up in various geographic locations. Each of the seven fellows were paid stipends through the Gender, Sexuality, and Feminist Studies (GSFS) program and the Feminist Resource Center at Chellis House, something that allowed those who could not afford to take unpaid internships to participate. Students had varying degrees of experience with both the academic field of gender studies and also creating art; some were feminist-identified art majors who had little prior involvement with gender studies while others were GSFS majors who did not necessarily consider themselves artists.

The group's diversity in terms of life experiences and intellectual and artistic training informed our conversations, as well as the art that emerged out of them, in deep and profound ways. In fact, at the end of each of our two-hour-long weekly meetings, it seemed there was always more to say. Perhaps that is because in Middlebury College's first Public Feminism Lab, we had a lot of ground to cover. What does "public feminism" even mean? What can CPCs and public feminism illuminate about one another? How might we articulate the relationships among abortion justice, reproductive rights, and Reproductive Justice—and where do CPCs fit into this articulation? What can happen to our art, our politics, and our feminism when art becomes our way of *doing something* politically? How can feminist and queer theory, art, and activism be useful to one another? What, after all, does it mean to make feminist and queer art? What makes art "feminist" and/or "queer"?

Our goal, of course, was not simply to grapple with these questions through the use and production of words but to figure out what our responses could *look like* aesthetically. As such, in each meeting we discussed the assigned texts for the week, which included theoretically complex academic articles, films, and news coverage related to crisis pregnancy centers as well as feminist reflections on art and feminist art exhibits. Doing so gave us precise language to use to discuss fellows' art in progress. In fact, each meeting began with students sharing art they had created since our last gathering, and engaging with responses to it. This process allowed each artist to strengthen and transform their art so that it was more in line with the artist's individual goals as well as the collective goals associated with the exhibit.

Ultimately the fellows produced more than fifty original pieces of art, spanning a variety of mediums: sculpture, acrylic paint on canvas, photography, collage, embroidery, 3D installations, film, AI-generated imagery, watercolor, and graphic design. Each piece of art was accompanied by a developed artist's statement that translates ideas about Reproductive Justice, abortion, and CPCs that we addressed through the lab. To our great surprise, more than 250 people—at our small liberal arts college with a student body of approximately 2,500—showed up for the opening event of "Visualizing Reproductive Justice: A Call to End Fake Clinics." This number far exceeds attendance at

[FIGURE 1: Positions, Isabel Perez-Martin]

the vast majority of campus events, including various events focused on Reproductive Justice that took place right around the same time as the exhibit opening.

The success of our exhibit opening speaks to the galvanizing nature of art and therefore its use for Reproductive Justice activism.

[FIGURE 2: Regulated or Unregulated?, Emily Ribeiro]

Our desire was to create an exhibit that could speak to people who are unsure how they feel about abortion as well as those who believe that they are ardent supporters of Reproductive Justice. As it turns out, neither group is likely to know much about CPCs, despite their centrality to the successes of the antiabortion movement. The exhibit did more to create buzz about CPCs on campus and in the broader community than any of the many things my students and I have done over the course of my seven years at Middlebury College—including teaching about CPCs in my classes, publishing my research on CPCs (in academic journals and such high-profile

[FIGURE 3: To Be Seen as a Woman, Alexis Welch]

venues as the *New York Times*), writing op-eds in the campus newspaper, and protesting the presence of Middlebury's CPCs at an annual
on-campus student activities fair.

The director of Middlebury's CPC attended the exhibit's opening
event and after penned an op-ed in the local paper declaring that

they were being misrepresented by our exhibit. Someone stole a piece of art in the exhibit, and after a fellow used the app YikYak to ask for information about the missing art, the art was anonymously returned. The student newspaper covered the event. Several faculty—across various departments—brought their classes to the opening exhibit event and related academic talk on the world-building power of feminist and queer aesthetics. In the weeks leading up to the exhibit opening, I gave a public presentation on campus about CPCs, two student fellows and I gave a guest lecture about CPCs in a public health class, and fellows tabled multiple times. One fellow led the most well-coordinated, well-attended, and well-covered student protest of the CPC at the campus student activities fair yet. Energy—or anxiety, especially for administrators and the campus communications office—was high.

In many ways, I see the campus and community buzz surrounding the exhibit as a reflection of the power of both feminist- and queer theory–informed art and art-infused activism. I also see the exhibit's success as enabled by past anti-CPC organizing on campus and as enabling future action. To ensure that our exhibit was a means rather than an end, so to speak, we took several steps: We worked with the Archives of Dissent, a digital archive of campus-based feminist activism, to archive past and current anti-CPC organizing on campus. We invited a Vermont state representative to the exhibit opening, and she not only attended but expressed her commitment to introducing legislation to regulate CPCs in Vermont. During one fellow's participation in the lab, she founded a coalition to work across New England liberal arts colleges to ban CPCs from campuses. While the Public Feminism Lab provides a model for simultaneously crafting theory-informed art and art-infused activism, ultimately what it illustrates is that we can find joy, pleasure, and fun even when things are enraging, horrifying, and shocking. In fact, the greatest lesson we learned from the Public Feminism Lab is that we have to.

Part IV *Fighting at the Frontiers of Criminalization*

RICKIE SOLINGER

Before *Roe v. Wade,* law enforcement staked out offices and rooming houses where they thought abortions were occurring and conducted raids after they'd collected enough license plate numbers and furtive snapshots. Today the tools and processes of criminalization are more sophisticated, involving elements such as electronic surveillance. We see a patchwork of both eager and reluctant actors—police and prosecutors, scared medical professionals, and stymied faculty members who want to provide resources to their students on abortion-hostile terrain—forced to do their jobs under a regime that has significantly broadened the definition of criminal behavior.

Law professors Aziz Z. Huq and Rebecca Wexler define our phones as "the new battleground," a danger zone, a place prosecutors and others can access our most private information, such as our attempts to find medication abortion and record our menstrual cycles. The authors show how since *Dobbs,* law enforcement is empowered in some states to get this kind of information, and they lay out the limits and the possibilities for protecting "digital privacy" now.

Patty Skuster (whose essay engages with Suzanne Valdez's in part III, "Strategic Action for Securing Access") considers prosecutors who have signed pledges not to prosecute individuals for violating abortion restrictions, but who are nevertheless drawn into prosecutions of people most likely to pursue self-managed abortion as well as their helpers. Many people in this category, she argues, are already targeted by law enforcement because they are poor, people of color, young, LGBTQIA2S+, the undocumented, and others who occupy highly vulnerable statuses. How do prosecutors view their pledges when the experience of "getting an abortion" has changed so radically for so many? This question raises another: How do individuals within the entire "ecosystem of pregnancy criminalization" remake themselves into knowledgeable actors in the wake of *Dobbs*? Dana Sussman describes a crucial new resource, *Confronting Pregnancy Criminalization*—a manual prepared to train thousands of physicians, nurses, midwives, criminal defense attorneys, prosecutors, social workers, policymakers, child welfare workers as well as nursing, medical, and law students to become educated responders to reproductive health matters under the *Dobbs* regime.

Dr. Jamila Perritt focuses on how the new criminalization is creating much more fraught conditions for physicians, who may or may not be well-versed as knowledgeable post-*Roe* actors, and thus may serve their patients less well. Perritt focuses on patients facing medical emergencies such as miscarriages—again, especially people in the most vulnerable categories. These patients may find themselves targets of "suspicion" and prosecution, even as they face poor access to health care. They may experience heightened fears about merely seeking care, even—or especially—in emergency situations where they might, under *Dobbs*, be denied or reported. Another group with rational fears under the new criminalization are undocumented immigrants, who have always faced deportation if found to have committed crimes of "moral turpitude"—a category of crime that now may include abortion. Indeed, immigrants may even face heightened suspicion if they experience pregnancy loss or an ectopic pregnancy. Asees Bhasin details some of the many ways that reproductive capacity now endangers immigrants, an impact that clarifies *Dobbs* as in part a population-control strategy. Bhasin also provides a view of the ways immigrants and allies are fighting back.

Texas has pioneered in targeting abortion-allies in the new era, people who may provide information about how to get an abortion or provide a ride to a medical facility. We must even ask, today, how must a professor at a Texas (or other abortion-hostile location) university comport herself under SB8 and *Dobbs?* What information about campus and community resources can she safely provide to students? At what point is she stepping into the territory of aiding and abetting? This is Alison Kafer's question, which she addresses in part by pointing to the strategic innovations of disability justice activists, disabled students and faculty, and disabilities studies.

26 The Digital Battleground in the Fight for Reproductive Rights

AZIZ Z. HUQ AND REBECCA WEXLER

Dobbs v. Jackson Women's Health Organization led to a spate of new restrictions on reproductive choice. In this essay we illuminate how the digital domain will become a vital battleground in the fight for reproductive rights. Our aim is to sketch reasons that those concerned with reproductive choice should pay attention to what's happening on the technology front—and in particular the way that search tools, social media platforms, and companies dealing in digital data respond to *Dobbs* in the coming years.

Why the Digital Environment Matters to Reproductive Choice

The digital environment matters for two main reasons: (1) online tools provide vital pathways to information and services, but (2) digital data is also a powerful tool for prosecutors and others bent on squelching reproductive choice. Let's take these points in turn.

Effective reproductive choice requires some literacy about sex and bodies. Where schools don't provide that knowledge, internet-mediated information fills the gap. It does so imperfectly, of course. The information available will often depend on what search firms like Google and social-media platforms such as Twitter,

Facebook, and Instagram choose to prioritize and hence draw to users' attention. It cannot be assumed that firms will prioritize accurate information. In the past, platforms have throttled online access to sex education materials, designating them "inappropriate."

Increasingly, actual medical services can also be obtained online, namely via telemedicine. Since 2000, federal law has permitted the use of mifepristone for early nonsurgical abortion in health-care settings. On December 16, 2001, the Food and Drug Administration (FDA)—the federal agency responsible for regulating medications— permanently lifted a requirement that certified clinicians could dispense mifepristone solely in a health-care setting, hence allowing prescription in the course of a telemedicine appointment. Although that rule change would likely be reversed under a Republican administration, it is likely that online provision of medication abortion by non-US-based organizations would continue. In the wake of *Dobbs*, we saw an increased resort to digital tools offering reproductive care. Providers also responded to *Dobbs* by prescribing pills to patients further along in pregnancy than the ten-week limit set by the FDA, by making pills available to women who are not pregnant but feel they could need them someday, and by deciding not to verify that patients are in states that permit abortion. All of these services are facilitated by digital access.

But even with government endorsement, online paths to medication abortion are not secure. Access to telehealth-based medication abortion, like information generally, is subject to the vagaries of content-moderation policies of search engines and social media. An informational or a provider site can be shut down if an internet service provider (ISP) decides to block it. Private companies that provide hosting and security services for websites that offer information and services can also decide to withdraw their own services. Furthermore, the universe of digital data created by pregnant persons, potentially pregnant persons, or providers can itself be exploited to identify and punish those involved in reproductive care. Some of this data comes from the online search activities and digital provisions of reproductive care just discussed—but not all. Indeed, there is a surprising range of quite mundane activity that can generate data capable of being used for restrictive purposes.

States' ability to stifle reproductive rights, especially in an era of medication abortion and remote medicine, turns on their ability to identify who is seeking such care. Digital traces, created not just via a person's use of the internet but also by wearable tools, phone-based applications, or online transactions likely all will become fodder for antiabortion prosecutors in the post-*Dobbs* era. Indeed, the Supreme Court's ruthless suppression of one kind of privacy—the privacy right of reproductive choice—creates an incentive for state actors to intrude on another kind of privacy, in respect to digital data and online activities. The first and most obvious worry for many pro-choice advocates as the *Dobbs* decision loomed in early 2022 hinged on period-tracking apps, such as Flo and Clue. Obviously these tools can provide potentially critical evidence for prosecutors hostile to abortion. But they are just part of a much larger body of data that can be used against people.

Consider first the variety of medical data, including that maintained by primary care providers, hospitals, and even school nurses, which might equally single out people seeking abortions. Generally all the government needs is a court order to acquire that data, even if it's covered by the federal privacy statute HIPAA. And since antiabortion police and prosecutors will be seeking to enforce criminal statutes, there's little doubt they can get such an order. Moreover, the range of data that could aid antiabortion prosecutions runs far wider. This is a consequence of the wide dispersion of digital devices that gather and record data about our movements, our actions, our behaviors, and our bodies. Thanks to new techniques of "machine learning," it is often possible to exploit large pools of information to surface hidden and seemingly unrelated data points: it has been more than a decade since the retailer Target elicited howls of protest for analyzing customer purchasing data to predict (accurately) which visitors were pregnant. Since then, not only have machine-learning tools improved, but our tolerance has grown for recommenders (on Amazon and Netflix, for example) that mine our past behavior to shape our future conduct.

What kind of data might states use to target abortion beyond medical and health data? Consider fitbits, which collect weight, activity, heartrate, sleep, and locational data. The company promises to share it only "for legal reasons, or to prevent harm"—both exceptions that a prosecutor could argue apply in an abortion prosecution. Locational data generated by cell phones and other wearable devices might also be used to infer travel out of state to secure care. Imagine, for example, a Missouri or Indiana prosecutor seeking data about people who cross their state's border into Illinois and travel to a facility that provides reproductive care. (Or imagine if that same prosecutor seeks information from a sister state that has an automated toll system on whether a particular vehicle took that path.) A 2018 Supreme Court decision in *Carpenter v. United States* holds that a warrant is required when the state asks a cell phone company for data—but again, warrants will be easy to get for law enforcement officers intent on extirpating abortion.

These threats to digital privacy won't be limited to states that prohibit abortion. Even in the first months after the *Dobbs* decision, criminal and civil restrictions on abortion alike were already spilling over into other states. Texas's 2021 ban on medication abortions, for example, was explicitly aimed at out-of-state providers. Some of the first suits under Texas's vigilante law were filed by Illinois and Arkansas residents. And Nevada prosecutors have subpoenaed California-based Facebook for digital data to prosecute a pregnant woman who sought abortion care.

Finally, the changing landscape of digital privacy will bring to the fore a group of influential yet shadowy actors called data brokers. These firms buy and sell personal data, including information that might be leveraged by antiabortion states. Since *Dobbs,* there have been calls for data brokers to limit the flow of information that might undermine reproductive choice. At least initially, however, data brokers did not change their behavior.

The Changing Politics of Big Tech

Digital companies' decisions about abortion will be highly consequential. They could either choose to cooperate with antiabortion states by shutting down the flow of useful information via content-moderation rules and by handing over inculpating data. Or they could entrench the flow of health information and carve out new kinds of privacy against the inference of pregnancy or abortion.

The ensuing battles will also scramble ideological front lines. Feminists have long had an ambivalent relation to privacy against government intrusions. A generation ago, they struck a major blow against the scourge of domestic violence by resisting the idea that constitutional privacy immured the home from view. Today, however, the script is flipped. Those who once fought liberal conceptions of the home as a private space will likely scramble to carve out new, digital private spaces for reproductive choice. At the same time, this era raises new questions about the relation of government to big tech. For many liberals and progressives the problem of tech hinges on the concentration of private power. This poses for them challenges to important values, ranging from the nation's democracy to a child's dignitary claim to control photos they've taken. Democratic polities have powerful cause to rein in private power when it runs rampant.

Yet when, as now, state power is flexed in regressive and cruel ways, it is natural to look to civil society—including firms—as a countervailing force. The decision of Apple, Amazon, and IBM to exit the market for facial recognition tools may not have stopped police from using those instruments. But they likely slowed the spread and blunted the efficacy of such tools. Even as conservatives decry state intrusions on liberty and celebrate free speech online, it is likely to be pro-choice forces urging Google and Facebook to shield pregnant people and to insulate their reproductive choices from the state's baleful gaze.

What Can Be Done?

Of course, this is not the end of the story: there are plenty of things that individuals, organizations, and even states can do to shore up digital privacy post-*Dobbs*. Individuals have a good deal of control over how their activities online and their choice of portable devices expose them to the risk of abortion-related surveillance. Choosing to exercise digital privacy rights by opting out of certain apps, stopping third-party tracking, and seeking the privacy of a VPN or a Tor browser are all expensive options. Self-help is likely to be least available for those who need that help most. The most effective interventions on the digital privacy front therefore have to be structural in nature. Indeed, implicit in what we've explained so far is the possibility that antiabortion states can move aggressively to use the digital environment to stifle choice: they can use compulsory process to acquire information; they can buy it from data brokers; and they can pressure tech firms to facilitate prosecutions, or make the acquisition of accurate medical information more difficult. But what can pro-choice states do by way of response?

The initial pro-choice state response to *Dobbs* was halting and incomplete in respect to digital privacy. Quickest off the mark, California and Connecticut enacted laws that limited law-enforcement cooperation with abortion prosecutions. They shored up data-privacy rules for providers. And they permitted countersuits against out-of-state vigilante plaintiffs. In September 2022 the California Legislature also voted to enact a measure that protects medical records from out-of-state antiabortion subpoenas. But these laws are still hazardously incomplete. Apart from the limited category of medical records in California, their privacy measures are toothless in the face of warrants and court orders from antiabortion states. A state-law right to delete data stored by, say, Google or Meta does nothing to stop a Texas or Alabama court from ordering those companies to ignore the request and hand the data over to law enforcement instead. Nothing prevents antiabortion actors from using subpoenas for locational information or commercial transactional records to identify abortion providers and patients, say, in Connecticut as a means to shame and threaten them into inaction. And nothing in the California and Connecticut responses to *Dobbs* does anything to staunch the growing threat of verbal and physical stalking and harassment against patients and providers—which can happen both online and in offline contexts.

Pro-choice states, however, have options to do better. They can, indeed, draw on well-worn legal devices to fashion both a sword and a shield that would robustly protect reproductive choice and digital privacy. Start with the sword. Tort law has long prohibited outside malicious interference with certain special relationships, like employment relationships or medical care. States should create a civil action that empowers pregnant persons and their reproductive care providers to sue anyone who interferes with their access to care. That would include suits against out-of-state actors who threaten, harass, and intimidate pregnant patients and their care providers. And it could also reach the data brokers who continue to traffic in abortion-sensitive data.

Another option for pro-choice states would be to create what is called an "evidentiary privilege," like the lawyer-client one, to shield abortion-related data. When you confide with a lawyer, no one—not even law enforcement—can force them to spill your secrets. Privileges also block courts from compelling disclosure of those private communications. And they bar the use of a warrant to break into your lawyer's office and seize their papers. Privileges can thus be a stout legal defense against both subpoenas and police searches. Indeed, they are stronger in some ways than the protection offered by the Fourth Amendment. A state statute or common law rule could create a privilege covering any information that reveals a person's reproductive health choices. This includes internet searches, locational data, social media communications, medical data, biometric data, related financial records, and more. Next, make the privilege applicable to all antiabortion subpoenas, warrants, court orders, and judicial proceedings. This would set up a zone of privacy around reproductive choice, like that already in place when we deal with lawyers. Importantly, this zone would cover many of the sources and the species of digital data discussed above, including data brokers.

Ideally the US Congress would enact such a privilege to apply in courts nationwide. In that case, if a Texas prosecutor or vigilante plaintiff somehow got their hands on the data despite state-level protections, the federal privilege would stop them lawfully using it in any antiabortion court proceeding—including trials, sentencing, or even pre-trial proceedings to keep someone in jail. Of course, federal action faces hurdles, and states shouldn't wait for gridlock on Capitol Hill to abate.

Conclusion

The August 2022 Kansas referendum on abortion access—as well as constitutional amendments in California, Vermont, and Michigan in November 2022—made clear that there is a deep well of latent public support for action to protect abortion. The antiabortion lobby has played its hand. Now those who believe in reproductive freedom must stand up to the cross-border bullying by something more than the piecemeal and incomplete responses we have to date seen. And the digital domain must be an essential part of that strategy.

27 Law Enforcement Discretion for Self-Managed Abortion Helpers

PATTY SKUSTER

The two police officers lived on separate ends of the African continent, but they shared a path to abortion rights advocacy. I learned this as we chatted over coffee during a break between sessions. Together in Toronto for the International Law Enforcement and Public Health conference, we would later appear together on a panel about partnerships between abortion providers and police. Both had served as doctors at police hospitals in countries where people end their pregnancies with sticks, chemicals, blunt force trauma. Like other African doctors-turned-abortion-rights-champions, they had provided care for people who suffered injury, bleeding, and infection after abortion. Both doctor-officers felt strongly that their governments needed to do more to help people get abortion care, without risk to health and life.

I was in Toronto on behalf of my employer at the time, the global abortion rights nonprofit Ipas. The officers were there to share their cadet-training programs and curricula on abortion, the aim of which was to stop the criminalization of abortion seekers and providers. Back then, I didn't think my work spotlighting the police partnerships with abortion providers had much relevance in my own country. I knew criminalization was a Reproductive Justice issue—scholars and advocates like Dorothy Roberts, Lynn Paltrow, and Michelle

Goodwin had written about criminalization of pregnancy, particularly among members of poor and Black communities. Attorney activist Farah Diaz-Tello had made me aware of arrests related to self-managed abortion. I knew police could be helpful by enforcing buffer zones around abortion clinics. But it was 2018 and abortion was legal. Broadly speaking, law enforcement officials had no particular interest in abortion.

Then, in the weeks and months after the *Dobbs* decision, elected Democrats—including law enforcement officials—became eager to demonstrate their abortion moxie. Dozens of elected prosecutors at state and local levels vowed not to prosecute abortion cases. They primarily serve blue cities within red states, where previability abortion is or could soon become a crime. Unlike the African police officers, many of the elected prosecutors are inexperienced with abortion in their professional lives. The harm of recent criminal abortion laws has not yet fully played out.

The abortion bans had some dire immediate outcomes, as abortion clinics closed in states where the bans took effect. Abortion providers and clinic staff were not inclined to take on legal risk associated with providing abortion, even in locales with abortion-supportive prosecutors. But I suspect these are the individuals whom the prosecutors had in mind when pledging not to prosecute—the licensed and trained health-care workers who provided abortion care before bans came into effect. In an earlier statement pledging to exercise discretion in response to proposed bans, the prosecutors noted the doctors, nurses, and other clinic workers who could face criminal liability, along with the patients ending their pregnancies. The 2022 elected prosecutors' statement, with nearly a hundred signatories, noted that criminalizing abortion will not end abortion, but it will end safe abortion. What the prosecutors miss is that, even where abortion is banned, people are safely self-managing their abortions.

The presence of a medical professional is not required to make an abortion clinically safe. In fact, before the advent of modern medicine, people were ending unwanted pregnancies with the help of friends, family, and experts in the community, with varied degrees of safety. It was the influence of doctors over regulation of abortion over the past couple centuries that pushed forward the medicalization of abortion, ensuring that abortion is legal only when provided by a health-care provider.

In recent decades, early abortion has been moving away from medical professionals' exclusive authority, with the increasing use of self-managed abortion with pills, without clinical supervision. Medication for abortion was first discovered by women in Brazil, who noted the label on the ulcer drug misoprostol warned of miscarriage as a side effect. In the same era a pharmaceutical company began to develop another abortion drug, mifepristone. Since the 1980s, pregnant people have self-managed their abortions with medicine, and with the help of community groups, hotlines, friends, family members, activists' websites, and others. Evidence shows that self-managed medication abortion can be safe. Just this year the World Health Organization included in its guidelines the approval of self-managed abortion as a method early in pregnancy.

The shift away from in-clinic abortion is accelerating in the United States as state legislators impose bans on abortion. Even in jurisdictions with prosecutors who have pledged their support, abortion clinic operators and medical professionals have declined to take legal risk and have closed abortion clinics. With bans on abortion some people will travel to another state to end their pregnancy. But many Americans lack adequate time or money to travel or have other reasons to avoid the formal health-care system. Self-managed abortion may be a good option for them. People seeking abortion may do so online. Some will look for help from friends, family members, or other members of their communities. In the context of abortion bans, the work of self-abortion helpers will be essential to ensuring large numbers of people will be able to get the abortions they need.

Research from around the world shows that contrary to the prosecutors' understanding, abortion can be clinically safe, even if legally banned. Abortion criminalization does give rise to legal risk—risk of arrest or prosecution. Unwilling to take on legal risk following the *Dobbs* decision, abortion clinics closed in states where it is banned. Not only are abortion providers known to authorities, but they also are unlikely to take the personal and professional risks that come with arrest and prosecution. Law enforcement officials will be challenged to uphold their pledges in the face of abortions that may not take place in the way they imagine. For pregnant people who have abortions, the need not to prosecute is clear—no matter the context, prosecutors must refrain from charging people with crimes for decisions related to their pregnancies. In addition, to enable abortion care in this era of abortion bans, law enforcement officials must refrain from criminalizing those individuals most likely to take on legal risk, including self-managed abortion helpers.

The people most likely to face legal risk are individuals who are already targeted by law enforcement authorities. Prosecutors announced their support for abortion amid a national crisis of mass incarceration, where millions of poor, Black and Brown Americans are locked behind bars or live in communities subject to police surveillance, harassment, and control. It is not the 2022 abortion bans that will lead to criminalization, it is a system of racist structures and individual racist bias that already punishes people for helping others get the abortions they need. The same structural racism contributes to lack of preventive care, which results in Black women experiencing disproportionately high rates of abortion. The highest need for abortion may be in the very communities that are targeted for criminalization.

For decades before the *Dobbs* decision, people have been criminalized for self-managing their own abortion or helping. The organization If/When/How: Lawyering for Reproductive Justice has documented more than sixty cases of people criminally investigated or arrested for ending their own pregnancy or helping someone else do so. Given the challenges with such research, the true number is likely much higher. People of color were disproportionally represented and were charged with a range of laws—from mishandling of human remains to practicing medicine without a license. The laws under which people experience criminalization related to self-managed abortion haven't changed with post-*Dobbs* abortion bans. However, the number of people who need to self-manage their abortion and who will take legal risks while helping others will increase.

To support abortion, law enforcement officials must not criminalize people who self-managed abortion or those who help, particularly within communities that face the most legal risk. Like Americans who faced legal consequences in connection with abortion, it was people who faced discrimination and experienced vulnerability because of poverty, age, or social status who faced arrest and prosecution for abortion in the two countries where the African police officers worked. They were training police recruits to understand abortion as a health and human rights issue, rather than a criminal one. A similar shift among law enforcement officials could help Americans get the abortions they need in light of inhumane abortion policies in the United States. But such a change must be integrated into other efforts to decriminalize unjust and health-harming laws—laws that prohibit drugs or sex work, for example, and give power to police and prosecutors to inflict violence and control over communities that face structural discrimination and individual racism at the hands of law enforcement authorities.

In the face of an inhumane and discriminatory legal system, the role of law enforcement in the context of abortion bans, as other harmful laws, is to reduce the violence and harm they inflict upon criminalized communities.

28 *Preparing Criminal Defense Attorneys to Fight for Reproductive Justice*

DANA SUSSMAN

Pregnancy Justice (formerly National Advocates for Pregnant Women) is uniquely positioned to understand how pregnant people, regardless of pregnancy outcome, are policed by the state. Pregnancy Justice has long understood that more arrests and prosecutions would be looming in a post-*Roe* America. Our amicus brief to the Supreme Court in the *Dobbs* case laid it out in stark detail. Drawing on our decades-long experience defending people charged with pregnancy-related crimes, we predicted that if the Supreme Court overturned *Roe* and *Casey*, more pregnant people would face prosecution and other punitive state action because of pregnancy, both in the abortion context and beyond. *Roe* and *Casey* not only articulated a fundamental right to abortion, the Supreme Court opinions also made clear that pregnant people, and not fetuses, are people, with full constitutional rights. Without such protections, state action once considered rights violations—from denial of a person's bodily autonomy to surveillance and incarceration, all in service of the government's "legitimate" interest in "prenatal life" as Justice Alito put it in *Dobbs*—are now permissible.

Since its founding in 2001, Pregnancy Justice has defended people who have faced criminal charges, from felony child neglect to murder, for experiencing a pregnancy loss, having an abortion, or exposing their fetus to some perceived or actual risk of harm, all purporting to be in the name of protecting "fetal life." We have documented more than seventeen hundred cases of pregnancy-related criminal cases or forced medical interventions, from 1973 to 2020, in which pregnant people's rights are ignored and dozens of cases in which pregnant people face decades-long prison terms for experiencing a pregnancy loss or having an abortion. All of these cases occurred, of course, before the *Dobbs* decision (and we don't yet have a tally of cases that occurred in 2021 or the first half of 2022 before the decision came down). The rate of these cases is rapidly accelerating—Pregnancy Justice documented 413 such cases from 1973 to 2005, and more than 1,350 such cases from 2006 to 2020, representing a threefold increase in less than half the time.[1]

The concept of "fetal personhood," once a relatively fringe ideology, has moved into the mainstream and is used both to justify laws that ban abortion and efforts by prosecutors and courts to criminalize pregnant people. However, defending "fetal life" is just another mechanism to maintain patriarchal and white supremacist power by controlling women and all people capable of pregnancy, singling them out and making them more vulnerable to state control and prosecution than nonpregnant people. This is particularly true for pregnant people of color and poor pregnant people. The *Dobbs* decision is infused with fetal personhood ideology, and Justice Alito's opinion rests on the principle that the government's "interest" in protecting what he describes as "prenatal life" is legitimate and can justify complete bans on abortion without any exceptions.

In late winter and early spring 2022, with the *Dobbs* decision looming and our prediction that pregnancy-related criminalization would continue even more aggressively on its current upward trajectory, Pregnancy Justice focused our efforts on trying to give the actors within the ecosystem of pregnancy criminalization the information and tools they need to interrupt this cycle of criminalization. These actors include health-care providers and hospital-based social workers, who often initiate the call to law enforcement or other state authorities, turning a site of care into a site of criminalization; medical examiners who may be confronted with providing a report or drawing conclusions about a fetal loss that could be used in a criminal prosecution; police officers and prosecutors who hold inordinate power and discretion; and criminal defense attorneys who may have never taken on a pregnancy-related case.

Partnering with the law firm Schulte Roth & Zabel, who donated over six hundred hours of pro bono time to develop this document, we published *Confronting Pregnancy Criminalization* on June 23, 2022 (the day before the *Dobbs* decision was published) with an online webinar attended by more than five hundred people. Since launching, and since *Roe* being overturned, we have used the guide to train thousands of doctors, nurses, midwives, criminal defense attorneys, prosecutors, social workers, policymakers, and child welfare workers as well as nursing, medical, and law students. The guide draws on Pregnancy Justice's more than two decades of experience defending these cases, overturning convictions, and galvanizing public opinion. It contains chapters focused on each discipline and provides practical guidance to those disciplines on how to confront and end pregnancy-related criminalization. The guidance for criminal defense attorneys has the potential to be the most impactful, as so many people who face pregnancy-related charges are poor, eligible for indigent defense, and are often provided a court-appointed attorney who does not have the resources, time, and in some cases interest in mounting a substantial defense.

The guidance reminds criminal defense attorneys that people facing prosecution for acts or omissions that create perceived risks to their pregnancies are often in incredibly vulnerable positions: their bodies are used as evidence against them; they may feel stigmatized, dehumanized, violated, and dismissed; they may have confided in medical professionals or sought medical care only to have their confidential discussions with their caregivers and their medical records turned over to law enforcement. The guide reminds criminal defense attorneys that in many cases the criminal charge is based on the erroneous assumption that a woman engaged in acts or omissions that harmed the fetus. Defense attorneys should challenge the causal link between the alleged behavior and the alleged harm to the fetus in as many ways as possible, in light of the fact that miscarriages are extremely common and can be caused by myriad factors. Proving causation between a pregnant person's acts or omissions and a miscarriage is virtually impossible, and a court should be made aware of this in no uncertain terms as early and often in the process as feasible. This may include retaining experts like forensic pathologists and ob-gyns to challenge any causal links allegedly based on the evidence.

While the focus of these cases will often center around the evidence, criminal defense attorneys are encouraged to not assume that the prosecution is actually authorized under the state's law. Every argument possible should be raised before and at trial and should be preserved for appeal. If the client is charged with child endangerment, child abuse, feticide, or under a general murder statute, it may be possible to argue that the prosecution extends beyond the plain language of the statute because the statute does not define "child" to include a fetus or that the statute either explicitly excludes pregnant women or does not explicitly include the acts of pregnant women in relation to their own pregnancies. In many instances states may have considered—but rejected—an expansion of the statute to include fetuses under the definition of children. In such cases, argue that your client had no notice of potential prosecution under the state's construction of the statute in violation of her constitutional right to due process under the Fourteenth Amendment as well as the relevant provision of the state constitution. In most cases, but for the pregnancy, the conduct itself would not be considered criminal. There is no comparative liability for men. For example, while all states and the federal government criminalize possession of illicit drugs, most states do not explicitly criminalize drug *use* and evidence of drug use on its own is rarely sufficient to sustain a possession charge. As such, a father's drug use (absent additional circumstances) would not be criminalized or monitored in a comparable way to that of a pregnant woman.

Where permitted and appropriate, defense attorneys can seek attention from local and national media. Attorneys often shy away from media attention but, as we have seen consistently in our cases, public outcry and organizing can be an effective tool to put pressure and scrutiny on law enforcement. Public outcry not only puts pressure on the prosecution, but it can also alert the community and other stakeholders to what is happening. Defense attorneys should seek amicus briefs even at the trial level, even if it's not typical practice. Amicus briefs function to bring national attention to a case and draw in other avenues of help for the defendant. They also have been critical for establishing the dangerous medical and public health implications of the criminalization of pregnancy. Amicus briefs should be collected from a variety of groups, prioritizing local groups, especially medical groups, human rights organizations, and experts generally.

This work requires allyship, collaboration, and an all-hands-on-deck approach. Our work is strengthened when we work across disciplines in furtherance of our vision of a world in which all pregnant people are treated with compassion, dignity, and respect, and that one's status as pregnant is not exploited in furtherance of systems of oppression that maintain white supremacy and patriarchy.

29 *What's Next for Doctors and Patients*

Care, Compassion, and Criminalization in
a Post-*Roe* World

JAMILA PERRITT

I got the call in the wee hours of the morning. The nurse was on the
phone. I was the obstetrician on call. A pregnant woman had arrived
to the hospital via ambulance. Would I come and evaluate her?

When I arrived, I saw right away that her clothes were covered in
blood from the waist down. She was six weeks pregnant and had begun bleeding a few hours ago. In between her tears (and the staff's
poking and prodding), she shared her story and answered our questions.

Yes, she knew she was pregnant. She already had an appointment
scheduled to start her prenatal care.

No, this was not her first pregnancy. She had three healthy children and was looking forward to growing her family with the addition of a fourth.

Yes, she was healthy and, no, she didn't have any medical conditions or problems . . . until now.

She denied recently experiencing violence or trauma.

We spoke about what was happening. I explained that this was
likely a miscarriage, and that the pregnancy would not continue to

full term. I spoke about how commonly miscarriages occur, especially early in pregnancy (10–20 percent of known pregnancies end in miscarriage). We talked about her options for care. I explained that for many people, their bodies manage the process on their own, passing the pregnancy safely and completely. For others, the bleeding or cramping can be heavier than expected and they may want or need medical intervention to complete it. In her case, her blood count was already very low and this heavy bleeding was worrisome. I recommended that she have a dilation and curettage to prevent even more blood loss and possibly death (sometimes called a D&C, this is a suction procedure where the pregnancy tissue is removed from the uterus, completing the miscarriage). When she heard the news, she was sad and afraid. But she was resolved. She wanted to be there for her other children. She would have the D&C.

We began prepping her for the operating room and contacted the anesthesiologist on call so that we could provide her with the medicine she needed to keep her comfortable throughout her care.

We ordered labs, did an ultrasound and exam, and signed consent forms. We moved quickly to get ready to head back to the OR. When the anesthesiologist arrived at the bedside and began reviewing her chart, he was kind and compassionate. At first. He explained the medication he'd be providing, asked a few additional questions, and continued to review her medical record.

Within minutes, however, his attitude changed. He became visibly upset and left the room. While reviewing her chart, he noted that the ultrasound I had performed at the time of her arrival showed cardiac activity. He stated loudly and angrily that he would not participate in her care in any way as long as there was still a "heartbeat." He said he would care for this patient if she was having a miscarriage, but he was "morally opposed" to abortion. So he refused to take care of her.

It didn't matter that this pregnancy was nonviable. It didn't matter that this person stood in front of us losing blood as her condition was rapidly becoming critical. It didn't matter that the recommendation for a D&C was in line with standard care practices. It didn't matter that the patient had been given the options for care and this was what she chose to do. It didn't matter that she was actively bleeding.

None of that mattered. She didn't matter. We would have to call someone else.

We contacted the backup anesthesiologist first. We contacted the head of the anesthesiology department next. No one else willing to participate in her care was available.

Our options were few: wait until she got "critical enough" that her surgery constituted an "emergency"; perform serial ultrasound evaluations, waiting until there was no longer cardiac activity to then proceed; or move forward with the D&C without the additional anesthesia.

I had to explain all of this to the terrified, grieving mother in front of me. We would not be able to care for her the way we knew we could and should because the doctor responsible for safely administering anesthesia objected to participating in her care. Moreover, I had to explain that he was protected and supported by the hospital (and the federal government) in this decision, but she was not supported by any of these entities in hers. Indeed, the "Conscience Provisions," collectively known as the "Church Amendments," enacted in the 1970s allows individuals and entities that object to performing or assisting in the performance of abortion or sterilization to opt out of doing so if it would be "contrary to the provider's religious beliefs or moral convictions."

She decided to move forward with the D&C without the additional anesthesia. We would give her what we could for pain. We would care for her the best we could so she could go home and be with her family.

We did. She did.

This was more than ten years ago. I cared for her at a time when *Roe* was considered the "law of the land." I cared for her in a "blue" state, where abortion was legal and access to care was assumed to be ensured for every person who needed one. But this was not the case for this person. And she is not alone. For many the promise of *Roe* was never a guarantee, and assurances of equal access to this previously constitutionally protected care fell short. Even before the recent Supreme Court ruling in *Dobbs,* people seeking abortions faced numerous barriers to accessing care, not just the "moral objection" of providers. Legislative restrictions, financial obstacles, and social stigma abounded, pushing abortion out of reach for many.

As an obstetrician and gynecologist who has provided comprehensive reproductive health care for more than fifteen years, I have supported thousands of people throughout their pregnancies. I have caught their babies at birth centers, in hospitals, and once in the backseat of a car! I have held their hands as they cried with the joy that comes with birth and from the grief that comes with death. I have helped them build their family through adoption and infertility care. And I have helped them navigate accessing abortion care when building their family wasn't the right decision for them. I can tell you, firsthand, accessing abortion care has never been an easy endeavor for any person. And this road is even steeper for people of color, young people, undocumented people, and other communities who have been, and continue to be, marginalized from care. This was where we started with abortion access. And then came *Dobbs*.[1]

As I write this, we approach six months since the Supreme Court eliminated the federal protections afforded by the *Roe v. Wade* ruling. Although the ruling on June 24, 2022, was a blow, it was not a surprise. Abortion rights and social justice advocates have seen the writing on the wall for decades now as reproductive rights have been stripped away bit by bit since *Roe v. Wade* was decided in 1973. The thing that abortion rights supporters feared most, the overturn of *Roe,* came to pass and states moved swiftly to eliminate or severely restrict access to abortion, making it all but impossible to obtain.

Yet we know that when abortion is restricted, people will continue to access that care in whatever way they feel is best, legal or not, including seeking ways to self-manage their own abortion.[2] Unlike the era pre-*Roe,* self-managed abortion is medically safe and effective when people have access to the information and resources they want and need. The real risk of self-managed abortion is not medical, it is legal. In fact, a recent study by If/When/How identified sixty-one cases of people criminally investigated or arrested for allegedly ending their own pregnancy or helping someone else to do so from 2000 to 2020.[3] It is important to note that although criminal investigations in these cases occurred in twenty-six states, self-managed abortion has historically only been a crime in seven states; currently, only two states consider self-managing one's own abortion a crime. These cases show us what many in the Reproductive Justice community have long known—criminalization occurs regardless of the law, not because of it.

When I am asked about what it means to be an abortion provider in a post-*Roe* America, how I understand and face this future we are hurtling toward, I consider all of the contexts that people find themselves in, because the decision to be pregnant or not, to parent or not, doesn't occur in a vacuum. It never has and it never will. Individual and community experiences with abortion, contraception, and pregnancy interact in a complex web that is shaped by the social, political, and historical context in which we live and operate in this country. We cannot understand or even begin to address reproductive health inequities like abortion access without understanding and acknowledging the contexts in which they occur. And the context that we live in has turned many medical facilities into sites of criminalization.

For politically or ideologically motivated prosecutors and legislators, the goal has always been to end *all* abortion, self-managed or otherwise. The law is simply one tool used to surveil, target, and criminalize people to this end. Moreover, the laws are discriminatorily and unequally applied.[4] People of color, specifically Black and Brown people, those living in poverty, LGBTQIA2S+ people, undocumented individuals, and young people bear the brunt of this inequity. In fact, in the If/When/How study the majority of those criminalized were living in poverty, and people of color were disproportionately targeted.

As a doctor, one of the most concerning issues reported was the clear role that health-care providers played in initiating and facilitating criminalization of people for their pregnancy outcomes. The If/When/How report showed that almost half of all people criminally investigated for suspicion of managing their own abortion were reported to law enforcement by health-care providers or social workers when they sought care. This occurs despite the fact that there is essentially no way to tell the difference between someone who has self-managed their abortion with medication and someone who has experienced a miscarriage. There are no exams, no bloodwork, no medical tests or clinical workups that can make the determination. Unless the patient discloses that they have managed their own abortion, it is difficult if not nearly impossible, to detect. So, in the absence of self-disclosure, the impetus for reporting rested on the providers' *suspicion* of "wrongdoing." And this suspicion is frequently fueled by bias—both implicit and explicit.

We have long known that bias negatively impacts quality of care and contributes to health inequities. Whether health-care providers are calling the police on their patients out of an explicit desire to punish and criminalize behavior that they find unacceptable or immoral, or simply because of ignorance about their legal requirements related to mandatory reporting, participation in and facilitation of criminalization causes harm. It robs people of their agency and bodily autonomy in health-care decision making. It keeps people from seeking care when they need it. It disrupts the patient-provider relationship by pitting patients against their health-care providers. People come to us seeking care, and instead they receive punishment. It doesn't matter the intent. The impact is clear.

I think of the patient I cared for so many years ago often, especially lately as we grapple with the future of reproductive health care in this country and its impact on patients and providers alike. I wonder how her care would look different today. Would she still come to the hospital when the bleeding began? Or would she be too afraid that someone would call the police because they suspected she self-managed her care? I also reflect on my own behavior. Would I proceed with the D&C, despite the law, in a state where abortion is now banned? Or would I wait until she was close enough to death before moving forward? How close is close enough? How many lives will be lost in the waiting?

As health-care providers, we are asking ourselves many hard questions. What does a way forward look like that centers compassionate, person-centered care for the communities we serve? What does resistance look like in these places and systems where we are being asked to withhold care, to protect ourselves instead of our patients? What would and could it mean for doctors, those who often hold the most power in medical systems, to refuse to participate in criminalizing those we care for and claim to care about? The unraveling of abortion access did not occur overnight, and the rebuilding and reimaging of a new system of care that serves us all will not be quick or easy. But rebuilding will be worth it. I believe that it is possible to create a new model of care where patients and providers are partners in care, not adversaries or opponents. It will take us all to get there.

30 *Surveilled, Criminalized, and Deportable*

The Disproportional Impacts of *Dobbs* on Immigrants and the Fight against Reproductive Injustice

ASEES BHASIN

Immigrants have historically been, and continue to be, subjected to grave reproductive injustices. When they desire parenthood, they are confronted with accusations of hyperfertility and of giving birth to "anchor babies." When they seek to access abortion care, they encounter key structural barriers. In this essay I analyze the impact of the Supreme Court's ruling in *Dobbs v. Jackson Women's Health Organization* on immigrants' reproductive agency and discuss the strategies currently being deployed in resistance.

The criminalization of individuals suspected of having abortions is terrifying in and of itself, but there are additional consequences that undocumented pregnant people face in this context. Immigration law dictates that one of many grounds for deportation from the United States is if the undocumented person is convicted of a crime that is either an aggravated felony or one of "moral turpitude." Immigrants convicted for aggravated felonies or crimes involving moral turpitude (CIMT) may be deported without a hearing in front of an immigration judge, may be disqualified for relief such as asylum, may become permanently inadmissible to the United States, and may face up to twenty years in prison if they reenter and are apprehended. The Immigration and Nationality Act has a long list of conduct that could be possibly considered as an aggravated felony. For instance, murder or any other "crime of violence for which the term of imprisonment is at least one year" are considered aggravated felonies. A person receiving an abortion may be charged for either of these offenses. In addition to being a possible aggravated felony, it could also be construed as a CIMT, a term that has been criticized for being vague and nebulous.

Although there is a dearth of case law interpreting whether receiving an abortion is indeed a CIMT, a 1946 decision by the Board of Immigration Appeals in *The Matter of M* plainly stated that the crime of abortion was one of moral turpitude. A closer read of the statute in that case shows that it defines the crime of abortion as one that required the "procurement of abortion" (the defendant was charged for performing an abortion), and it is hard to find historical evidence where receiving an abortion was construed as a CIMT. Nevertheless, due to the significant overlap in antiabortion and anti-immigration ideology, we can expect to see states restricting abortion pass explicit guidance or legislation on how to regulate or prosecute immigrants seeking abortions. Similarly, conservative judges may interpret abortions as falling within the purview of CIMTs, thereby making those who are undocumented immediately deportable.

The criminalization and consequent deportation of immigrants post-*Dobbs* is not merely speculative but is a reality that is already unfolding. In April 2022 twenty-six-year-old Lizelle Herrera was arrested in the Rio Grande Valley for self-inducing an abortion and was charged with murder. This led to her arrest and imprisonment in a detention center with a bond of $500,000. Although the district attorney in charge ordered charges to be dropped after fierce protests by advocacy groups, similar incidents in the future will not be surprising. For instance, legislation is being introduced in Texas that will empower DAs to prosecute abortion-related crimes that may occur outside their jurisdiction. While this is merely one out of several bills that have been introduced countrywide to punish and deter abortion, it is safe to assume that we can expect an exponential increase in abortion criminalization. This punitive regime will not only impact abortion care but open up medical events such as pregnancy loss and ectopic pregnancies for investigation and criminalization due to their resemblance to self-managed abortion. In turn, undocumented immigrants may be deterred from receiving care, compounding the lower rates of prenatal care and higher rates of pregnancy complications that already afflict immigrants.

Pregnant people in immigration detention have always faced significant hardships in accessing abortion, even though many of these pregnancies were caused due to rape and sexual violence faced while crossing the border. Immigration and Customs Enforcement (ICE) only funds abortions in cases of rape, incest, or danger to the mother's life, and survivors of sexual violence are often unaware of these exemptions or are unable to articulate that they fall within these categories. Furthermore, as seen in the *J.D. v. Azar* litigation, immigration officials prevent immigrants in detention from receiving timely care, forcing them to jump through legal hoops, such as counseling requirements at religiously affiliated "crisis pregnancy centers." The reality on the ground is harsher after *Dobbs,* with several asylum seekers finding themselves in detention facilities situated in states where abortion is illegal. While the Biden administration has announced plans to instruct detention centers to ensure that immigrant women in custody continue receiving abortions by transporting them to states where the health procedure is legal, there will still be delays in providing care, and detainees may defer care because they distrust the government and medical establishment.[1]

Seeking out-of-state care is not only impossible for immigrant detainees but also for those immigrants who are not in detention but lack legal status. It is practically impossible for those living in border states to get abortions. Border securitization and surveillance makes intrastate and out-of-state travel extremely dangerous for undocumented people by putting them at risk for being apprehended, detained, and subsequently deported. Even for those living in nonborder states, out-of-state travel is undesirable since we've seen several instances of immigrants entering deportation proceedings after being stopped at traffic lights. In recent times, a growing number of immigrants are forced to wear electronic monitoring devices or ankle monitors as they await outcomes in immigration proceedings. For people under this type of surveillance, leaving the state to receive an abortion may be impermissible, or impossible without raising the awareness of immigration enforcement officials.

In addition to opening immigrants up to the risk of criminalization and deportation, *Dobbs* has impacts on laws governing areas other than reproductive rights. In *Dobbs* one of the majority's principal objections to *Roe v. Wade* was that the Constitution made no reference to the right to abortion and that the right was not protected by any constitutional provision including the Fourteenth Amendment. Justice Thomas's concurring opinion in this case implored the Court to reconsider other precedents that implicated the substantive due process clause and were "demonstrably erroneous." In addition to jeopardizing outcomes in cases such as *Loving, Griswold, Lawrence,* and *Obergefell,* following such guidance in *Dobbs* would also endanger *Plyler v. Doe,* a case that held that the Fourteenth Amendment ensured that all children, regardless of their immigration status, had a constitutional right to a free public education from kindergarten to twelfth grade. Perhaps picking up on the Constitution's absence of any mention of undocumented children's right to education, after a draft opinion in *Dobbs* was leaked, Texas governor Greg Abbott said that he would resurrect a challenge to *Plyler* due to the educational expenses of educating migrants.[2]

While the assaults on immigrants' rights are grave and egregious, they have been met with strong pushback with those fighting for Reproductive Justice and immigrant justice, among others. Abortion funds and local organizations such as Frontera Fund and Mariposa Fund provide financial and logistical support for immigrants seeking abortions by providing them with financial and logistical support. Helpline organizations such as Repro Legal Helpline and Repro Legal Defense Fund have also been helping individuals understand their reproductive options while managing legal risk. Reproductive Justice and immigrant rights organizations are playing a crucial role in emphasizing the intersectional impacts of *Dobbs,* particularly on undocumented people. Many such organizations have been working on abortion access for many years, and advocating for the passage of legislation such as the Health Equity and Access under the Law (HEAL) for Immigrant Families Act, the Equal Access to Abortion Coverage in Health Insurance (EACH) Act, and the Women's Health Protection Act (WHPA). They have also advocated for lifting the Hyde Amendment that bans the use of federal funds to pay for abortion care except in a few limited circumstances.

Post-*Dobbs,* while some of these legislative pushes have become even more urgent, these groups have also been putting pressure on the Biden administration. This includes demands to make abortion accessible in all detention facilities and to ensure the right to travel without the fear of apprehension particularly in regions affected by border patrol activity. Organizations such as the National Latina Institute for Reproductive Justice (NLIRJ) have been highlighting the links between border securitization, immigration enforcement, and reproductive surveillance. Preempting an increase in abortion-related detention, they have started deepening their work around deportation defense and are emphasizing cross-collaborative work with bail funds, and organizations that work to get people out of prison. Recognizing the interconnectedness of oppression, they have also started working with advocates and nonprofits in Mexico, particularly since Mexicans have experience providing care in an environment that restricts abortion access and because they are currently faced with several Americans traveling to their country by crossing the border to seek medication abortions.

A high priority for organizations such as the National Asian Pacific American Women's Forum (NAPAWF) and their state-based chapters has been to emphasize the cultural and linguistic diversity within immigrant communities. They have been fighting for language access and have been providing public information disseminated in the aftermath of *Dobbs* in several languages and dialects. NAPAWF, noting that "AAPI" is a large catch-all category, has also been advocating for the disaggregation of federal data so as to understand which groups are most affected by policy decisions and require most assistance.

In conclusion, as the ripple effects of *Dobbs* become clear, the disproportionate impact of this decision on immigrant communities should be prioritized, all while acknowledging that these injustices are not new and have been perpetrated against immigrants for decades. Despite this, immigrant communities and advocates with help from local, state, and national organizations have continued to resist, fight back, and advocate for greater health-care access for their own communities and for all others.

31 Using Disability and Access Statements to Get Resources to Students in Texas

ALISON KAFER

I am one of many faculty working at public universities in states with governors and legislatures hostile to reproductive, sexual, and gender freedom. In the wake of *Dobbs,* SB8 (the Texas law that allows for civil lawsuits against those who "aid and abet" abortion), state investigations into families with trans youth, and political attacks on the teaching of race, gender, and sexuality, what are professors at places like the University of Texas to do?

According to our institutions, very little. The official *Dobbs* guidance offered to UT faculty consists only of a general statement issued by HR that "free speech rights are protected" on campus. As at other universities in states with abortion bans, we have been informally reassured that principles of academic freedom are still in effect, but that reassurance often hinges on troubling notions of "aboutness": to the extent that abortion and reproductive health care are discussed in our courses—that our courses are "about" these issues—then we can continue to include them as subjects of study. But the students most in need of support are often *not* in courses where abortion or Reproductive Justice are expected topics of discussion. It seems less clear that the university will support anyone in astronomy or engineering who decides they want to address student concerns about abortion access.

My sense that the university's support has limits is exacerbated by the "off the record" guidance I've heard from leadership: faculty should discourage conversations with students about reproductive health care, at most referring them to counseling and mental health services, the student health center, or the Title IX office. We lack the proper "training" to discuss such issues with students, and doing so opens us (read: the university) to unnecessary risk. This guidance, that we refer all students elsewhere, is a familiar move to those of us who teach about sexual assault ("interrupt students to tell them about mandatory reporting if you think they are going to disclose") and those of us working in disability studies ("students should take any conversation about their own disabilities to the disability services office or the counseling center"). We are told our role is to teach about issues in the abstract, not as they pertain to anyone in the room, or, worse, to report: "if you see something, say something." Being disabled, being a survivor of assault, being unexpectedly pregnant: each is an experience that does not belong in the college classroom, an experience best met by shame, surveillance, removal, and silence.

As a mode of resisting these imperatives, I turn to the *disability and access statement*—a tool disability studies scholars and disabled faculty have long used to refuse this kind of academic gatekeeping. I encourage all faculty concerned about the impact of abortion bans to adapt and mobilize these syllabi statements in support of Reproductive Justice in our classrooms. We can use the strategies of disability justice movements to make Reproductive Justice interventions in our institutions, regardless of what our classes are "about."

In stark contrast to university-generated language about accommodations, these more radical access statements recognize inaccessibility as a structural problem, one requiring collective action and systemic change. The "problem," in other words, isn't disabled students but an academy that requires a strict adherence to limited ideals of performance, communication, participation, productivity, and achievement. Disabled activists and scholars actively resist the stigmatization of disability by acknowledging the presence of disability and disabled people in our classrooms. My statement opens: "All students are welcome in this course, including students with learning, emotional, physical, cognitive, and/or hidden disabilities, illnesses, injuries, and health statuses, regardless of diagnosis." I then explain how I came to these positions, emphasizing that because access to supportive medical care, disability documentation, and diagnosis is hampered by racism, sexism, homo- and transphobia, and anti-immigrant and antiwelfare policies, I do not require such documentation in my courses. Disabled activists and scholars call for a broader understanding of the ways our lives affect our learning.

And for many of our students, ableism is not the only factor behind the university's inaccessibility; the barriers they encounter are not only "about" disability. In recognition of these facts, my access statement also includes information about changing one's gender markers with the registrar's office; locations on and near campus where students can find assistance with food, clothing, and shelter; and contact information for local sexual assault hotlines. If "access and accommodations" are about making sure students have what they need to perform well academically, then providing information about basic needs is an essential part of such frameworks. Disability justice provides a theoretical and pedagogical framework for understanding why "accessibility" includes information, for example, about gender-affirming care and immigration: trans and/or undocumented students cannot devote their full attention to their studies if they are concerned about being captured by the state or if their capacities are being challenged. The same is true for students grappling with an unwanted pregnancy, or unable to find reliable birth control, or in need of prenatal care.

What I am suggesting is that this kind of crip/disability justice approach to "access and accommodations" offers a way for all faculty, *even those teaching courses not "about" abortion and reproductive care,* to provide life-changing resources to our students. In what follows, I share excerpts from my current access statement, including a few brief annotations to explain my thinking and mark opportunities for extended conversations in class.

Accessibility, Disability, Equity, and Inclusion [excerpts]

Stress and uncertainty about the bodily autonomy, health, and well-being of yourself, your family, and your communities can negatively impact your ability to complete your studies.

Reproductive health, rights, and justice has been an essential component of many iterations of disability rights and justice movements. Many disability activists, theorists, and community members have argued that accessibility includes reproductive issues, in part because sick, mad, deaf, and disabled people are particularly affected by abortion bans and cuts to reproductive health care.

> Stressing that disability justice frameworks define "access to reproductive care and information" as a necessary component of "disability access and accommodations" offers an intellectual framework for including these kinds of resources in all courses, not only those "about" disability or reproductive politics.

For local resources on these topics, consult:

- The Gynecology Clinic at University Health Services offers a range of reproductive health services, including pregnancy tests and emergency contraception (often known as "the morning after pill"). Their website also offers information about which forms of emergency contraception work best for different body sizes. **Emergency contraception—which remains legal in Texas**—is sometimes available over-the-counter and in-person at local pharmacies, but call to confirm.

> I added this clause after hearing colleagues express fear about sharing emergency contraception (EC) information in the wake of SB8 and *Dobbs*. If they are unclear about the legality of EC, then undoubtedly many of our students are too.

- *EC4EC,* the Bridge Collective, and Every Body Texas are local organizations that will deliver free "Repro Kits" (two doses of emergency contraception, two pregnancy tests, condoms, lube packets, and an instruction and resource guide) to anyone in the greater Austin area (the Bridge Collective is for immediate needs; Every Body Texas is ideal if you are planning for the future).
- If you have recently experienced **sexual assault and need emergency contraception,** contact Eloise House at SAFE Austin.
- Students who are pregnant, **who need to terminate a pregnancy,** who have recently given birth, who are nursing, and/or who are parenting are protected under Title IX, a federal civil rights law that prohibits discrimination on the basis of sex— including pregnancy and parental status—in educational programs and activities. For assistance in requesting resources, accommodations, and other support, contact the Title IX Office.

> One way universities nationwide are responding to *Dobbs* is by expanding their services to student parents—necessary work, long overdue— but this messaging often downplays the fact that students seeking abortion are protected too.

- The Lilith Fund and Fund Texas Choice are the two **abortion funds serving Central Texas;** Jane's Due Process focuses on teens. The National Network of Abortion Funds maintains a list of other funds in Texas and nationally, and needabortion.org offers a range of resources for Texans. All of these sites provide information about accessing abortion pills and/or travel out of state.

> This entry is the one that feels the most important. Naming abortion explicitly is a way of resisting the stigma of abortion: *students who have abortions are valued, integral members of my class.*
>
> Given SB8's focus on those who "aid and abet" abortion, the mere provision of information is not without at least minimal risk. Local abortion funds have been advising supporters to use general language. Rather than advising someone directly ("you could do X," "you can go here"), instead be more abstract: "people have found X resource helpful."

- The Repro Legal Helpline and Repro Legal Defense Fund are available for those who have concerns about or are being investigated, detained, arrested, or questioned for having an abortion, experiencing pregnancy loss, or other reproductive health issues.
- Here is information on maintaining digital privacy when researching reproductive health care.
- If you need child care, UT offers a limited number of slots in its on-campus facilities. If you need a lactation room, consult this list of campus locations. Consult this page for **additional resources and information for student parents.**
- Advocates for Youth, Amaze, Our Bodies Ourselves, and Planned Parenthood offer fact sheets, videos, and other **sex ed resources** for students.

Almost 90 percent of incoming undergraduates at UT are Texas residents, which means that most of them have gone to school in a state that prioritizes abstinence-only curricula; requires parental consent for education about sexual health, family violence, child abuse, and sex trafficking; and has supported challenges to Title X clinics and their provision of birth control.

ATTENDANCE: If you need to **miss class due to a family emergency, illness, a medical procedure, and/or travel out of state for a medical procedure,** please let me know as soon as you can. I do not need proof, documentation, or a detailed explanation—just let me know when you will be gone, how long you expect to be out, and when you expect to return. Consult the resources list above for more information about accommodations, including those through Title IX.

If you are experiencing difficulty with childcare and it will cause you to miss class, please let me know as soon as you can. In an emergency it may be possible to bring your child to class.

RECORDING: Any class recordings are reserved only for students in this class for educational purposes and are protected under FERPA. The recordings should not be shared outside the class in any form. Violation of this restriction by a student could lead to Student Misconduct proceedings. I will not record any of our sessions without your explicit permission; I ask you to do the same for me and your classmates.

UT's legal team encourages faculty to include this section on our syllabi because of concerns that students' "personally identifiable information" is being captured during Zoom sessions. But perhaps this policy can also provide at least some protection to students in the wake of SB8's "bounty hunting" dimensions. Although I would hope no one in my courses would be inclined to surreptitiously record or disseminate recordings of others discussing reproductive health care, students will at least know that doing so violates UT policy.

. . .

Statements like these are not enough, and there is a huge gulf between giving students a list of resources and getting them the actual resources and support they need. But perhaps they can create an opening into other ways of being together, of refusing the silence of the university, of making space in our classrooms for the lives we lead outside them. I share the above excerpts—incomplete, imperfect, in flux—as an act of solidarity, as a small move toward thinking outside the legalistic frames of the institution, and as an invitation to collaboration. Please create your own, send me yours, share them widely.

Part V *Protecting Abortion Access in the Face of Fascism*

KRYSTALE E. LITTLEJOHN

As the essayists decry throughout *Fighting Mad,* people already faced obstacles to getting an abortion before the Supreme Court decision to end *Roe.* Allowing states to create their own rules only exacerbated financial and other access barriers. Against this backdrop, activists and others on the ground fight tirelessly to mitigate the costs of the decision. This part of the book brings contributors together to highlight both the financial and logistical obstacles posed by the most recent iteration of the assault on Reproductive Justice and to shed light on promising approaches that address the broad spectrum of needs for people seeking abortion.

Sociologist Tracy A. Weitz draws attention to the often unspoken ways that money shapes access to abortion. Weitz makes visible the uneasy relationship with money that undergirds so much of abortion access and provision—from prohibitions on federal Medicaid coverage for abortions, to discomfort about paying for abortions, to a refusal to adequately compensate staff involved in providing abortions. By vocalizing the unspoken, Weitz shows how money matters and offers an agenda for creating change. Organizer Elizabeth Gelvin and advocate Gabriela Cano complicate the access story further by detailing the struggles that Louisianans and Oklahomans face when seeking abortion care, whether or not they can secure financial access. Through Gelvin's eyes, readers get a sobering glimpse at the tireless work and coordination that goes into successfully facilitating abortion access in the face of all kinds of disasters—whether these catastrophes are wrought socially (via restrictions) or naturally (via weather disasters). Gelvin's essay shows that people need access in all kinds of circumstances and under all kinds of conditions. Cano's essay offers a visceral accounting of the obstacles that Oklahomans faced before and after the fall of *Roe*—from abortion barriers posed by lack of access to childcare to those posed by increased surveillance and criminalization. Even as states enact restrictions to constrain abortion access, these essays show that abortion defenders and advocates jump into action to find new ways of paying the costs without creating new ones.

Obstetrician-gynecologist Jody Steinauer elucidates an overlooked cost of the *Dobbs* decision to allow states to ban abortion: physicians in states with abortion bans may not get the training they need to adequately support patients seeking abortion. From knowledge on how to counsel patients, to psychological and moral harms, Steinauer shows that the costs are many and the stakes exceptionally high. Alongside detailing the harms of abortion bans for medical education, Steinauer offers several concrete strategies that can serve to maintain the integrity of training programs and meet the needs of learners and future patients alike.

Rafa P. Kidvai, Repro Legal Defense Fund (RLDF) director at If/When/How, adds important insight into the range of costs that accompany seeking an abortion in the context of expanding criminalization. Building on the discussion of the harms of criminalization, Kidvai draws out the financial costs of criminalization and the crucial role played by organizations like the RLDF to provide legal support to people facing prosecution for their abortions and pregnancy outcomes. Although the financial costs associated with criminalization can impede people's ability to mount a strong fight, Kidvai explains that those costs can be preemptively managed, and criminalization can be challenged via multipronged community activism.

Sociologist Katrina Kimport picks up on this thread and shows how some employers have stepped in with promises to help facilitate travel access across state lines to work around some of the risks posed by criminalization. However, the story is not as simple as providing financial assistance and waiting for people to come—or go. When considering abortion travel, it's particularly important to make sure that the needs of all people needing abortion are met. Abortion travel is a work-around, not a solution in this case. Following Kimport's overview of employer responses and their limits, Odile Schalit, executive director of the abortion access fund Brigid Alliance, shows what it looks like—and what it takes on the ground—to provide vital practical support for abortion access. Brigid Alliance's work shows that bringing dignity, love, and respect to every abortion care interaction requires not just financial support but also attention to the wide range of human needs that people have when traveling for an abortion.

Lastly, journalist, author, and lawyer Jill Filipovic rounds out this part of the book with an interview with Dr. Rebecca Gomperts. For decades Gomperts has engaged in innovative work to provide abortion care for people living in places with restrictive abortion laws. From providing access to abortion on a rented boat, via Women on Waves, to providing access to information and abortion-inducing medication via other ventures, Gomperts's work has showed the tremendous power of facilitating access to abortion with the available tools, whatever they are and wherever they may be.

Together, the essays in this part underscore the reasons for hope and the power of on-the-ground resistance to create change in the face of the myriad financial and logistical obstacles posed by unjust restrictions.

32 *Let's Talk about Money and Abortion*

TRACY A. WEITZ

Abortion is an economic issue. In the United States, capitalism shapes both the need for abortion and people's ability to access it. This tension with capitalism touches people seeking to end their pregnancies, the workforces providing the care, as well as everyone contributing their labor to ensure people can choose whether and when to have children. This fraught relationship between abortion and financial resources is further strained by the Supreme Court's June 2022 decision eliminating legal protection of abortion in *Dobbs v. Jackson Women's Health Organization,* which has stressed all those needing as well as those seeking to ensure access to abortion. This essay follows in the tradition of the reproductive health, rights, and justice movement in calling for a frank and transparent conversation about money and abortion in the public sphere.

Even prior to *Dobbs,* economics constrained access to abortion care. Indeed, the *Dobbs* decision is simply a new chapter in a longer story of abortion, money, and stigma. Beginning in 1976 and every year thereafter, the federal government has imposed the Hyde Amendment on the federal budget. This amendment prohibits federal Medicaid from paying for abortions. While sixteen states use their own funds to provide coverage, the remainder of the states require people of limited income to pay for that health care themselves.

Research estimates that between 20 and 25 percent of people do not obtain a desired abortion because of this restriction.[1] Likewise, decades of research documents that the struggle to gather the money to pay for the abortion is one of the greatest barriers to care and, even when successful, causes significant psychological stress as people make decisions to delay rent, utilities, and child-rearing expenses.

To fill in for the failure of the federal government, nonprofit organizations known as abortion funds (some national, some local, and some institutional) help pay for the cost of abortions as well as the costs associated with travel and lodging when seeking an abortion away from home. The best estimate is that in 2021 these organizations contributed over $80 million to cover costs that Medicaid would pay if not for the Hyde Amendment.[2] Most of these resources come from a few philanthropic institutions that give their funds anonymously to avoid being linked to the effort. In the wake of *Dobbs,* advocates have called for individuals and philanthropic institutions to increase their giving to abortion funds, but the demand for financial assistance far outstrips the resources donated. It remains to be seen if this call to action will be heeded as the impact of *Dobbs* becomes normalized over time.

Even in states with Medicaid coverage for abortion, the system is far from perfect. Notoriously a poor payor for health care, state Medicaid reimbursement rates for abortion services fall well below the full cost of providing care. This differential is worse for abortions later in pregnancy when the cost and complexity of the care increases. Consequently, few health-care providers offer late abortion care to people relying on Medicaid. And other providers tap abortion funds or philanthropy funders to cover the gap between the rate that state Medicaid pays and the price of the abortion. The result is that even in states where abortion is legal and Medicaid covers the service, many communities lack an accessible abortion provider.

Despite adequate payment for abortion as the number one need for people experiencing an unwanted pregnancy and the providers who offer this care, money rarely tops the agenda when abortion makes it into private or public conversations. In 2018 a research team at New York University updated the abortion questions in the General Social Survey (GSS).[3] Considered the most scientifically rigorous public opinion survey, the GSS collects information and maintains a historical record of the concerns, experiences, attitudes, and practices of US residents. Rather than continue to ask people simply whether abortion should be legal or is moral, the new abortion questions asked people about what kinds of help they would offer if a close family member or friend decided to have an abortion. Options included providing emotional support, making arrangements, paying for those arrangements, and paying for the abortion. Not surprisingly almost 90 percent of people said they would offer emotional support and nearly three-quarters would help with arrangements like a ride or childcare. These numbers included many people who were morally opposed to abortion. But buried in these positive results is a sad story about money. Even among people who strongly supported legal abortion, fewer than half would help pay for the abortion. In other words: "I'll drive you to the clinic but don't use my money to pay for the abortion."

Why the general discomfort with money and abortion? Scholars of abortion stigma have long argued that it has its origins in the legacy of the illegal abortion provider who extracted high financial costs for offering illegal services by colluding with women in severing the association of sex and motherhood. At the time of legalization, one of the first disagreements in the abortion rights movement was over whether abortion providers should be not-for-profit entities as entrepreneurial physicians established practices with the intent to make money by meeting the new demand. As such, there has been a general negative association between abortion providers and profit.

Opponents of abortion have mobilized this discomfort to disparage those who offer abortion care. They refer to abortion providers as the "abortion industry" and accuse Planned Parenthood of misusing government resources to gain extensive profits from performing abortions.

Because of the ongoing taint of money in abortion, people may feel uncomfortable talking about the business realities associated with providing abortion care. Unlike other health care, people want abortion providers to offer the service out of a sense of duty. Both the people who need and the people who provide abortions are supposed to be willing to sacrifice to prove that they understand the moral weight of the abortion decision. To manage the taint of abortion stigma, economic sacrifice is justified and expected.

Just as the burden of failing to talk about gathering the money for abortion falls disproportionately on people of color, who are more likely to be enrolled in the Medicaid program, our social failure to talk openly about money in provision also impacts the same communities. In recent years journalists have documented the union-busting practices of some Planned Parenthood affiliates. To keep the cost of services low and thus accessible to people in need, Planned Parenthood suppresses the wages of the nonlicensed clinical staff, many of whom are people of color. Echoing the demand for sacrifice, these individuals are told by leadership that improvements in their wages will come at the expense of clients. This practice pits low-wage workers against low-income clients. Despite abortion opponents' narrative, Planned Parenthood abortion clinics are not making a profit; however, they have been bullied into not demanding higher payments, revenue that could be directed to raise the salaries of the abortion-care workforce.

This culture of silence combined with the expectation that everyone in the abortion experience engage in sacrifice means advocates for abortion access are unable to discuss realistically both what it will take to make abortion equitability available and the role that public funds must play to achieve that outcome. Talking freely and unself-consciously about money is a necessary first step in winning the abortion culture war. No one should be able to claim to be "pro-choice" if they do not support governments and insurance companies paying, and paying well, for abortion.

It is time to act. Strap in and get ready to have uncomfortable conversations with friends, family, coworkers, and political allies about why money matters and why abortion should be paid for and covered appropriately in all health insurance, including Medicaid. In that spirit, I offer the following thoughts:

1. Abortion access supporters and advocates in states with Medicaid coverage need to prioritize efforts to raise state reimbursement rates for abortion care, especially for abortions later in pregnancy.

2. Philanthropic donors that support abortion funds need to publicly acknowledge their support and demand that other donors join them in funding this critical work.

3. Abortion providing institutions need to allow researchers to study the actual costs of abortion care when clinical staff and clinicians are compensated appropriately for this work.

4. Wages for licensed and unlicensed staff working in abortion care should be reflective of the social value of this work and collective bargaining should be encouraged.

5. State and federal grant funds should be available to abortion providers to offset the costs of providing care regardless of the IRS business designation of the entity.

6. Political organizations that support abortion rights need to deny funding support for candidates who do not actively work to repeal the federal Hyde Amendment or raise state Medicaid reimbursement rates.

7. People who have abortions need to be supported to share their stories of the challenges that limited access to money plays in their ability to exercise their human rights.

8. Legal academics need to author scholarship regarding how denial of financial coverage for abortion is a civil rights violation.

9. Litigators need to file legal challenges to financial restrictions on abortion using new theories and novel plaintiffs.

10. Everyone needs to get comfortable talking about money and abortion. No one should have to financially sacrifice to end an unwanted pregnancy or work in abortion care. Abortion is a basic human right, full stop. Join me in expanding this agenda and in talking about money and abortion as we rightly should.

33 *Pre*-Dobbs *but Post*-Roe

Funding Abortion in Louisiana in Early
Pandemic Years

ELIZABETH GELVIN

*You can fund abortions all day long, but if you can't get to the clinic, what
good is it?*

The early days of pandemic were rife with fear and confusion. Our
job (as the client services team of the New Orleans Abortion Fund)
was to provide stability, information, and access to abortion care to
the best of our abilities. Our responsibility was to keep the line open.
Our duty was to redefine, led by the self-identified needs of our clients, what holistic abortion access support could look like for each
client who called our line. Before 2020, the New Orleans Abortion
Fund focused its work on covering financial gaps or in some cases the
full cost of abortion procedures for people in Louisiana and our
neighbors in surrounding Gulf South states. The helpline was available for clients to call directly, seven days a week, to seek support in
English or Spanish language.

March 2020 came crashing in, and it quickly and dizzyingly became apparent to some of us that this pandemic would be with us for
a long, long time. Everything had to change. Everything that we built

had to meet the needs of those requiring travel support and contour to the unique safety measures necessary for said travel—both within the state and across state lines. We had to not only book bus tickets and arrange for Ubers, but we had to provide PPE (masks, hand sanitizer, face shields). It was our duty to not just get people from point A to B but to listen intently to people's needs and preferences for how they sought to travel, for how they gauged their risk and the risk of their families' safety.

The first practical support case my team took was in April 2020. Two kids (both over eighteen years of age, a client and her companion) traveled by bus to New Mexico. I believe it was their first time leaving the state—as it is for many. The bus was stalled or broke down at least once on the trip there, and heading home was treacherous too. Sure, it was a long week and a half for those of us on this side of the phone. It was a lifetime for those two kids. They made it back safely, and I have never stopped exhaling my sigh of sheer relief.

So here we are and there we were. The maligned, mythologized state of Louisiana: a state whose history is steeped in the transatlantic slave trade, the domestic slave trade, Jim Crow, mass incarceration, mass surveillance, disaster capitalism, and disaster resistance. Strike that, just call it resistance—all resistance is against a disaster, be it white supremacy, capitalism, violent infrastructure by design— including draconian limitation on abortion access.

In those first two years defined by the COVID-19 pandemic, the client services team supported roughly a thousand Louisianans (and our neighbors in Gulf South states) each year in access to abortion care—at clinics in Louisiana and across the United States. We covered procedure costs, plane tickets, gas money, train and bus tickets, food stipends. Our team of fifteen client services volunteers grew to nearly thirty, and each volunteer provided deep, person-driven care. They listened to needs. They listened to fears. They rejoiced in clients' successes and safety. They pinned down details, they devised and presented options, and they held each other through each passing week. They made sure pregnant children had headphones to listen to their favorite songs, or a stuffed animal to hug on the long journey ahead. They arranged for money orders to arrive at clinics, for Uber rides to safely transport people, for calls confirming safe arrival at the clinics and safe returns back home. They mailed care kits to each client who sought one—menstrual pads, heating pads, cotton underwear, comfy socks, good quality masks, and emergency contraception.

In summer of 2020, Hurricane Laura devastated the city of Lake Charles and southwestern Louisiana, and Hurricane Zeta, though far less ferocious, impacted New Orleans and surrounding areas. In late summer of 2021, Hurricane Ida devastated the cities of Houma, New Orleans, and much of southeastern Louisiana. For those impacted by Laura, our work shifted into ensuring people make it safely to care and safely back home—whether home was a structure or a community, or, God willing, both. We went out to Lake Charles and Lafayette to bring emergency contraception, condoms, pregnancy tests, and informational materials. We kept our line open, through hotspots and battery packs, when members of the client services hotline team lost power from Zeta here in New Orleans, to ensure that people had a place, a person to touch in with if they needed it—*that they would never be alone.*

In 2021 new (yet age-old) crises emerged. In the wake of Hurricane Ida the city of New Orleans lost power for roughly ten days (depending on your neighborhood or ward). I had left the New Orleans Abortion Fund three weeks prior to Ida making landfall, but I knew that a Category 4 hurricane would mean pressing, urgent challenges to the access of basic needs, including reproductive health and harm reduction resources—as it is every hurricane season, as it is in the face of every climate crisis.

Alongside shifting into survival mode ourselves, some members of the former client services team focused our energies on other ways to support our communities, in mutual aid disaster response networks, as neighbors, in the care networks that we rely upon to keep each other safe. Some of us, despite lack of electricity, stayed committed to providing emergency supplies to more severely impacted regions in southeastern Louisiana, for that is health and Reproductive Justice—it is not just paying for the cost of an abortion . . . it is ensuring that people have tarps for their roofs, warm food for their bellies and souls, mold remediation supplies for their homes, water for drinking and washing, Narcan for their loved ones who use opiates, diapers for the babies, and more.

Here are a few things I know for certain:

1. Everyone should have access to abortion care at any point in pregnancy—regardless of location, age, race, religion, income, citizenship, or any other quality of their personhood.

2. People should have access to nonstigmatizing abortion care even if by basis of their family, community, upbringing, or faith practice *they claim they are an exception from the reasons why abortion is "wrong."* Those who seek an abortion should receive abortion care, point blank. I will always hear the voices of the people who had abortions calling me later on, days or weeks later, asking if God hated them. Baby, I can't speak for any God. But as you exist on this earth, you are loved. And if you somehow read this, hear it like I told you then—the God I worship may or may not be the same God you worship, but my God loves you so very, very much . . . and I have a sneaking suspicion that maybe, just maybe, your God and my God may be the very same God.

3. The fight for bodily autonomy and reproductive sovereignty began when human bodies first came on stage. The fight for

health justice began when capitalism, white supremacy, patriarchy, transphobia, ableism, and other modes of oppression began waging violent wars on people's bodies. Alone, we tackle them piecemeal. Together, we destroy all barriers standing between your body (perfect) and your personhood (perfect), and whatever you dream for your life and the life of your loved ones.

4. The American South is not a lost cause. People for whom *Roe* never stood have been living in the future, not the past. The understanding of what's at stake when *Roe* doesn't stand and the skills needed to navigate that landscape with wit, wile, creativity, bravery, and grace have been honed in the South and the Midwest for decades. People in the South and Midwest who have sought and provided abortion care have been paving the way for us in this post-*Roe* time for decades. They've given us the tools. They've shown us how to survive. It is our duty to honor the lessons they've given us and use them to build a new world that they've always known is possible.

34 *We Take Care of Us*
Continuing the Fight for Abortion Access in Post-*Dobbs* Oklahoma

GABRIELA CANO

Since the fall of *Roe,* my stress has festered into nightmares where I'm incarcerated by the state of Oklahoma, forced to carry a pregnancy against my will. And when I wake up, I remember the real nightmare is still unfolding. Unable to access abortion care, which has now been criminalized, Oklahomans are forced to carry pregnancies against their will in a state with the country's highest rates of maternal mortality. On the ground, Oklahomans and their families are desperately fighting to access care, either navigating legal risk and a race against time to self-manage abortions at home or scraping together enough funds to leave the state. Advocates and loved ones—myself included—are terrified of the legal risks we face every time we help someone access care. I continue the fight, but the gravity of the crisis haunts me.

Even before *Roe* fell, we understood legality never meant accessibility. For decades, Oklahomans have been subject to some of the most antagonistic abortion restrictions in the country, including bans on insurance coverage, a ban on both telehealth and self-managed care, a mandated waiting period of seventy-two hours, mandated antiabortion counseling, and parental consent and notification requirements for those seeking care who are under eighteen years old, all while 95 percent of our counties lacked clinics.

We also understood that abortion restrictions were inextricably connected to countless other ways in which the state inflicted harm. In Oklahoma a criminally botched pandemic response continues to erode access to food and health care, while state-made environmental disasters contribute to worsening housing insecurity. We consistently suffer the highest rates of domestic violence homicide, child abuse, and sexual violence in the country, while those in power block survivors' access to care and inflict much of the abuse themselves. Families are struggling to afford basic necessities like groceries, utilities, medications, and childcare. Here, experiencing domestic violence, a drug overdose, or a miscarriage can land you in prison for years.

With the highest incarceration rate of any democracy in the world, Oklahoma inflicts harm at levels that are difficult to process. Then in May 2022, Oklahomans lost access to legal abortion. A series of bills not only banned abortion "from fertilization" but also created a mechanism for community policing through a $10,000 bounty against anyone supporting a loved one in accessing care. All four remaining clinics were forced to immediately shut down, turning away patients who had already traveled hundreds of miles to access lifesaving care. Clinics, advocates, and patients alike struggled to make sense of contradictory, sloppily crafted statutes whose vagueness threatened to criminalize any move they made.

Then in June, *Roe* fell and a dozen neighboring states woke up to Oklahoma's nightmare. I've spoken to Oklahomans who have sold personal belongings and taken out loans in hopes of saving enough money to flee the state for care. I've spoken to parents who faced severe fetal diagnosis and pregnancy complications, but no childcare access and mounting travel costs prevented them from receiving timely care. I've spoken to survivors of violence whose ability to obtain an abortion was a vital step toward safety from traumatic and deadly situations. I've spoken to Oklahomans trapped in the hamster wheel of trying to save up for a procedure whose cost is exponentially increasing with each day you spend saving. I've spoken to Oklahomans who do not consent to carrying a pregnancy in a state that is continually inflicting trauma upon its residents, the effects of which we are still struggling to process. And despite the countless risks, networks of Oklahomans across the state are fighting to gain back control of our bodies and futures by any means.

With no time to even process the devastation, Oklahomans jumped into action. We disseminated resources on self-managing abortions at home, on accessing funds to flee the state, and on combating state surveillance. Artists created spaces for sharing stories and raising awareness of what was happening on the ground. Advocates for harm reduction and abortion access worked to expand access to emergency contraception as well as safer use and safer sex supplies to nearly every county in the state. Grassroots advocates launched a billboard campaign across the state to raise awareness of the ongoing criminalization of pregnancy outcomes, sharing resources and ways to join the fight. Local abortion defenders have joined forces with national reproductive rights organizations to sue the state for enforcing these deadly bans. To meet the rising need of Oklahomans fleeing the state, Oklahoma's abortion fund collaborated with activists to expand its reach, fundraising to support not just Oklahomans' procedure costs but also rising travel costs.

Oklahomans are working tirelessly, but we're struggling. Clinic staff have lost their jobs, advocates and supporters and those seeking care are worried about criminalization and surveillance, Oklahomans continue struggling to access care, and community members feel silenced and unsure if it's safe to publicly support the right to care. Sometimes it feels like we're trapped inside a building actively collapsing into itself with no help or relief in sight.

We're tired because the fight for Reproductive Justice and abortion access is a deeply personal commitment for so many Oklahomans, myself included. At twenty-two, I experienced a pregnancy after rape and the fight to access care almost killed me. I experienced the deep stigma that thrives in the face of unchecked attacks against abortion access, where the only stories we hear blame and dehumanize those seeking care. My desperation grew with every barrier I faced, but stigma kept me isolated and unable to seek support. The barriers I faced seemed so insurmountable, I acknowledged to myself that suicide might be the only way to regain agency over my own future. Years after I was able to access life saving care, abortion—proven again and again to be one of the safest procedures on earth—is banned in Oklahoma, with more than fifteen other states either completely banning or severely restricting access in the face of legal uncertainty.

I'm tired. It's a struggle to process the hopelessness and rage I carry. I worry incessantly about the possibility of a safety misstep that could put me, my community, and my loved ones in serious risk. But to me and other Oklahomans devoted to supporting access, the stakes have never been clearer. There are community members right now being harmed, put in deadly situations, facing barrier after barrier in the fight to access abortion. So many will be unable to access care and forced to endure a pregnancy with no support or resources in one of the deadliest states for pregnant people and families. Oklahomans and their families will be pushed deeper into cycles of poverty, of lack of access, of generational trauma and violence. Oklahomans will face traumatic medical emergencies. Oklahomans will be murdered by a state with the highest rate of domestic violence homicide and maternal mortality in the nation. Oklahomans will suffer disastrous mental health crises, including suicidality and suicide attempts, all while those in power refuse to include mental health in their performative "health of mother" exemptions.

Resistance is our only option. I want to end this nightmare and rebuild a world in which we feel safe. I'm committed to the work of cultivating networks that are deeply supportive and trusting, connected by a shared vision of liberation. Networks that center the needs, experiences, and leadership of Black and Indigenous Oklahomans, of those historically targeted by surveillance and criminalization, those currently detained and imprisoned, those criminalized for using drugs or surviving violence. Networks that elevate the stories of people in states like Oklahoma, where extremist abortion bans are putting our loved ones in dangerous, desperate, and deadly situations.

Let's continue assessing our risks, strategizing for our collective safety, and preparing for the waves of devastation and criminalization we know are already here. Let's ensure every space of complacency is disrupted. Our collective voice will not be silenced, even by threat of violence. We'll continue stating, as loudly as we can, that abortion is one of the safest medical procedures in the world and something you have the option of self-managing at home. We'll continue ensuring Oklahomans have the information and resources they need to access abortion and continue caring for themselves and their families.

We're building a world where we're safe to make our own choices about our future, and where our choices are met with access and support. A world with ample safety, resources, connections, and support. Where we have the space to collectively process the complexity of our experiences and where our stories are honored.

To get there, I commit to supporting any Oklahoman seeking abortion, at any time and for any reason.

35 Dobbs *and Medical Education*

JODY STEINAUER

Access to patient-centered abortion care is critical, and medical education is critical for ensuring this access. Now that states are allowed to ban abortion, physicians and learners are being forced to violate our core professional value of patient-centered care. Training institutions in states with bans may not be able to ensure that their learners gain the medical knowledge and clinical skills needed to care for patients, and these learners will experience moral distress from not being able to provide patient-centered care. Not only will *Dobbs* harm patients currently living in states with abortion bans, it will continue to affect future patients cared for by insufficiently trained and emotionally affected physicians.

Obstetrician-gynecologists must have the skills to provide abortion care; it is our professional obligation to do an abortion in the setting of an emergency if no one else is available, and abortion and pregnancy-loss care are core components of our specialty. The Accreditation Council for Graduate Medical Education (ACGME) requires obstetrics and gynecology (ob-gyn) residency programs to include abortion training. Although abortion training is not required in any other specialty, it is critical that residents in other specialties—especially family medicine, internal medicine, pediatrics and emergency medicine—learn about abortion care.

Physicians of many specialties are often the first to tell a patient their pregnancy test is positive, therefore that practitioner must have counseling skills. They provide care in primary and urgent care settings and must be trained to provide patient-centered care to people who have had an abortion and have questions about symptoms or desire confirmation of abortion completion. The patients may have self-managed their abortion outside of the formal medical system—for example, by accessing medication abortion through online pharmacies, had an in-clinic abortion in the community, or left the state to access abortion care elsewhere. It is especially critical that in restrictive states these physicians honor patient confidentiality and do not report them to law enforcement.

To ensure adequate physician knowledge, the Association of Professors of Gynecology and Obstetrics recommends all medical students graduate with a "deep and thorough understanding of abortion" and are able to provide compassionate, nondirective, pregnancy options counseling, including having the knowledge to explain abortion methods and rare complications. Thus all medical schools and residency programs that include clinical care of reproductive-aged people who can become pregnant should include abortion education, and many residency programs (especially family medicine) should include abortion training, as physicians of diverse specialties include abortion care in their practice.

State abortion bans mean that many medical students and residents are at risk of insufficient training to safely provide critical aspects of reproductive health care. As of December 2022, six months after the *Dobbs* decision, in the (then) twelve states with current bans, there are more than eleven hundred ob-gyn residents being trained and more than thirty-five thousand medical students being educated. A recent paper estimated that up to 44 percent of ob-gyn residents—more than twenty-six hundred residents in 128 programs—are in states considered likely to ban abortion. When residents are trained in abortion care, they learn skills needed for abortion care and many other common clinical scenarios, such as ultrasound, pain management, and techniques for many intrauterine procedures. They also include the skills needed to care for people with pregnancy loss. Ob-gyn residents in programs with integrated abortion training graduate better prepared to offer both medical and procedural management options for people with miscarriage compared to residents in programs with elective or no abortion training.

In addition to the impacts on clinical skills, these bans will cause potential psychological and moral impacts on physicians and learners. "Moral distress" is the emotional state that occurs when one is unable to carry out what they believe to be the ethically appropriate action, often due to external circumstances. In the post-*Dobbs* world, physicians experience moral distress when unable to counsel about or refer for abortion care, when prohibited from doing an abortion, or when forced to wait until a patient becomes sick before being allowed to do their abortion. Moral distress can lead to burnout and long-term moral injury, and for our learners, who experience higher levels of moral distress, this may lead to their leaving a specialty or the profession altogether.

What can we do to try to lessen the training impacts of these bans? Medical schools and residencies must prioritize teaching about abortion; there is no reason that didactic education should end under bans. Training hospitals in states with restrictive laws must maximize legal abortion care within their institutions, ensuring care for people with medical conditions that qualify for abortion within their state, both to decrease harm to these patients and improve clinical training. They must improve pregnancy loss care, ensuring that patients can access all management options including outpatient uterine aspiration, which is often the patients' preference. This will improve patient care, and because there is substantial overlap between skills used in pregnancy loss and abortion care, this will help ensure competence in abortion skills.

The ACGME policy, as revised after *Dobbs,* continues to require clinical experience in abortion care, but now says that "if a program is in a jurisdiction where resident access to this clinical experience is unlawful, the program must provide access to this clinical experience in a different jurisdiction where it is lawful." The Kenneth J. Ryan Residency Training Program (the Ryan Program) in Abortion and Family Planning, a program founded in 1999 by Dr. Uta Landy, and now under my leadership, has supported 113 US residency programs to integrate abortion care. After the Texas law SB8 was passed in September 2021, the Ryan Program began supporting Texas-based programs to partner with programs in less restrictive states so their residents can do an abortion-focused away rotation. Since *Dobbs,* we have expanded the program and have matched all Ryan Programs in restrictive states with host institutions. Although we can accommodate the Ryan Program residents, there will be insufficient sites to train the many ob-gyn residents who need to travel, not to mention residents in other specialties such as family medicine. The Ryan Program has also partnered with Innovating Education in Reproductive Health, an online hub of sexual and reproductive health curricula, and the Council on Resident Education in Obstetrics and Gynecology to create a national curriculum that, once piloted and revised, all ob-gyn residents will have to complete before graduation.

Medical schools and residency training programs must facilitate strategies to mitigate moral distress and help learners navigate these ethical challenges. Educators should be trained in recognizing and responding to learner moral distress to support learners through these challenging times. The literature about moral distress suggests that faculty sharing their own emotional experiences and curricula supporting learners' self-reflection and discussion may lessen the distress. In addition, supporting learners to advocate for patients and for patient-centered policies may help. Medical schools and residency programs should include advocacy training for learners in health policy, the public health impacts of abortion restrictions, and ethical obligations around abortion care.

The *Dobbs* decision came at a time when abortion had been integrated into medical education more than ever before. Medical Students for Choice, an organization focused on supporting medical students to advocate for abortion education, has continued to grow and is now in more than two hundred US medical schools and in twenty-eight countries. The American Medical Students Association, a US-based organization of more than thirty thousand students, demands abortion education. The Ryan Program community continues to expand, primarily because programs are desperate to have the designation due to medical student applicants' desire for abortion training.

Abortion training integration in obstetrics and gynecology programs has steadily increased since the 1992, when only 12 percent of ob-gyn programs had training, to more than 60 percent of programs in 2020. Family medicine residency training has also increased, and the Reproductive Health Education in Family Medicine (RHEDI) program supports this training in family medicine in the same way the Ryan Program does in ob-gyn. Complex Family Planning, a fellowship that was created in 1991, became an accredited fellowship in 2020 and a board-certified ob-gyn subspecialty in 2018. Along with Drs. Landy and Darney, I coedited *Advancing Women's Health through Medical Education: A Systems Approach in Family Planning and Abortion.* This textbook celebrates and documents efforts to integrate abortion in health professions education within and outside of the United States. Now that we have successfully integrated abortion into many levels of medical education and into reproductive health care, *Dobbs* threatens to move us backward.

Now that abortion is considered a core part of obstetrics and gynecology and more than ever before in family medicine and in the profession of medicine in general, even though we face challenges, we will work hard to continue to advance training. Learners will continue to demand training and to advocate for patient-centered, just care. And educators will fight to ensure that our learners receive the training and support they need so they can practice within the core professional values of medicine and so that their future patients will receive the high-quality care they deserve.

36 Repro Legal Defense Fund (at If/When/How)

RAFA P. KIDVAI

In April 2022, a few weeks before the leaked US Supreme Court opinion in *Dobbs v. Jackson Women's Health Organization,* a Starr County, Texas, woman was arrested for allegedly "self-inducing" an abortion. For organizers and legal advocates this case stood for much of what we already knew about abortion prosecutions: a misinformed medical provider making a report to the police, and a prosecutor with no legal authority to prosecute, could turn someone's life upside down. It also highlighted how women of color and immigrant communities are disproportionately at risk of being stigmatized and targeted by the state. All this while *Roe v. Wade* was still in effect.

Months later, when the final opinion was issued and *Roe* was overturned, we braced ourselves for a potential "wave" of criminalization of those seeking and providing abortion care. And although the stark growth in abortion stigma and the rapidly changing legal landscape shows us that abortion care is in fact increasingly under threat, it is imperative we remember people were being criminalized for ending their own pregnancies even when the constitutional right to abortion was in effect.

If/When/How—a national organization working to transform the Reproductive Justice law and policy landscape through advocacy, support, and organizing—found that between 2000 and 2020 there were sixty-one documented cases where people were criminally investigated or arrested for self-managing their own abortion (i.e., an abortion managed outside of the formal medical system) or helping someone else do so. These cases are likely a very small sliver of the actual number of people targeted by the criminal, family, and immigration systems for accessing abortion care. Yet they provide us with critical information about the mechanics of state violence and how people are punished for managing their own abortions.

People often self-manage their abortion because of a lack of meaningful access to clinical care, or because it is the care that feels right to them. With the rise in abortion stigma and the constantly changing state of clinical access, self-management is often the only available option. And even though the advent of medication abortion has made self-managed abortions more accessible and medically safer, the legal risk remains significant. In June 2021, in recognition of the legal risk, If/When/How launched the Repro Legal Defense Fund (RLDF) to ensure the people criminalized for their abortions and pregnancy outcomes could fight their cases from the outside and put up stronger defenses. By covering bail, bond, and other pretrial costs, we could attempt to diminish some of the violence of incarceration, while increasing the chances of better legal outcomes. As any public defender or criminal defense attorney will tell you, the criminalized person's emotional well-being *and* case outcomes improve drastically when someone's liberty isn't a prosecutor's main bargaining chip.

By covering attorney's fees, expert witness and investigation costs, providing access to counselors and mitigation specialists, and paying for commissary or the costs associated with remaining connected to loved ones, the RLDF can ensure someone's financial circumstances aren't a barrier to putting up a strong fight. Because let's be clear—being prosecuted is intentionally costly, and depleting an individual and community's emotional and financial reserves is an essential part of the state's violent strategy. Therefore, when the Starr County case came to light, the RLDF was lucky enough to have been prepared for yet another self-managed abortion prosecution. Within twenty-four hours the RLDF secured release while If/When/How's legal team worked to convince prosecutors that the prosecution itself was unlawful. Of course, none of this would have been possible had activists on the ground not fiercely organized and made their presence known to cops and prosecutors. In essence, a multipronged strategy that demanded a thoughtful coalition between organizers and lawyers locally and nationally—a true community effort.

In every case the RLDF worked on, we learned that stronger, safer communities are in fact the answer to a future free from surveillance and control. That medical providers, family members, and close friends are the ones that most often report individuals to law enforcement is alarming. That cops and prosecutors initially charged individuals with murder or homicide in nearly half of the cases where criminalization took place conveys just how stigmatized abortion care is in this country. Those most likely to be the target of criminalization continue to be those facing the most significant forms of interpersonal and structural oppression. This is a clear indicator that the fight against abortion criminalization must be in solidarity and partnership with related social justice movements because our struggles are inextricable. This requires truly listening to and centering the voices of Black and Brown people, immigrants, poor people, people with disabilities, sex workers, substance users, survivors of intimate partner violence, and queer, trans, and gender nonconforming people.

Prior to the existence of the Repro Legal Defense Fund, the majority of cases of abortion criminalization ended in guilty pleas, while approximately a quarter were dropped or dismissed by either the prosecutor or court.[1] We are hopeful our next wave of research will show that getting people out of jail and funding strong defenses will mean fewer people are convicted. However, the very fact of an arrest—conviction or not—causes lasting irreparable harm. People lose custody of their children temporarily or permanently. They face immigration consequences like detention and deportation. They lose jobs, housing, and close relationships. Their mental health suffers as they try to survive and navigate the horrors and trauma caused by incarceration and separation from their loved ones. We have a long way to go and some scary times to come, but through our collective efforts to fight white supremacy and patriarchy, we can work toward a world where no(body) is criminalized.

37 Employer Abortion Travel Benefits Are Important, but They Aren't Enough

KATRINA KIMPORT

The US Supreme Court's decision to overturn the constitutional right to abortion in its *Dobbs v. Jackson Women's Health Organization* decision paved the way for states to make abortion illegal. Many states did just that. The result is that *millions* of women and other people who can become pregnant now live in states where abortion is banned.[1] Almost as quickly as states banned abortion following *Dobbs,* a number of private employers publicly announced that they would pay travel costs for employees in states prohibiting abortion to leave their state to get abortion care. Large international companies, including Starbucks, Tesla, Microsoft, JPMorgan Chase, the Walt Disney Company, and Walmart—the largest private employer in the United States—announced that they were committed to helping employees access health-care services that are not available locally.[2]

Some employers were explicit in their support of reproductive rights while others took a more seemingly neutral tack, affirming commitment to equal access to health care for all employees and for coverage of travel expenses in any instance where travel was required to access care. Reddit and BuzzFeed reported they would offer stipends to cover travel. Warner Brothers said it would expand benefit options to cover transportation expenses. Nike said it would cover both travel and lodging. Other companies described a cap on travel, with Zillow, for example, saying it would reimburse up to $7,500 in travel costs.[3]

The public statements were well-received by supporters of abortion rights. These companies were stepping up, insisting that their employees have access to legal abortion services and the ability to manage their fertility. They were publicly applauded for engaging in a politically and socially contentious issue, even as it was clear that such a benefit had savvy business underpinnings. Offering to pay abortion travel costs could help companies retain and/or entice employees in a competitive marketplace. Yet while the accolades are not misplaced, work-arounds to unjust laws are not sufficient for protecting people's access to abortion care. A look at the experiences of people who leveraged travel work-arounds to get abortion care when *Roe* was still the law of the land highlights the limitations of work-around solutions. Even before *Dobbs,* all but seven states and the District of Columbia banned abortions after a point in pregnancy.[4]

For a research study starting in 2017, I interviewed thirty women who had to travel across state lines to obtain an abortion before *Dobbs.*[5] They traveled not because of safety or an absence of clinical skill but because providers in their home state were legally prohibited from offering them care. Their experiences demonstrated, most simply, that having to travel was deeply burdensome—financially, logistically, and emotionally. Women had to pay for transportation, lodging for multiple days, and food. Some took out loans from family, friends, and banks to cover these costs. The logistics too were often overwhelming. They had to find flights or a reliable car, plan a route, find hotels, secure childcare for children who stayed home, figure out pet care, and negotiate time off from work. And, perhaps most threatening to their privacy, they often had to disclose to their employer why they needed time off. For some women this meant exposing themselves to antiabortion sentiments. Several women reported experiencing harsh social disapproval of their abortion decision from coworkers and even their human resources representative when they explained why they urgently needed time off.

Even when the financial and logistical costs were sorted, these women were still left with staggering emotional costs from traveling to get the abortion care that they needed.[6] They described the stress of going to an unfamiliar city and having to be away from their support networks. One woman expressed her simple wish that she could have slept in her own bed instead of a hotel bed. Being away from basic comforts was stressful for most of the women I talked to. Moreover, knowing that their travel was compelled by the law—and not a medical reason—exacted an even greater emotional toll. Several described feeling cast out of their home state and discussed the effect it had on their sense of community and belonging when they returned home. To be sure, some of the women I interviewed endeavored to make lemonade from the lemons of having to travel. They took time to appreciate the beauty of their destination city, for example. And all appreciated the compassionate and high-quality care they received at their destination facility. But the reality of travel necessitated by legal restriction was irreducibly burdensome.

These women's experiences traveling for abortion care demonstrate that travel work-arounds come with costs, but that does not mean that companies paying for employees' abortion travel is without benefits. Abortion travel coverage will enable some people to have the abortion they want and cannot obtain otherwise. Indeed, travel is expensive and few Americans have the emergency funds urgent travel requires. Private employers funding employees' abortion travel also shares the costs of navigating around abortion bans and means less burden on abortion funds. State abortion bans have already dramatically increased the demand on abortion funds as people seek travel to states where abortion remains legal. Actions like employee abortion travel benefits can take some pressure off these already spread thin funds.

Yet private employers' efforts to blunt the injurious effect of abortion bans on their employees cannot eliminate the myriad costs of being forced to travel for abortion care. Work-arounds like what employers are offering may enable some individuals to get abortions they couldn't otherwise, but not without notable costs. Employers paying for travel only alleviates the financial burden of travel—and perhaps not even all of it if costs related to childcare and pet care, for example, are factored in. Employees who travel for abortion care will still have to navigate the logistics of out-of-state travel and will still have to experience the emotional costs of travel. They may also encounter abortion stigma in the very process of accessing their employee benefit. These costs cannot be accounted for and they cannot be recouped.

Looking at the experiences of people who had to travel across state borders for abortion care because of legal restrictions prior to the *Dobbs* decision, we can see how funding abortion travel can contest unjust restriction on abortion access. But employer support is a work-around. It is not a panacea. If we want to ensure abortion access and reproductive autonomy for all, we must confront the root issue: people need local, legal, and accessible abortion care. Our society must work to ensure that they get it.

38 *Getting People to Abortion Care, Whatever It Takes*

ODILE SCHALIT

I am asked with some frequency if we at The Brigid Alliance knew that *Roe* was going to be overturned when we launched roughly four years before the *Dobbs* decision. While that writing may have been on the proverbial wall, our focus was largely on the facts on the ground: that abortion was already inaccessible for many. The protections *Roe* enabled were never enough to ensure equitable access to care for everyone. *Roe* left huge gaps for people with low incomes; people with disabilities; Black, Indigenous, and other people of color; people with limited access to health-care providers, including many people living in the most rural areas of our country; and people in states whose legislatures have been chipping away at abortion rights for years. Recognizing that travel was becoming one of the primary barriers to abortion access in 2018, with some 90 percent of counties in the United States at the time without providers, our founders and I set out to build an organization that would practically and immediately address the widening gap between abortions seeker and providers. In this sense we have been preparing for *Roe*'s fall since our inception.

In August 2018 we opened our services in New York with a focus on providing logistical and financial support to people who needed to travel to New York City for abortion care after the first trimester of pregnancy. And from that first moment, we knew we couldn't be an organization simply paying for abortion travel. We had to become an organization providing *practical support* for all of our clients' needs: transportation, lodging, meals, childcare, childcare reimbursements, referrals for emotional or legal support, or language interpretation, and an organization that brings dignity, love, and respect to every interaction we have with people we would exist to support.

Beginning with a focus on New York meant we could pilot our program in our own backyard, in a state with good laws and poor access. Some New York state residents must travel ten hours to the nearest in-state provider. Others must leave the state altogether, traveling to Colorado, Maryland, or Washington, DC—a serious hardship for people working to make ends meet, for young people or mothers with no childcare support. Since 75 percent of abortion-seekers have lower incomes, it's obviously crucial to make abortion geographically accessible. That's where we put our focus: who is not getting where they need to be and how can we get them there. We aimed to meet the practical and immediate needs of the many folks for whom traveling such a distance was logistically, emotionally, or financially impossible.

We further decided to focus on abortion care later in pregnancy, as our partners indicated that spotty access meant many people had been unable to get early care because of barriers, including the scarcity of providers, the high cost of procedures, the enormous stigma associated with abortion, and the logistical complexities that arise from the distances one must travel and length of time away from home the travel entailed. Other groups tried to address these barriers, but the financial and staffing costs of supporting people traveling across state lines for multiple daylong appointments was beyond the capacity of most organizations. The Brigid Alliance understood the desire and need for us to step into this arena. Developing a service for long-distance travelers will be our truest lesson in the value and breadth of providing practical support.

We began the process of designing our program by learning from the movement and also from communities full of extraordinary, mostly grassroots and often volunteer-run reproductive health, rights, and justice organizations. We quickly learned about the challenges we faced supporting the travel of abortion-seekers, managing the growing capacity and health of staff-based organizations, dealing with the dearth of resources to serve people requiring later abortions, contending with the ubiquitous antiabortion movement. We came to understand the necessity of developing an intersectional approach as well as the infinite joys and importance of collaboration. We were finding the heart of our organization and building into and within the preexisting network.

After four months of fielding countless referrals for people traveling from New York and other northeastern states, to the rare providers in DC, Maryland, Colorado, and New Mexico, and conversing with providers nationwide, we pivoted to become a national practical support organization supporting people traveling from anywhere in the country to their nearest available later-abortion provider. Today The Brigid Alliance is a core component of abortion-access in the United States, a compensating element for the gross absence of a pro-abortion health-care system.

We have not stopped growing. Each year we have doubled our staff and doubled our budget. And every year we've faced additional crises: the COVID pandemic, more aggressive abortion bans, worsening natural disasters, Texas's SB8 law, and the *Dobbs* decision. All of these events have exacerbated access issues, emphasizing the importance of the availability and adaptability of our services. After SB8 and the leak of the *Dobbs* decision, we expanded our mission, investing time in developing Apiary for Practical Support, an organization I cofounded in 2019 with Diana Parker-Kafka, executive director of the Midwest Access Coalition, and Marisa Falcon. Apiary supports current and new practical-support organizations, in the capacity-building process. Brigid's client services team designed new systems for easy and safe referral pathways between different organizations. We also took time to heal and connect with one another, recognizing that this work is full of heart and soul and brain power and can be exhausting on a deep level. We added more coordinators to our team and more structure to our overall organization to support the strength of its foundation in recognition of the years ahead.

After *Dobbs,* in the midst of a historic crisis in access, thousands more unwillingly or dangerously pregnant people are forced to continue government-mandated pregnancies unless they can manage to get to abortion providers. Abortion bans that have gone into effect since *Dobbs* will likely quadruple the number of people who need to travel for abortion care and will increase the distance they must travel by hundreds of miles. As the crisis worsens, surging numbers of people need our services. In the first month after *Roe v. Wade* was overturned, we received 50 percent more referrals. Now we are urgently scaling up our work on a number of fronts to ensure that the quality of the services we provide meets the needs of this larger group. For example, we've hired four additional client coordinators, increasing our capacity from serving 125 individuals per month to 200 per month. In five years we've grown from a team of two to an organization of fifteen, including seven coordinators who are true experts. We are also strengthening our organizational infrastructure with additional administrative and operational personnel, and we are investing in technology to enhance the security of our operations and to otherwise serve our growing number of clients and staff.

Perhaps most important, we are further deepening connections with local and regional groups to provide holistic support for an increasingly diverse array of clients. This time we're reaching out to community-based groups, outside of Reproductive Justice, to increase our visibility among groups that may encounter people in need of our services. We want to be able to make sound referrals to them when and where needed. As a key part of the effort to deepen our partnerships, we are adapting our client-services model to create regionally focused teams supporting staff serving clients traveling to states in the Northeast, the mid-Atlantic, and the West—the three areas we decided to target after *Dobbs*. Today two to three Brigid staff coordinators are dedicated to each region, investing in stronger relationships with a smaller number of local partners and clinics, developing specific knowledge of the hotels, transportation options, and other services available in their regions, serving our clients with expertise.

Deploying this expertise to meet the needs of clients from a variety of backgrounds, including young people, undocumented immigrants, and survivors of abuse, requires emotionally present and well-trained coordinators—thus our expanded training program. We are also focusing on developing creative approaches to our work. For example, when we learned that a Swahili-speaking client was traveling to a clinic that had no interpreter, we found a vendor who would allow us to set up a translation service on our client's phone.

Today we are doing unprecedented work; adapting to our new reality hasn't been easy. But what we've accomplished has been incredible, in the context of the daily assault on reproductive rights. Although it's hard to feel excitement, I do feel immense pride. I'm proud of our incredible, growing team of coordinators, of the depth of the services we provide, and of the impact we've made and are continuing to make in the lives of thousands of people who have sought our services. Before, Brigid operated in the background, without drawing attention to ourselves. Post-*Dobbs*, that's no longer an option. This moment calls for everyone who believes in abortion rights to be bold and unapologetic. Brigid won't stop until abortion is borderless, burden-free, and accessible to all. It will take all of us in the abortion rights movement working collectively to achieve that vision. There is a long road ahead, but I firmly believe we will get there, and that a better future awaits us.

39 *Jill Filipovic Interviews Rebecca Gomperts*

Abortion rights are at a crisis point in America. In June 2022 the US Supreme Court overturned *Roe v. Wade,* the 1973 decision that legalized abortion nationwide. Feminist activists, who have long struggled to make abortion more accessible to poor and rural women by way of abortion funds and political advocacy, are now looking toward a future in which far fewer American women are entitled to safe, legal abortions in their home states. Some are trying to come up with strategies to help women safely end their pregnancies outside of the formal health-care system.

Enter Rebecca Gomperts.

Gomperts is one of the world's most radical abortion rights activists, although she doesn't necessarily see herself that way. In her view, she's a medical doctor who took an oath to help people in need. And that means providing safe abortions to people who need them— whether the state allows it or not.

Born in Suriname, she grew up in the Netherlands and studied conceptual art at college before turning to medicine. In the early years of her medical career, during which she sailed around Latin America as a ship's doctor and environmental activist with Greenpeace, Gomperts saw the heavy toll that unsafe abortions exact on the lives of women. In 1999 she founded Women on Waves, a mobile abortion clinic that brought the procedure to women around the world by way of a rented boat that sailed to countries with restrictive abortion laws and distributed miscarriage-inducing medications to women in need.[1]

Seeking to reach more people, Gomperts founded the nonprofit Women on Web in 2005, which uses telemedicine and the internet to distribute misoprostol and mifepristone—the two-step medications that safely induce abortions—and information on how to use the pill combination safely and effectively, so that a person anywhere in the world could essentially self-induce a miscarriage privately in their own home.[2] In 2018, Gomperts began a related venture, Aid Access, working with abortion providers specifically in the United States to provide medication abortion by mail in an increasingly restrictive America.[3] In early 2022, Gomperts spoke with the *New York Review* about her work to provide abortions when abortion is outlawed, the connection between abortion bans and the rise of global authoritarianism, and why American women should start stocking up on abortion pills now. What follows is an edited transcript of our conversation.

Jill Filipovic: *What was the transition from Women on Waves to Women on Web? Why make that shift?*

Rebecca Gomperts: What happened after the first ships campaign, and especially the one in Ireland, was that we started getting many emails from pregnant people all over the world who were asking, "When is the ship going to be here?" And we didn't even have a ship. We just rented the ship. We started thinking, well, we have to do something else—and it's just pills, so it should be possible to send them by mail. A lot of legal research was done on how to do this in a sustainable and a legal way, and we found the loopholes. And so that's how Women on Web started in 2005.

Jill Filipovic: *And what are the typical legal loopholes? I would imagine it differs from country to country, but generally, in countries that restrict abortion access, how is it legal to provide abortion-inducing medications to women?*

Rebecca Gomperts: What is interesting is that [misoprostol and mifepristone] are just medicines, and they're actually on the essential medicines list of the World Health Organization.[4] People around the world are allowed to order medicines for their own use from other places. The pills themselves are not illegal, because they can be used for all kinds of indications. Swallowing the pills is not breaking the law either—it's only when women are pregnant that they're potentially breaking the law.

It's also very hard to prove somebody intentionally had a miscarriage. And the abortion pills themselves essentially induce a miscarriage, it's very similar, and in the really rare event that somebody needs medical care, aftercare, it's not possible to prove it was intentional.

What we've seen, though, is that in some countries doctors are putting women under a lot of pressure to "confess" that they used medicines themselves to try to induce an abortion.

From the perspective of the organization, Women on Web is based in Canada, and there is no abortion law against this in Canada. And the doctors who are working for Women on Web are doing so from countries where it's allowed to prescribe the medicines from a distance.

Jill Filipovic: *Can you talk about how wider access to misoprostol has affected the ways abortion rights activists work and abortion providers offer services?*

Rebecca Gomperts: It's been very exciting to be part of that revolution from the beginning. My work started in 1999. Misoprostol was available in some countries, especially in Latin America, but there were very few women who actually knew it was used for abortion. The first safe abortion hotline giving information about misoprostol was launched in 2004, during the Women on Waves campaign in Portugal, because misoprostol was very easily available over the counter there. And then that work took us to Latin America, where we trained all the local women's rights organizations.

There was a division at that time between the medical professionals and the feminists, and a lot of doctors were not very supportive of the use of misoprostol—especially feminist doctors, because many of them believed that it let doctors off the hook and that doctors had to be willing to provide abortion services instead of putting the responsibility back on women. We thought something else: that actually it's extremely empowering for women to do this themselves. And the feminist groups did also. The training of the feminist groups really changed things—to put this knowledge in the hands of women, where it belongs.

It's been very interesting to see that revolution unfold itself and spread over the whole of Latin America, with so many groups involved in training one another, and the growth of underground networks that get the pills and provide them to women—it *has* been a real revolution. And it's women who have taken control and power over this very important medicine for women's health.

In Africa it was a little bit different, but in countries like Indonesia and Pakistan, where we also trained women's organizations, we saw the same things happening.[5]

Jill Filipovic: *You mentioned that some women seek medication abortion out of empowerment, and some seek it out of disempowerment and essentially a lack of other options.*
Rebecca Gomperts: That also has to do with the enormous medicalization of this process. A miscarriage usually doesn't need any medical

treatment or oversight. But the United States is a very medicalized society. For example, in the Netherlands, home birth is the normal way of giving birth. That is absolutely not the case in the United States. When you look at the number of caesarean sections in the United States, it's so much higher than in other countries in Europe, and that has to do with the medicalization of the female body. And that is connected to the way the United States is also a very litigious society.

Jill Filipovic: *Given that we in the United States do have a relatively litigious society and one with pretty sophisticated law enforcement, are there particular legal issues that come with working here that you haven't faced working in other countries where abortion may be restricted?*

Rebecca Gomperts: No, not really. I think the difference is that when we're working in another country and face a legal complaint—and we have already had some court cases—we can trust the legal system to be fair. And so, we won those cases. In the United States the problem is that it's so expensive to go to court, and there's no legal aid, or very bad legal aid, for those who can't afford it. There is so much legal injustice in the United States that is not the case in other countries where we've been working.

Jill Filipovic: *With the law in Texas that allows any citizen in the country to sue anyone who "aids and abets" an abortion, are you concerned about legal liability or vulnerability there?*

Rebecca Gomperts: I'm not working in the United States. I am a doctor registered in Austria; I do my medical practice in Austria. I adhere to all the laws in Austria, and, most of all, to my medical oath. It's very simple: when there are people in need of urgent, time-sensitive medical care, as a doctor you don't have the luxury of saying, "I am not going to help you." That is what you're trained to do.

There are many international human rights agreements that protect the right of women to have access to the medical care they need, and safe abortion specifically. These international agreements over-rule local laws if those laws are in violation of the human rights law. The human rights law is the only law that I need to comply with.

Jill Filipovic: *Internationally, where are you seeing progress on abortion rights and access?*

Rebecca Gomperts: Progress is everywhere except for in the United States, to be honest. No, that's not true: there are some other places where there are real challenges. Poland, for example; Hungary is another, Turkey, and Russia. And what they all have in common is that they're countries that are really struggling with the rule of law and with democracy in general. These are countries where democracy has been undermined systematically.

In countries where democracy is stronger or the political situation is moving toward more democratic governance, and where human rights are more respected, they all move toward legalization of abortion—like Ireland, Northern Ireland, Gibraltar, Thailand. South Korea has legalized abortion, Argentina has legalized abortion, Mexico has legalized abortion. It's also a sign of what is happening in general in these countries. Women's rights are a very clear indication of where a society is headed.

Jill Filipovic: *Why do you think that is? What's the connection between women's rights and either a pro-democracy movement or a shift toward antidemocratic, authoritarian governance?*

Rebecca Gomperts: The connection is that in countries that restrict abortion access, all rights are being violated or undermined. In Hungary there is no free press anymore. All the press is controlled by progovernment owners or companies, or by the government itself. So it's not just women's rights. It's that all the freedoms are affected.

But another link you see in Russia, Poland, and Hungary is the influence of Eurocentric, pro-natalist movements—where they want more white babies born, and the way to do it is to control women's bodies and use them as political instruments. By forcing women to have babies they don't want, you keep people poor. And people who are poor have no voice, they have no say.

Jill Filipovic: *Do you know of any efforts to pressure companies like Google and Facebook to make medically accurate and useful information about medication abortion more available to women?*

Rebecca Gomperts: Oh, yes. YouTube and Facebook have banned Women on Web so many times, but we always fought it, and because we had access to the news media, we were able to solve it. That is easier. The Google algorithm is a little more hidden, and it has only been a problem since the COVID-19 pandemic began: it was actually part of an effort to make unscientific information about COVID harder to find. But it's extremely difficult to fight it because nobody understands how the algorithms actually work. It might be something that we would eventually start a court case over. But that is what people don't realize: it's Google that is filtering people's access to information.

Access to information about the pills is less of a problem than getting access to the pills themselves. The algorithms are making it much harder to find the places where you can obtain these medicines.

Jill Filipovic: *How can women who are searching online tell the difference between reputable telemedicine abortion services and any random person who sets up shop?*

Rebecca Gomperts: That is the problem. One of the issues is that people have to be educated in using the internet: for instance, you could Google to see if there is any other information about such a site—have other people written about it on social media, on Reddit, say—because that is where you can find information about these sites and whether they're reliable or not.

There are certainly many sites that are not reliable, but there are many that are. Plan C [an organization that assists people in finding abortion-inducing pills online] has done a study on the websites that are offering abortion pills and found that they offer real medicines. The problem is they don't always provide information on how to use them; there's no oversight, no supervision from a doctor. That matters because, for example, Aid Access always provides extra doses of misoprostol, since research has shown that repeated doses help to complete the procedure, and result in a higher success rate, especially later in pregnancy. And many of these other sites don't do that.

Jill Filipovic: *What kind of medical oversight or supervision is necessary to complete a medication abortion oneself?*
Rebecca Gomperts: Not much, but people need to have the information: how to use the medicines, and when to look for medical care if there are complications. That's it. And that information is pretty widely available—really specific knowledge that we have built up over the years, which the websites selling the medicine don't give. This includes advice about using the medications orally rather than vaginally, the slightly higher risk of complications if a person has had multiple previous caesarean sections, and the signs of ectopic pregnancy.

Having a good help desk and medical oversight can, in exceptional cases like ectopic pregnancies, be lifesaving. But there shouldn't be any doctor having to prescribe this drug treatment; it should be a medicine that is available over the counter.

Jill Filipovic: *In places like the United States and Hungary, what should women be doing now to prepare to protect and advocate for ourselves, and for other women who may have fewer resources and may be more vulnerable?*
Rebecca Gomperts: Of course, people should organize to stop these regimes from doing what they do, but that is not so easy, and

what they're up to is happening already. So I'd say: make sure that people have as much information as possible about medication abortion, and make sure that they have stocks. Get as many pills as you can, I would say. And buckle up.

Jill Filipovic: *So women should have misoprostol and mifepristone on hand, whether they're pregnant or not?*
Rebecca Gomperts: Absolutely. The shelf life of mifepristone is really long. So yes, get it and make sure you have it on hand.

Jill Filipovic: *What can American feminists and abortion rights activists learn from your work, and from the work that activists have been doing for so many years in countries that have long had these restrictive legal landscapes?*
Rebecca Gomperts: What I've found very interesting from our work with groups all over the world is that initially there's a lot of self-censorship and fear, because the laws are often very unclear and people are afraid they can be prosecuted—especially in the United States. Removing that self-censorship is really important.

You need to do things publicly that challenge these laws in order to discover that you shouldn't be too afraid of them. The people usually targeted by the law are the really vulnerable ones who do not have networks of support, but if you have a community and you work together, you can do a lot you didn't think was possible.

Part VI Resisting Religious Tyranny

RICKIE SOLINGER

State and religious institutions are promulgators of dense and often conflicting bodies of law and policy. The clashes between state and religious regulations around the world have been fierce across centuries, the causes of wars, millions dead, mass migration, endless brutalities. The United States was, of course, founded on the principle of the *separation* of church and state, the prohibition of an established religion, a formal commitment to diversity of opinions, religious and otherwise, all features of a democracy.

Today the US Supreme Court has disapproved of these foundational tenets, as majorities have empowered secular law to enforce religious-based regulations; established "Christian exceptionalism" as the basis of secular law; and prohibited behavior (abortion, and in some states, speech) that conflicts with the particular creed of Christianity that six members of the Court chose to elevate as the law of the land. The essays in this part of the book object fiercely to these developments. Each offers ideas that lie at the heart of one faith commitment; a discussion of what the state is willing to trammel, using what precise authoritarian logic. The religious teachers and leaders authoring these essays rely on foundational religious texts and also on the US Constitution to explain the dangers of *Dobbs* and the true meaning of religious liberty.

Toni Bond focuses on *Dobbs* as a direct attack on democracy as it denies individuals the right to make their own moral decisions. She especially decries the sharp and ongoing attacks on the reproductive dignity of people whose forebears' reproductive capacities were defined as a source of profit, eugenic degradation, cheap or free labor, in the name of white supremacy. Bond explores "liberation" as a religious value, a secular and individual goal, and a "basis for action." A group of seven Muslim organizations offers a statement that defines *Dobbs* as a threat to the Muslim ideal of *maslaha amma,* or the general good, a key tenet of which is religious diversity. This document ties Muslim ideals to foundational ideals in the US Constitution, especially the commitment to honor both religion and diversity.

Rabbi Danya Ruttenberg identifies key passages in Jewish texts that establish abortion as a matter of religious freedom, a permitted decision and even, under some circumstances, a matter of obligation and responsibility. *Dobbs*'s reliance on particular Christian concepts such as "fetal life" to support abortion bans, Ruttenberg argues, violates Jewish law and spiritual obligations and constitutes an offense against individual dignity. Gillian Frank and Neil J. Young give us a fresh, long view of antiabortion coalition-building among Catholics and evangelical Christians from the 1950s forward. They show that this cross-religion cooperation was not simply an expression of political tactics, but that the sometimes-uneasy coalition consistently and effectively promoted the merging of religious and social conservative issues, now celebrated in *Dobbs.*

Pastor Laurinda Hafner explores how abortion decision-making helps us understand what it means to be "faithful" and describes her participation in a novel lawsuit brought by a number of religious leaders in Florida, against state legislation HB5, which, the suit claims, violates freedom of speech, free exercise of religion, and separation of church and state. Here, as in all of these essays, *Dobbs* as an expression of state power is an enemy of the rights of persons of faith and others, threatening to make us criminals for exercising our religion and our nonreligious beliefs.

40 *The* Dobbs *Decision, God, and Moral Conscience*

TONI BOND

Central to reproductive and sexual justice is recognizing people's humanity. When you recognize the humanity of an individual, you also acknowledge their human dignity. And, when you acknowledge their human dignity, you recognize their human capabilities. A lens of Reproductive Justice looks at what people are actually able to do and to be. It requires creating the conditions that ensure people can do more than just survive but can thrive because their humanity is acknowledged, and their human dignity is respected.

Respecting Human Dignity and Capability

The ruling in *Dobbs v. Jackson Women's Health Organization* underscores Supreme Court justices lack of respect for the human dignity and capability of women and pregnant-capable people to make moral decisions about their reproductive autonomy. The *Dobbs* decision was much more than a direct attack on the humanity and moral agency of every individual who is faced with the decision of whether to become a parent. It was also another affront to the reproductive dignity of Black, Indigenous, people of color who have historically had their bodies, reproduction, and sexuality monitored, controlled, and surveilled by governmental and private actors. The US debate

[261]

over reproductive and sexual autonomy—whether women and pregnant-capable people can make decisions about whether to carry a pregnancy to term—is a forced adherence to prescriptive patriarchal norms rooted in Christian exceptionalism and white supremacist ideology. These norms valorize male control and dominance over bodies that can reproduce.

Fundamentalist evangelical clergy and politicians engage in hermeneutical sleights of hand with their misinterpretations of biblical text assigning meanings of fetal personhood (Psalms 139:13–16, Job 10:11–12, Jeremiah 1:5) to scriptures that are more allegorical in meaning such as Davidic prayers about God's knowledge of the innermost thoughts of humans and for help against certain enemies or laments about the human condition and questioning God's presence in the midst of suffering. The Bible actually does not address abortion specifically. Although, as religious anti-choice proponents have shown, it can be relatively easy to convolute biblical text to support reproductive oppression.

Planting the Seeds to Erode Democracy

Conservative Supreme Court justices delivered a much more damning blow to democracy that goes well beyond overturning *Roe*. Organized religion has played a central role in attempting to determine the point at which life begins in the abortion debate. The jeremiad of anti-choice Catholic and evangelical religious leaders has been that life begins at the point of conception. The designating point at which an embryo becomes a life is not based upon scientific data but rather when these religious traditions believe the creation of an individual human soul occurs. By returning the authority to the states to determine personhood or fetal rights, the Court all but delivered the power to conservative anti-choice legislators to make laws grounded in their particular religious beliefs about when life begins, thereby abrogating women's and pregnant-capable persons' First Amendment right to religious autonomy. It also plants another stake in the ground toward codifying Christianity as the one and only religion in the United States.

The Court's opinion erroneously argued that philosophers and ethicists have been unable to justify the right to abortion using the point of viability outlined in *Planned Parenthood of Southeastern Pennsylvania, et al. v. Robert P. Casey*, the 1992 landmark case that upheld *Roe v. Wade*. A number of philosophers have crafted compelling arguments in support of the right to abortion. The American philosopher Judith Jarvis Thomson in her 1971 essay, "A Defense of Abortion," argues that the fetus's right to life does not override a woman's jurisdiction over her body.[1] In other words, one person's right to life does not entail the forcible usage of another person's body to sustain their life.

The American philosopher Bertha Alvarez Manninen put forth a Kantian ethical argument in "A Kantian Defense of Abortion Rights with Respect for Intrauterine Life" wherein she drew from German philosopher Immanuel Kant's formula of humanity arguing that the "formula of humanity precludes compelled gestation."[2] Kant's formula of humanity states that "rational nature exists as an end in itself . . . [a]ct in such a way that you use humanity, whether in your own person or in the person of any other, always at the same time as an end, never merely as a means."[3] Manninen argues that while respect for the fetus's "potential personhood" requires "appropriate care and esteem," the fetus's status does not trump a woman's well-being and personhood.[4] In applying Kant's formula for humanity, Manninen is clearly arguing that the woman must not be used merely as a tool to meet the survival ends of the fetus. The woman, also being worthy of dignity and respect as a person, is an end in herself.

Conclusion

No other form of health care makes access to health care contingent upon morality. You do not have to be a good person to have a root canal performed by a dentist. If you go to the emergency room complaining of chest pains, medical staff will immediately triage you, complete an EKG, draw blood for lab work, perform x-rays, and perform every other examination possible to determine whether you are having a cardiac event. It is only with reproductive and sexual health care— contraception, obtaining abortion care or health care for transgender and gender-diverse individuals such as basic physical exams, preventive care, and health-care concerns and needs around transitioning medically by using hormones or having surgery—that morality issues are raised.

Religious scholars and leaders have a unique role to play in this current political moment. There is diversity both within and among faith traditions. There is, in fact, no singular one point of view on abortion. In fact, it was a network of more than two thousand faith leaders called the Clergy Consultation Service who helped more than 250,000 women obtain abortions from 1967 to 1973.[5] Religious scholars and leaders must help navigate the way to reclaiming the moral high ground around abortion access in particular, and for reproductive and sexual autonomy and liberation more broadly. Conservative, anti-choice religious voices are deeply entrenched in a form of Christian exceptionalism that is grounded in white supremacy. Political leaders have used arguments of religion and moral conscience to set the moral compass, both domestically and globally, through state and federal policies such as religious refusals and religious exemptions that allow health-care professionals and institutions to refuse to provide certain reproductive health services such as abortion and sterilization without facing legal, financial, or professional consequences.

Across the reproductive health, rights, and justice movements, leadership must intentionally make space for those religious voices who can speak to the historical strategy of anti-choice religious conservatives to promote an agenda of Christian exceptionalism and white supremacy that is cloaked in theological and ethical concerns for the unborn. That historical perspective must go back to 1978, when anti-choice religious leader Paul Weyrich used abortion as a rallying cry not for moral reasons but to rally religious supporters behind efforts to keep then President Jimmy Carter from winning a second term in order to preserve school segregation. Weyrich and others anti-choice leadership chose abortion as an organizing message because they believed it would be an effective religious crusade around which to organize religious people. However, it is important to note that the Southern Baptist Convention actually passed resolutions in 1971, 1974, and 1976 (after *Roe*) affirming women's access to abortion for a myriad of reasons and that the government role in that decision should be limited.

The role of religion in the struggle for reproductive health, rights, and justice must be one of liberation. Liberating women and pregnant-capable people's bodies from all forms of oppression includes speaking truth to our God-given free will, standing in the gap for those who need access to the full spectrum of reproductive and sexual health care, and fighting for access to safe abortion. It means lifting up the true meaning of evangelicalism, which means to bring forth the good news of the liberation of God's people and reminding us that social justice is an important part of that message of good news, which includes access to all forms of health care. This is the work that religious scholars and leaders must carry forth at the intersections of religion, faith, and reproductive and sexual justice. We must talk about and affirm individual moral reflection and decision-making around the use of contraception, whether to carry a pregnancy to term, premarital sex, sexual orientation, and even the use of assisted reproductive technologies.

Any action by the government or private actors to interfere with that individual free will, agency, and moral decision-making stands in the way of justice, kindness, and humans' relationship with God, all of which are central to ethical reflection for people of faith.

41 *Open Letter from Seven Muslim American Organizations*

This is an open letter written on behalf of a coalition of the following Muslim American organizations: Muslim Advocates, KARAMAH: Muslim Women Lawyers for Human Rights, HEART Women and Girls, American Muslim Bar Association, Muslim Wellness Foundation, American Muslim Health Professionals, and Muslim Public Affairs Council.

American Muslim women are diverse in race, ethnicity, and cultural background. In fact, American Muslims are the most diverse religious group in the United States. We are united by a belief in God and the Prophet Muhammad, but we are a minority religious community comprising a wide range of spiritual practices and political opinions. In this way we are true to our Islamic heritage; the "nations and tribes" of Muslims around the world have always followed a diversity of *fiqh* schools and cultural norms.

Many Muslims today don't realize this because so much of our collective memory has been interrupted by colonial thinking, but one of the reasons so many *fiqh* schools could thrive and grow is because premodern Muslim governments did not have the authority to declare a particular *fiqh* opinion correct over all the others—and even less to enforce it over the entire population. When classical Muslim rulers forced a rule on the people, it had to be justified as serving the general good (*maslaha 'amma*). This is also what protected non-Muslims living in safety under Muslim rule for so many centuries—they could follow their own religious laws as long as such laws did not conflict with the general good.

Similarly, the Constitution's Establishment Clause ("Congress shall make no law respecting an establishment of religion") prohibits lawmakers from giving ("establishing") one religion priority over another—and that includes favoring a particular religious view over others. In short, the Constitution insists that our public lawmaking stay religiously neutral. An important principle of valuing religious diversity emerges from both Islamic history and US constitutionalism. When a state takes sides in a religious debate, it can have devastating consequences. From the Crusades to the Spanish Inquisition, history shows us that individual religious freedom—not to mention human lives—can be lost when a regime endorses one religious doctrine to stifle others. The founders of the United States recognized the same danger. Working in the shadow of the Protestant-Catholic wars of Europe, they paid special attention to protecting religious practice from government overreach. As a result, religious practice in the United States is refreshingly diverse, encompassing a range of religious beliefs and practices about everything from the environment to marriage to abortion. But this may be under attack.

Consider the Mississippi abortion ban (the basis for the *Dobbs v. Jackson Women's Health Organization* decision). By defining life as beginning at conception, this law adopts the religious belief of some Christians who believe that all abortion is immoral. But not all American Christians, nor Americans of other religions, share this belief. In other words, by picking one religious belief and enshrining it into law, Mississippi (and now many other states) is infringing on constitutional protections for American religious diversity. An interfaith coalition recently made this argument in an amicus curiae brief to the Supreme Court, arguing that Mississippi is trying to use state power to impose a particular view of when life begins, thus stifling "the diversity of views within and across religious traditions" on the morality of terminating pregnancy.

We should not assume that what might be prohibited for Muslims is what the state should prohibit for every inhabitant. Among the signatories to that brief were several Muslim legal organizations. These signatures followed deep reflection and deliberation by organizations whose members hold a wide range of Islamic beliefs about abortion. Their conclusion is consistent with the lesson from Islamic history that governments should not declare a particular religious view correct. For believers, these decisions and discussions are best left to individuals in consultation with their muftis, rabbis, priests, or other spiritual advisers, faithful to their respective understandings of scripture. It is clear that reasonable minds—including pious, God-conscious minds—can differ on the morality of abortion. Sharia itself, with its diversity of *fiqh* opinions on the topic, allows Muslims to follow different rules about the permissibility and timing of abortion. The centuries-long tradition of Muslim lands hosting religious minorities reminds us that we should not assume that what might be prohibited for Muslims is what the state should prohibit for every inhabitant.

In other words, Muslims who oppose the [*Dobbs* decision] on these grounds of religious liberty are not compromising Islamic values by doing so. We can look to our own history to see that it is quite Islamic to insist that a state should not select one religious view (even if it is one we happen to hold ourselves) and force it on the very diverse population of the United States. In short, you can be a Muslim who is religiously opposed to abortion and nevertheless think that [the Supreme Court] should not impose this view on everyone living [in the country]. In our view [*Dobbs*] not only compromises the Constitution's protection of religious diversity among Americans but also threatens an Islamic principle of honoring religious diversity. That same principle is consistent with the idea that a secular state should resist enacting laws based solely on the beliefs of one religion. We should applaud, not condemn, Muslims who are fighting against that impulse. Today the crusade to enshrine religion into state law is being fought over abortion rights; tomorrow it will be something else.

42 *The Torah of Abortion Justice*

RABBI DANYA RUTTENBERG

Four thousand people in front of the Capitol at the Jewish Rally for Abortion Justice, demanding that the Senate codify abortion rights with the Women's Health Protection Act.

Nearly a million dollars raised in five months through the Jewish Fund for Abortion Justice to provide travel funds and abortion care for those who need it immediately after the fall of *Roe.*

Immersion in the *mikveh*—the Jewish ritual bath—to ritualize the completion of an abortion, with all of the emotions (varied, depending on the person immersing) that go with it.

More than a thousand Jewish communities across the United States participating in an annual Repro Shabbat, learning and speaking about abortion and Judaism, telling abortion stories, dismantling stigma.

The white supremacist Christian fundamentalist right has so hijacked the discourse around abortion—so thoroughly and strategically, over decades of work, messaging from key leaders, indoctrination at prayer camps, media empires, deep pockets—that it is understood by most swaths of American society that "religion" always equals "antiabortion in every way." Then, of course, as the story goes, those fighting abortion bans—and for the life, safety, and dignity of those whose freedom and humanity are being abrogated—are antireligious secular feminists screaming, "Get your rosaries off my ovaries!"

There may be truth to that, insofar as evangelical leaders have successfully made fighting abortion their rallying cry for decades, overturning *Roe* their crowning achievement (until they pass a national abortion ban, of course). And insofar as many in the reproductive freedom camp *are* secular, they take the right to do and be and believe whatever makes sense for them.

And yet. That's not the whole picture. That's never been the complete picture. I'm a rabbi who serves as scholar-in-residence at the National Council of Jewish Women, which includes two hundred thousand advocates on the ground fighting to preserve the right to abortion, to regain it where needed, and to expand access to care; the organization has supported access to contraception and abortion care since its founding in 1893. Our organization's Rabbis for Repro network includes more than two thousand Jewish clergy of every denomination who preach, teach, agitate, and advocate on behalf of everyone's right to a safe and accessible abortion. We fight for abortion justice not *despite* our religious beliefs but *because* of them. Our understanding of our obligation to engage in this work is grounded both in Jewish law and in a more expansive understanding of our Jewish mandate—which is, in part, our human mandate.

To understand the Jewish approach to abortion access, we must begin in the book of Exodus, part of the Hebrew Bible, which features a case of a person accidentally causing a miscarriage to take place—knocking over a pregnant person in a fight.[1] Exodus tells us that if the fetus is lost, but there is no other harm done to the pregnant person, they are obligated to pay financial damages only; the case is not treated as manslaughter. The "other damage" that would result in a more serious penalty would be the death of the pregnant person herself (or some other serious punishment relating to the damage caused). In other words, causing the termination of a pregnancy is not, in the Torah, considered manslaughter.

This passage has massive implications for the status of the fetus overall in Judaism, as we think about contemporary policy antiabortion lingo like "personhood." Interestingly, in the case of the accidental miscarriage, damages are managed as a community accountability process rather than in relation to the formal court system that the Torah discusses elsewhere. In any case, the difference in consequences makes the meaning clear: the fetus is regarded as *potential* life rather than *actual* life. This idea is underscored in the Talmud, a collection of rabbinic thought and culture that was codified around 500 CE or so. One statement declares that for the first forty days of pregnancy, a fetus is "mere water"—essentially, it has no legal status at all.[2] From the end of that forty-day period until the end of the pregnancy, it is regarded as part of the pregnant person's body—"as its mother's thigh," the Talmud says.[3] Here, again, the fetus is secondary to the adult human carrying it.

This becomes most clear when a pregnancy or labor endangers the pregnant person. According to a roughly two-thousand-year-old source called the Mishnah (the core of the Talmud), abortion is explicitly called for to save their life.[4] The life of the baby comes into consideration only once the head has emerged. But beyond life-or-death situations, Jewish law permits abortion in situations where carrying the fetus to term would cause "woe"[5] or "emotional pain"[6] and that includes risks to mental health[7] or to *kavod habriot* (dignity).[8] We have a text of a prominent eighteenth-century Algerian rabbi stating clearly that self-managed medication (presumably herbal) abortion is permitted by Jewish law, which nowhere indicates that the women who have been engaging in this practice should be consulting with any men— husbands or rabbis—before they decide to terminate a pregnancy.[9]

Abortion access, then, is a matter of religious freedom—and the First Amendment. Jews are permitted to terminate a pregnancy, and when our lives are at stake, we may be obligated by Jewish law to do so. Abortion bans are a violation of the Free Exercise Clause when government intervention prevents our access to abortion care. And abortion laws that enshrine specific Christian concepts—"fetal personhood," for example, or the notion that life begins at conception—trample over other understandings of when life begins and, as such, are a violation of the Establishment Clause. This doesn't affect just Jews but also Muslims, atheists, agnostics, and plenty of Christians who support reproductive freedom.

But it's important to note that on the Jewish side, our relationship to these ideas are about more than Jewish law—and, indeed, a feminist argument must interrogate the concept of rabbinic "permission" for abortion, particularly when those legal decisions have come pretty exclusively from men for over fifteen hundred years, up until perhaps the last couple of decades. There are many critical Jewish perspectives on abortion justice. For example, when we think about the increasing criminalization of abortion and pregnancy loss, we can remember that in Judaism, redeeming captives is considered a "great mitzvah," something that takes precedence over even supporting the poor.

And even more than that: many secular conversations center on the question of whether abortion is a right. But in Judaism we talk about responsibilities—to one another and to God. For me, defending abortion is about our broader ethical and spiritual obligations, as well as the specific ones prescribed by Jewish law. In the Hebrew Bible the Israelites who have been liberated from slavery are commanded to set up systems that ensure that even the most socially marginalized are enfranchised. The Bible's constant refrain to remember the "widow, orphan, and stranger" recognizes that those who are marginalized because of gender and status, because they are young and at risk, because they are immigrants or socially "other" in some other way, are particularly impacted by poverty and other harms. (Yep, that's ancient intersectionality.) Everyone must be included, cared for, empowered—and their rights must be protected.[10]

We know that abortion bans deepen every structural inequality in our society. They disproportionately affect people who are struggling financially, Black, Brown, and Indigenous communities, as well as young people, those in rural areas, undocumented immigrants, disabled people, trans men, and some nonbinary people. And we know that people who are denied access to reproductive health care are more likely to live in poverty and to remain in abusive relationships as a direct result of that denied care. We are obligated as Jews to create a more just society. Our work as Jews must always center those who are most impacted by abortion bans and follow the leadership of those working from within those communities.

Our own right to act out of our own self-knowledge must never be overridden. As Rabbi Becky Silverstein teaches, Jewish law holds that if someone is sick, they themselves are regarded as the expert on whether or not they are well enough to fast on Yom Kippur, our Day of Atonement—they are the expert on their own bodies' needs. As such, he argues, this principle also "authorizes as experts both pregnant people who want to end a pregnancy and trans people seeking gender-affirming care or the right to live as their true selves. It demands that we honor the self-knowledge of those individuals."[11] We must honor every person's self-knowledge. We must center those most impacted. We, as Jews, have an obligation to fight abortion bans and the criminalization of abortion in every way, from every angle— as an abrogation of our religious freedom and offense against the dignity of every single human being created in the image of the divine.

43 *What Everyone Gets Wrong about Evangelicals and Abortion*

GILLIAN FRANK AND NEIL J. YOUNG

In the wake of *Dobbs v. Jackson,* the Supreme Court opinion that over-turned *Roe v. Wade,* a familiar narrative has emerged. The story goes like this: white evangelicals didn't care much about abortion until the late 1970s. Around that time two prominent leaders of the soon-to-be-named "religious right," Paul Weyrich and Jerry Falwell, con-cluded that overtly racist politics would harm, not help, their quest for political power. They turned to abortion as a convenient wedge issue in the 1979 midterm elections to drive evangelicals to the polls and distract from the "real" motivations of the far right: stopping ra-cial integration and preserving the tax-exempt status of segregation-ist Christian schools.[1]

But this oversimplified narrative about abortion reduces the rise of the religious right to the cynical calculations of elite movement leaders—rather than to the actions of thousands of grassroots activ-ists, religious leaders, and conservative thinkers who spent nearly two decades building the networks and ideas that brought about the religious right.[2] It also disentangles abortion from a web of intercon-nected issues from the 1960s and 1970s, including opposition to the proposed Equal Rights Amendment (ERA) to the US Constitution, school prayer, school integration, changing attitudes about gender and sexuality, and the growing gay rights movement. Those issues were shaped directly and indirectly by racist ideas and attitudes and were part of a broader political realignment that moved white Southern evangelicals and Northern white Catholics from the Democratic Party to the GOP in this period.

Most important, this simplified history of abortion ignores the vast and decades-long, Catholic-led antiabortion movement and the coincident politicization of white evangelicals for nearly two decades before the 1979 midterm elections. Understanding this history is vital for making sense of the nearly sixty-year interfaith antiabortion movement that has led to this moment. Catholic leaders had long opposed abortion, becoming especially vocal in the 1930s, when the Great Depression led to an uptick in women seeking the procedure. By the early 1960s some evangelicals were beginning to view abortion as murder and a source of growing social and political concern. Twelve years before the *Roe* decision, a young woman wrote to the leading US evangelist, the Rev. Billy Graham, with the following question: "Through a young and foolish sin, I had an abortion. I now feel guilty of murder. How can I ever know forgiveness?" Graham, whose syndicated newspaper column "My Answer" reached millions of Americans, replied: "Abortion is as violent a sin against God, nature, and one's self as one can commit." Graham telegraphed evangelicals' unease with abortion, which would become increasingly political in the coming years.[3]

As state legislatures across the country contemplated legalizing abortion in the mid-1960s—buoyed by support from members of the medical and legal communities, as well as certain more liberal religious groups and, in particular, from the growing women's liberation movement—evangelical antiabortion voices also emerged in the debate. At the time, there was growing awareness but also a lot of ambivalence about abortion among these Christians. An article in a 1967 issue of the evangelical magazine *Eternity* captured this shifting terrain. It noted that the Bible was "strangely silent" on the question of whether the "unborn fetus"—not, tellingly, the "unborn child"—was a "living person with all the rights of life." To combat that silence, a smattering of evangelical ministers began participating in Catholic-led "Right to Life Sundays."[4]

But a real turning point occurred when a statewide referendum on abortion took place in Michigan in 1972. White Catholics there led the charge to oppose legalizing abortion. Crucially, they did so in a loose coalition with evangelical denominations, including Missouri Synod Lutherans, Dutch Reformed churches, and Southern Baptist Convention churches. These groups managed to get 60 percent of voting Michiganders to oppose abortion law reform by emphasizing that abortion was murder. The campaign codified a visual iconography that is now rote, with mutilated fetuses and endangered white babies at its center. The victory also marked the beginning of an important political coalition in the making between white evangelicals and Catholics who opposed abortion.[5] This type of religious cooperation was now possible because the meaning of abortion had changed for many evangelicals. Initially, most states proposed legalizing abortion only in "extreme cases": to save the life of the expectant woman and in cases of rape, incest, and fetal deformity or "carefully ascertained evidence of the likelihood of damage to the emotional, mental, and physical health of the mother." The Southern Baptist Convention passed a resolution in 1971 calling on Southern Baptists to "work for legislation that will allow the possibility of abortion under such conditions."[6]

Yet, in the wake of the 1973 *Roe v. Wade* decision, which (like the state of New York before it) allowed women to elect to have a legal abortion for any reason through the second trimester of pregnancy—before the point at which the fetus could viably live outside the mother's body—evangelicals came to see abortion differently. A statement from the National Association of Evangelicals immediately responding to *Roe* lamented that the decision "made it legal to

terminate a pregnancy for no other reason than personal convenience or sociological considerations." That idea grew in evangelical
circles as the number of legal abortions increased soon after. By 1975,
3.5 million women, or one in fourteen women of reproductive
age, had had an abortion.[7] That same year, a prominent group of
Protestants—including J.A.O. Preus II, president of the Lutheran
Church-Missouri Synod; Harold Lindsell, the editor of *Christianity
Today;* and Ruth Graham, wife of the Rev. Billy Graham—founded
the Christian Action Council to remind "non-Roman Catholic Christians that virtually all Christians have been against abortion from the
beginning and for the protection of human life." Quickly, evangelical
denominations and institutions adopted across-the-board opposition to abortion.[8]

These high-profile evangelical thinkers dovetailed with a groundswell of antiabortion sentiments from grassroots activists. Evangelical women entered the political arena by joining state-level campaigns against the Equal Rights Amendment. The anti-ERA
movement was a theological and political melting pot, bringing together Catholic anti-feminist leaders like Phyllis Schlafly with evangelicals across the country to oppose a range of perceived feminist
threats to the traditional nuclear family. Opponents of the ERA sin-
gled out abortion as particularly dangerous to family values. Evangelicals getting a political education from Schlafly and the multiyear
anti-ERA movement absorbed Catholic antiabortion rhetoric
that was increasingly being stripped of its most obvious sectarian
markers.

In 1977 this synergy was on display at the federally funded and
feminist-led National Women's Conference in Houston, as busloads
of conservative evangelical and Catholic women showcased a highly
refined political vocabulary to describe the ERA and abortion as intertwined threats to the divinely supported patriarchal familial
order.[9] Given the deep history of animosity and tension between

Catholics and evangelicals, this new political alliance was not always easy. To avoid alienating their congregants, evangelical antiabortion activists regularly made sure to remove Catholic imagery, such as the rosary and the Virgin Mary, from antiabortion literature. The Baptist Texas pastor Robert Holbrook, who founded Baptists for Life in 1973, ran antiabortion ads in Baptist newspapers that removed any references to the National Right to Life Committee, a largely Catholic organization that provided him with materials. Holbrook encouraged other evangelicals to develop materials that were published by their denominations, so as not to be perceived as Catholic. Still, despite these tensions, a viable new political alliance had been forged.

These developments set the stage for a large and coordinated white Catholic and evangelical antiabortion effort in the 1979 midterm elections. Both the (Catholic) National Right to Life Committee and the (evangelical) Christian Action Council worked through their particular religious communities to mobilize voters against politicians who supported abortion rights. In places like Iowa, Minnesota, and New Hampshire, a new crop of conservative, religious, antiabortion Republican candidates—who opposed more moderate candidates in their own party who supported legal abortion, as well as the Democratic Party's increasing embrace of feminist proposals like the ERA and legal abortion—defeated Democrats who supported legal abortion. The results were so remarkable that political observers at the time commented on the emergence of a new band of "single-issue voters" who made their political decisions solely on the issue of abortion. In other words, by the 1979 midterm elections there was already a large and growing antiabortion movement that had energized evangelicals for almost two decades. Conservative leaders tapped into this movement, creating new, politically minded religious groups—notably Falwell's Moral Majority in 1979, which mobilized voters behind Ronald Reagan's winning presidential campaign in 1980.

Antiabortion activism overlapped with racist political projects, which never receded for conservatives. Well beyond the 1980s, conservative politicians continue to reach white evangelical and white Catholic voters through racialized dog whistles and outright racist ideas, such as linking social safety nets to so-called "welfare queens," opposing busing and school integration, or invoking the specter of Black crime. Conservative antiwelfare initiatives dovetailed with the antiabortion movements' attacks upon tax-funded programs that especially helped women of color access reproductive health care. Images of white babies, meanwhile, emblazoned antiabortion literature in an effort to reflect the white faces that populated the segregated churches, which powered the antiabortion movement.

The powerful political coalition known as the religious right was not a last-minute manipulation of gullible voters in the late 1970s or a simple displacement of racist issues onto abortion. Instead, it reflected a decades-long coalescing of religious and social conservatives around a host of issues related to sexuality, gender and certainly race. At a moment when there are simultaneous attacks on African American voting rights, critical race theory, and abortion rights, it is crucial to understand that issues of race and reproduction are not and were neither separate nor proxies. Rather, they were and remain interlocking concerns within a far-right political movement devoted to eroding personal freedoms and democratic institutions.[10]

44 *Abortion and Faith in Florida*

THE REV. DR. LAURINDA HAFNER

As an ordained pastor for over forty years, there have been moments when I thought my heart would break for beloved church parishioners faced with unspeakable pain, fear, or challenges. One that continues to haunt me was a young mother of two. She and her husband were thrilled to be expecting a much planned and welcomed third child. She was in her tenth week, far enough along that family and friends had been told, the two children were anxiously awaiting a new sibling, and life was filled with anticipation and joy.

One quiet night, everything took a turn. I got the call that my parishioner had been rushed to the hospital because of serious blood loss and a fetus that if not taken by a D&C would probably result in her death. By the time I arrived, emergency measures were in place, my parishioner and her husband holding on to each other for dear life, and her question to me: "Will God ever forgive me if I go through with this procedure?"

She and her husband were part of a church community that would certainly be described as progressive: we supported the ordination of women, openly welcomed and affirmed those in the LGBTQIA2S+ community, and embraced Liberation Theology for those oppressed in Central America. We preached and taught and lived a theology of love and grace, not of sin and fear. Yet somewhere along the line, maybe after seeing "pro-life" billboards she had passed, or hearing antiabortion folks speak of the evils of abortion, she wondered aloud if God would ever love her again. Folks might be surprised at the theological conversation that ensued that evening. It was pastor and parishioner together wrestling with the eternal questions of good and evil, wrong and right. As I now look back on that occasion, I realize what a privilege it was to be with my parishioners, to speak of God's love, to offer up prayers and scripture, and most of all, the assurance that God was with them in this difficult moment.

Recently the unraveling of *Roe v. Wade* by the *Dobbs* decision has started what may be the downward spiral of the ability of clergy and parishioner to discern together what it means to be faithful in the face of difficult and complicated decisions surrounding abortion. As a pastor in Florida, the state's new abortion law House Bill 5 (HB5), passed by lawmakers during the 2022 legislative session and signed into law by the governor of Florida, is an entrée toward the restriction of clergy from helping a parishioner to make such a challenging decision. The freedom to provide spiritual comfort or support by clergy will be severely restricted or even against the law. As a pastor, I can't imagine a more important moment to be present and to share our faith than when faced with such decisions. Yet the very law that will restrict such a presence, such aid and comfort, and such guidance, has been endorsed, supported, and even driven by religious communities.

The fact that this bill was signed in a conservative Pentecostal church by the governor of Florida is evidence that it is religiously motivated. The question then becomes, *whose* religion? The religion of those who refuse to see the multitude of stories or humanity in each difficult decision around abortion? Or those whose sacred texts and theological understanding points to the fullness of life, freedom of choice, and one's free will in the love and grace of God?

To push that point legally, I have joined as a Christian with six other Florida clergy—including Jewish rabbis, a Buddhist, and a

Unitarian-Universalist—to file a lawsuit against the state of Florida. We are arguing that our ability to live and practice our religions' faith is compromised by Florida's post-*Roe v. Wade* abortion laws. It is our belief that this law, HB5, violates constitutional freedom of speech, the free exercise of religion, and the constitutional separation of church and state. Therefore we have individually, each on our own religious terms, filed a temporary injunction against the state of Florida to prevent the enforcement of HB5, citing religious freedom until our cases are heard. Saying Florida's strict new abortion ban is causing "immediate and irreparable injury to . . . fundamental rights and cherished liberties," our initial motion has asked a state court for a temporary injunction so that we can again "advise believers freely based on their own religious values and beliefs."

As a clergy person and member of the United Church of Christ, a denomination built on religious freedom and separation of church and state, it is my contention that this bill takes away my rights as a person of faith and as a religious leader. It requires my adherence to the strident, harsh voices of a faith I do not believe in and a religion that I do not practice. It further places a burden on my role as a religious leader in pastoral settings, preventing me from presenting the fullness of meaningful and faithful responses to important questions.

While this suit has been called a "novel legal strategy" as it takes exception to the notion that the "only 'religious' view on abortion is to oppose it," it is built on strong principles and constitutional promises. I'm most grateful that attorneys and clergy are working together to build a just, moral, and free society in which folks have personal freedom, a measure of self-determination, and the right to take personal responsibility for their actions. In my own Christian faith such religious freedom comes directly from the teachings of Jesus, who sought to undo the oppressive rules and laws of his day, so that all would live in a just and equitable society. Many of his teachings centered on the freedom of women to live fully, to be welcomed as equals, and to make decisions for their own destiny. As the sign outside our church said over a recent voting season: "Jesus trusted women. So do we. Vote pro-choice candidates."

As a Christian and ordained pastor, I deeply value the faith in which I was raised. My work in ministry, day in and day out is informed and profoundly shaped by the lessons that I have gleaned from our sacred texts and teachings about a God who loves each and every one of us. To that end, I believe women have an inalienable right to make their own moral decisions, guided by the wisdom of their own faith, and to rely on the tender mercies of a God of compassion and love. No institution established by humankind should supersede such God-given freedom. I am pro-choice, not in spite of my faith but because of it.

Part VII *Envisioning the Future*

KRYSTALE E. LITTLEJOHN

Even as the *Dobbs v. Jackson* decision inflicts fresh waves of pain with each passing day, the moment also offers an opportunity to imagine and create a more just future. In the contributions that comprise this part of the book, essayists from diverse domains offer inspiration for using this moment as another powerful inflection point in the centuries-long effort to resist reproductive oppression.

In the first essay I challenge approaches that pit contraception against abortion as if contraceptives can or *should* replace abortion care. Instead, I argue that reproductive freedom requires that people have access to all of the reproductive tools available to them, including abortion access whenever they want it and need it. Obstetrician-gynecologist Brian Nguyen tackles another important part of the reproductive equation, showing that although men are often overlooked in the fight for abortion, there are several intervention points that offer opportunities to incorporate men to build gender equity.

Dr. Lisa Harris offers her vision of a shift required to move the needle on support for abortion. She discusses the value of strategically leveraging the voices of doctors to meet the diverse needs of audiences making decisions about abortion. Even in the context of impending hostile legislation, there are voters who can come to see the value of supporting abortion if they are met with authenticity and compassion in the face of their questions and concerns. A powerhouse group of nurses, midwives, and health researchers—Amy Alspaugh, Linda S. Franck, Nikki Lanshaw, Daniel F. M. Suárez-Baquero, Renee Mehra, Toni Bond, and Monica R. McLemore—builds on the call to shift frameworks. They draw attention to the ways that dominant thinking about abortion prevents a nuanced discussion about the complexities undergirding pregnancy decision-making. To meet patient needs, they argue that health-care providers and researchers must reject false binaries operating in abortion and advance person-centered care that rests on dignity and respect for the patient regardless of their pregnancy outcome.

Law professor Melissa Murray shifts our attention to a different domain in need of rethinking, asking what it truly means to have women's rights adjudicated by a political process in the hands of the people. In a thought-provoking essay, Murray underscores the fundamental danger associated with returning abortion to voters in the context of partisan gerrymandering and a "distorted democracy" where voters have less power to exercise their will. Justina Trim-Nicholson, program manager at Collective Power for Reproductive Justice, shows that even in the context of increasing assaults on democracy, as outlined by Murray, we can all use our powers of discernment to notice when things are not as they seem. Although there is no doubt that the state of affairs is incredibly distressing, Trim-Nicholson shows that taking intentional steps to advance Reproductive Justice is indeed possible if we use discernment when facing rapid change and instability.

In the final two essays, Dr. Bria Peacock and Loretta Ross, visionary veteran activist, educator, and MacArthur fellow, ground the fight for abortion rights and Reproductive Justice in a reflection on the past and a transformative imagining of the future. Peacock writes about her meditations on the oppression of Black women as a Black doctor supporting Black patients and the revolutionary nature of her very role as a Black abortion provider. Her essay is a beautiful reminder that even as Black womanhood can be a lesson in the legacy of oppression, so too can it be a lesson in Black joy and freedom. Loretta Ross and Robynne D. Lucas, a recent graduate of Smith College, offer the final word and introduce the gift of a new vision for Reproductive Justice to guide us in the fight ahead. Drawing on Reproductive Justice and Afrofuturism, Ross and Lucas introduce Reproductive Justice Futurism to "articulate an emergent Black feminist theory of reproductive science and technology" that promises to shape the minds of all those who care about Reproductive Justice for years to come. As they argue, we must fight for the right to have a child, not have a child, parent a child in a stable and healthy environment, *and* dissociate sex from reproduction.

To conclude the volume, we as coeditors invite you to read on for inspiration, reflect on all that our contributors have shared in this expansive book, and join us in getting back to work.

45 *Even with Contraception, People Need and Must Have Access to Abortion*

KRYSTALE E. LITTLEJOHN

In eliminating constitutional protections for abortion in the *Dobbs v. Jackson Women's Health Organization* Supreme Court case, the majority drew on an argument about birth control that simply isn't true. Many people use it and believe it, however. In fact, lawyers used the same kind of faulty claim in the oral arguments that preceded the Court's disastrous decision to violate the reproductive autonomy of tens of millions of people who can become pregnant in the United States. The argument? That people don't truly need abortion because they have access to contraception. The number of people fighting to access abortion in the wake of *Dobbs* only underscores the illegitimacy of the argument.

In its egregious June 2022 decision, the majority argued that "reproductive planning could take virtually immediate account of any sudden restoration of state authority to ban abortions." That is, people could plan for abortion bans by planning their pregnancies—with contraception. This echoed comments made by Scott G. Stewart just six months earlier when the Court heard oral arguments in the case concerning the constitutionality of Mississippi's law banning abortions after fifteen weeks of pregnancy. Indeed, Stewart claimed that upholding Mississippi's law need not affect women's lives, because "contraception is more accessible and affordable and available than it was at the time of *Roe* or *Casey*," and "it serves the same goal of allowing women to decide if, when and how many children to have." In a July brief, Mississippi officials argued that "even if abortion may once have been thought critical as an alternative to contraception . . . changed circumstances undermine that view." The changed circumstances? Lower out-of-pocket costs for contraceptives, changes in contraceptive failure rates, and the availability of more effective birth control methods.

Although there is no doubt that contraceptive access has improved, which is good for reproductive autonomy, contraception is not a viable alternative to abortion. Put simply, people who have abortions use contraception and people who use contraception have abortions. That's not hard to believe when the average woman spends upward of three decades of her life trying to prevent pregnancy. Most women do practice some sort of birth control over their reproductive years, and yet one in four of them in the United States will have an abortion in their lifetime.

Only a tiny percentage of sexually experienced reproductive-age American women have never used any form of birth control. Women have overwhelmingly chosen to use an effective method such as the pill, a shot, or an intrauterine device (IUD) at some point in their lives (with almost nine in ten having done so). When examining contraceptive use more generally, 88 percent of sexually active, reproductive-age women who were not seeking pregnancy reported that they were using some kind of contraception during the month of the survey in 2016. When looking solely at women seeking abortion, however, about half reported using contraception in the month that they became pregnant in 2014.

At some point, many people stop using birth control even when they don't necessarily want to become pregnant. Why? Because tolerating birth control isn't easy, especially when women often have to carry that burden alone. Some people may begin using a method like the pill but switch to a method that doesn't require a prescription, because clinic access is difficult. Some people have challenges managing side effects. Some people grow tired of trying method after method for years without being able to find one that works for them, so they take a break from hormonal birth control altogether. As one woman I spoke with for my research put it: "I wish I didn't have to take a pill every day. I know there's other options, but I don't want to take those other options, either." One study found that 91 percent of women seeking abortion reported that not a single birth control method had all of the features that they believed were extremely important. All of this is sobering when you consider that women are expected to use contraception for so long. Expecting that they will be able to do so—without ever stopping—is simply unrealistic.

Just as important, even when people intend to use birth control consistently and correctly, they can face unwilling partners. In my research young women reported that while some partners often wanted them to use hormonal methods, others pressured them not to do so because they worried about side effects. Partner cooperation with condoms also posed serious obstacles. Some partners would outright refuse to wear condoms or even remove them during sex without women's consent. Emergency contraception provided a vital backup for women facing such experiences, thankfully, but women can't always count on it to work.

Women's experiences with nonconsensual condom removal point to the broader ways that the existence of contraceptive coercion undermines the availability of contraception as an alternative to abortion. A review article examining reproductive coercion found that women described experiences with partners preventing them from getting birth control or from being able to get refills of their pills. In these kinds of cases, women might become pregnant despite their interest in using effective birth control methods (and the widespread availability of such methods), because they simply do not have the ability to freely use them. Abortion is a crucial resource for them to maintain reproductive autonomy if they find themselves facing a pregnancy as a result.

Effective contraceptives are vital for helping people achieve reproductive autonomy, despite numerous imperfections and various challenges with consistent use. Even as we fight to ensure that people have access to abortion, so too must we fight to ensure that they have access to a wide range of birth control methods to help them prevent pregnancy for as long as they want to do so. Increasingly aggressive attacks by anti–birth control activists pose even more obstacles for people already trying hard to prevent pregnancy. Contraception is not a viable alternative to abortion, but it is crucial that it exists alongside it so that everyone can realize reproductive freedom. They should have the right to shape their futures and their families, freely using all of the methods that should rightfully be available to them.

46 Building Gender Equity by Engaging Men in Reproductive Responsibility

BRIAN T. NGUYEN

As an obstetrician-gynecologist, I'm trained to provide for the medical and surgical needs of women and their pregnancies. Yet after years of additional experience in this capacity and as a clinician-researcher, I've seen firsthand how crucial it is to advocate for involving men and male partners in sexual and reproductive health as a matter of gender equity. Many people assume that men have no role to play, or worse that they don't care, but my experience has shown otherwise. Several years ago, my team and I conducted a study where we interviewed and surveyed men in the waiting rooms of abortion clinics in Chicago, Illinois. We asked them about their feelings about their partner's abortion. We noted that even among men who disagreed with the decision to terminate an unintended pregnancy, many believed that there were important reasons to proceed with the abortion. They talked about wanting children but not being ready. They talked about wanting to prioritize their jobs and their education; in some cases, they wanted to prioritize their partner.

Yet when the Supreme Court's decision on *Dobbs v. Jackson* was released and protestors across the nation convened in public spaces to protest, there was a noticeable absence of a more visible and vocal male presence. This absence has always been striking because protecting abortion cannot be a "women's issue" or the burden of individuals with a uterus alone. Rather, protecting abortion requires educating and sensitizing all men to acknowledge the need for abortion and recognize how they can use their privilege and power to be allies and advocate for abortion.

While physicians have a role to play in fighting for abortion rights on the public stage, we also must recognize the necessity of incorporating the voices of our patients, their male partners, and other male-identifying allies. Physician advocates are frequently urged to tell trauma-laden stories to primarily white male legislators and politicians about their female patients and the struggles that some go through to obtain an abortion. We invoke narratives about the ubiquity of abortion—one in four women will have had an abortion by the time they reach the age of forty-five—and the possibility that their wives or daughters might need an abortion.[1] However, stories of how women suffer seldom change the attitudes of male politicians and others on their own. Perceiving themselves to be immune to the abstract risk of an unintended pregnancy, some of these men fail to recognize that abortion is essential. They instead see abortion as a frivolous choice or an unnecessary luxury. They remain silent in the face of attacks that seek to undermine women's right to determine the course of their lives. In order to change the beliefs and behaviors of men who are ambivalent about abortion, or outright hostile to it, long-term solutions that examine the root cause of men's patriarchal and misogynistic beliefs and behaviors are necessary.

While finding a comprehensive solution isn't easy, there are several points in a man's life that may spur him to consider his biological privilege and the structures that reinforce them—all of which are areas for potential intervention. Although it may be easy to disregard men's lack of action or awareness during these times as a failure of empathy, we should recognize the failures of a system that can change and facilitate more gender equitable beliefs and behaviors among men. These are just a few areas:

(1) Childbirth

Childbirth is one of the most powerful, life-changing events that an individual can experience. However, the medical system's acute attention to the birth rather than the couple experiencing the birth, or in some cases even the system's contempt for male partners, can affect men's engagement in the process and prevent them from stepping into protective, caretaking roles for their partner and child. Furthermore, when men are denied paid paternity leave or disincentivized to take their full allotment, their female partners assume childcare responsibility by default, with the widening gap in childrearing ability and gender roles reified further over time such that men lose awareness of the challenges of childcare, which can rival those of their own careers.

Including men in prenatal care initiatives and involving them in the birthing process can sensitize them to the disproportionate amount of personal risk taken by their female partners who become pregnant, regardless of their intent. Ensuring that men internalize the disproportionate burden of childcare via increasing their exposure and education during paternity leave or via reforming child support to emphasize the need for fathers to expend time rather than money alone may help men recognize the necessity of protecting reproductive choice and having abortion available as an option to their female partners.

(2) Sterilization

Even though vasectomy is a cheaper, safer, and more effective method of sterilization or permanent contraception than tubal ligation, it remains underutilized. When couples reach their desired family size, the female partner is more likely to undergo surgery, with few couples ever considering vasectomy as an option. Those who want to obtain a vasectomy are disincentivized by federal policies that provide coverage for tubal ligation to the exclusion of vasectomy.[2] Furthermore, men may be discouraged by their inability to find someone who can provide a vasectomy in their region, given that the majority of providers are specialists. In this way men are completely unable to participate in pregnancy planning such that their exclusion and disengagement becomes a social norm. When they're socialized not to take part in contraception and preventing pregnancy or the birth of a child more generally, it's logical that they would then consider the right to abortion as something that they need not advocate for.

(3) Abortion

Lastly, unaware of the dangers of pregnancy and the challenges of childcare, by the time men become involved in an unintended pregnancy, they may lack the empathy needed to recognize that the decision on the pregnancy's disposition should be that of their female partner. For men who are supportive of their partner's abortion, they may also feel the same stigma and shame felt by their partners. Yet without the same educational framing provided to their female partners by health-care providers and their peers, men may not recognize how commonly other men become involved in an abortion and thus how essential these services are. Changing this could lead to a fundamental shift in how men understand their role in fighting for abortion.

There are numerous other examples of times when a man's involvement in sexual and reproductive health issues could be leveraged toward building gender equity. For health-care providers, sexual health screenings, pregnancy care, childbirth, and family planning are all opportunities to engage men in conversations that lead to shared reproductive responsibility via male accountability. It is only through the repeated sensitization of men at times where they are the most likely to be engaged in both conversations with their female partners and the health-care system that they might come to recognize their privilege and the need for its redistribution, as manifested by their support for abortion and women's autonomy.

47 *Shifting Abortion Public Opinion*

A Case Study in Complexity, Compassion, and the Role of Doctors' Voices

LISA HARRIS

Dear Dr. Harris: I want to thank you for your opinion article that was in the Detroit Free Press *on October 30, 2022. I was hoping you could provide some additional guidance on Proposal 3. Until I read your opinion, I planned on voting no on Proposal 3. The reason is that it is morally wrong to kill people.[1]*

So began the email at the top of my inbox a week before Michigan citizens were to vote on Proposal 3, a ballot initiative to enshrine abortion rights into the state constitution. If passed, it would permanently prevent Michigan's 1931 abortion ban from being enforced, which had been a risk since the US Supreme Court overturned *Roe v. Wade* four months earlier. Proposal 3 opponents called it an "anything goes" abortion amendment, suggesting that it would allow unscrupulous doctors (along with high school counselors, massage therapists, and athletic trainers) to perform abortions at any time in pregnancy, until birth. As a doctor who provides abortion care in Michigan, I wanted to help calm worries about Proposal 3 and dispel erroneous claims by its opponents.

For many decades the voices of doctors like me were largely absent from public discourse. Stigma, harassment, and violence made it too frightening to have a public presence. As a result, authentic representations of abortion and those who provide it—our motivations, training and skill, compassion—were missing. Into that vacuum, abortion opponents fed the public imagination with stereotypes of abortion providers as greedy, predatory, dangerous, lacking compassion, and of course killers, as my op-ed reader suggested. Such images had law and policy consequences. In *June Medical Services v. Russo,* for example, the state and ultimately some Supreme Court justices argued for abortion restrictions by claiming doctors who provide abortion care were dangerous and indifferent to patients' well-being.

These flawed images needed correction, which felt especially urgent as the Proposal 3 vote neared. Years earlier I began a line of research to generate messaging recommendations for doctors who provide abortion care, to correct flawed images and generate more support for abortion care. That work, done in collaboration with strategic communications research expert Amy Simon and applied psychologist Phyllis Watts, PhD, taught me that effective messaging requires meeting your audience's needs—understanding their beliefs and values, building a bridge to them, and equipping them to make the shift you seek. It requires compassion for one's audience, not judgment or disdain—two things my younger self had often felt when engaging with people who didn't embrace abortion care. And it requires learning how to find a way through the immense polarization of abortion. Polarized issues trigger the brain's fight-or-flight responses, making it impossible to process new information. The way through polarization, I learned, is to lean into the emotional and ethical complexities of abortion. So I penned an op-ed that I hoped would meet the needs of undecided Michigan voters. It began:

Many of you see the complexities in abortion, and are carrying two opposite ideas in your hearts at the same time: that abortion means a potential human won't be born, and that a ban on abortion means that women may not be able to determine the course of their lives and their family's lives. Both things are true, and that is what can make abortion such a hard issue.

It used to feel dangerous for pro-choice positions to say what is obvious—that a human won't come into the world when I perform the abortion a patient requests. Or to share that abortion can feel like a kind of loss and raise genuine questions of life and death, things I've come to call "dangertalk." However, I noticed over the years that when I did engage in dangertalk, listeners softened a little and in fact seemed relieved. Focus group research participants sometimes visibly relaxed when I described experiencing two seemingly opposing feelings about abortion at the same time, the "tension of opposites." Some said they were grateful to have words to name their own conflicted feelings. This created space for their curiosity about what my patient care experiences were like, and why it was important to me that I provided this care.

In these moments dangertalk didn't feel dangerous at all; in fact, it opened doors to so many of the additional conversations I wanted to have: about the patients for whom I care, their lives and families, the safety of abortion, the compassion and skill of the teams with whom I work, and the consequences of an abortion ban. I was seeing those consequences as patients from Ohio and Indiana traveled to Michigan for abortion care and even for treatment of ectopic pregnancies that doctors in those states were now too afraid to treat in the wake of *Roe*'s overturn. I wrote about these things in the op-ed.

The reader's email went on: *Your article made it clear [that] in your practice, you take the decision to perform an abortion very seriously.*

Of course I take abortion provision, indeed all decisions about patient care, seriously. But again, decades of stigmatization, along with silence on the part of doctors means this is not self-evident. Audiences, I've learned, need reassurance that abortion care providers center patients' needs. In the op-ed I detailed how our care team always ensures patients have the time and information they need to make the decision that is best for them. And although it should go without saying, I also wrote:

> We never proceed with an abortion if a patient is uncertain, or needs more time. Sometimes, after meeting with our team, a patient leaves with referrals for prenatal care, choosing not to end their pregnancy. Our priority is for people to make the decision that is best for them, their family, and their health.

This reader trusted me to address his remaining worries about Proposal 3: *My concern with the current proposal is that it will make it too easy for a woman to have an abortion. Such as "I don't like the sex or the hair color of the child I am having." I would have liked to have seen a proposal with tighter controls. . . .* He went on to list a range of additional concerns, many of them the ones advanced by the "No on Proposal 3" campaign. Ultimately he asked for reassurance: *I realize that you can't make any promises, but could you give me assurances that if I vote for this proposal the issues I mention would not be a concern?*

There would have been a time when these questions infuriated me. I know that the idea that it is "too easy" for a person to have an abortion comes from, among other things, a kind of paternalism in which (some) women are thought not to be capable decision-makers or real moral agents. From misunderstandings of the reasons people make decisions to end a pregnancy, and neglect of the systems of oppression and material constraints that lead to abortion decisions, especially economic insecurity and the need to care for existing children (after all, most who end a pregnancy are already mothers, Guttmacher Institute data indicate). Nevertheless, his questions were genuine, and I answered them authentically. I saw in them a need to know there were medical and moral guardrails around abortion care. I saw him wanting to do the very best with his vote. I had compassion for him. So I wrote back:

> I am heartened that you are giving Proposal 3 such serious thought because it mirrors the seriousness I see in the decision-making of my patients.

I went one-by-one through his concerns, sharing medical evidence and personal experience. I ended by writing:

> I understand that supporting Proposal 3 is asking you to have an amount of trust or faith that both patients and doctors will make careful, serious decisions, for important reasons. Based on many years of caring for patients and many years of knowing the compassion and ethics of my colleagues—I feel confident all would be worthy of your trust.

Shortly afterward I received another note: *Dr. Harris, Thank you for the quick, detailed, and honest response to my questions. It has certainly changed my thinking with regards to Proposal 3.*

I don't know how this man ultimately voted. But by his own report my op-ed and our email conversation afterward changed his thinking. I share this encounter to offer anecdotal evidence that there are persuadable voters. And to offer evidence that doctors' voices, when shared in ways that meet audience needs—acknowledge the complexities of abortion, answer hard questions instead of pivoting from them, and when done with compassion—can be effective.

For those of us committed to abortion rights, it can be hard to have compassion for people who feel ambivalent about what we know is so vital. And it can be difficult to show audiences kindness and respect when we are not sure if they will do the same for people who may need abortion care. But my experience here, supported by focus group and survey research on what audiences need in order to support abortion rights points to a way forward.[2] Audiences have unmet needs for new kinds of conversations about abortion. Doctors' voices can help meet that need.

Michigan's Proposal 3 passed, with 57 percent of voters supporting it. The uncertainty and distress that I and so many other Michiganders felt in the months after *Roe* was overturned has faded, and we can now begin to plan for our responsibilities as a state where abortion access is protected. States without such protections have much work ahead, and the voices of doctors who provide abortion care will be essential in that work.

My reader ended his note by writing: *I have a daughter who is twenty-six and planning to get married soon. When she starts planning to have a family, I would want her under your care. Please stay healthy and safe.* Of course it's more important who his daughter would want caring for her than who *he* would want, but I was touched nevertheless.

48 Rejecting the Abortion Debate Binary Is Essential to Moving toward Reproductive Justice

AMY ALSPAUGH, LINDA S. FRANCK,
NIKKI LANSHAW, DANIEL F. M. SUÁREZ-BAQUERO,
RENEE MEHRA, TONI BOND, AND MONICA R.
MCLEMORE

In order to secure the future that people deserve, we as nurses, midwives, and health researchers believe it is necessary to reject an either/or position when it comes to abortion. Abortion is, importantly and without nuance, a fundamental human right. However, the dominant narratives commonly used to talk about the right to decide to continue a pregnancy or have an abortion are full of false binaries: pro-choice versus pro-life, bodily autonomy versus fetal personhood, and moral versus immoral. These dualities unnecessarily divide us because they prevent deeper conversations about the unique nature of pregnancy within our society. Furthermore, we know that using a both/and mentality, a hallmark of Black feminism and Reproductive Justice, creates the necessary space for multiple truths and a vital non-dichotomic position. We must stop assuming that decisions exist within silos: there is always more than one possible outcome, more than one discussion to be had, and more than one possible future to address the urgent reproductive health crisis in our country.

A legal compromise introducing viability should not dictate how we as a society think about abortion, even though viability was the primary issue in the *Dobbs v. Jackson Women's Health Organization* Supreme Court case that overturned *Roe v. Wade*. When *Roe* was argued, "viability" was *never* uttered. Instead, a Supreme Court clerk's suggestion led justices to accept the idea of viability as a *legal* compromise marking the point at which, in the words of Justice Thurgood Marshall, "the State's interest in preserving the potential life of the unborn child overrides any individual interests of the woman."[1] As we have learned from the experiences of countless marginalized groups, rights that are not universal are not in fact rights. They are conditional benefits that are inequitably distributed. The emphasis on viability in the abortion debate distracts us from the core human rights issue at hand: bodily autonomy, including the decision to continue or terminate a pregnancy, rests squarely with the pregnant person *at all times and in all circumstances*. As a human right, bodily autonomy is largely unquestioned outside of pregnancy and must therefore continue unabated in pregnancy and abortion care not as an option for some but a right for all.

Ignoring the needs of pregnant people is egregious, but it is not new. It has deep roots in chattel slavery and the oppression of Black people. Promoting the survival of the fetus at the expense of the pregnant person's humanity and autonomy was first noted in the United States in the whipping of pregnant, Black, enslaved individuals whose stomachs were protected through a hole dug in the ground.[2] Since then, the state has used the primacy of the fetus to justify state authority to restrict bodily autonomy and enforce distinct laws only over the bodies and decisions of pregnant people—especially pregnant people of color. Though taken for granted, separate and unequal laws for pregnant people compared to people who cannot get pregnant violate the human right to bodily autonomy and the guarantee of equal protection under the law. The beginning of life is a spectrum with few definitive markers. Defining when a fetus becomes a person and figuring out how to resolve pregnancies is best left up to those most intimately involved in each particular situation.

While simplistic binaries dominate political and popular discussions, only a minority of people (27 percent) believe abortion should be either legal without exception or illegal without exception.[3] The remainder of individuals, a plurality of respondents to a Pew Research survey, acknowledge that the context of the situation weighs into their calculus. This calculus can include the circumstance of the conception (consensual sex or rape), the kinship of those involved, the risk a pregnancy may potentially pose or is currently posing to the wellness and life of the pregnant person, and the health and gestational age of the fetus. Here again, these circumstances cannot be captured by a binary and serve as a reminder that every pregnant person and every pregnancy occurs within a unique context.

Like the public at large, health-care workers are heterogeneous in their views on abortion. For example, our recent research identifying obstetric, women's health, and neonatal nurses' attitudes around abortion found that one-third of survey participants expressed attitudes that placed them in an unsure category, meaning neither pro-abortion nor antiabortion. This category also included the largest percentage of participants who identified as Christian. Furthermore, among participants who reported having had an abortion, nearly one-quarter were in the unsure category and 10 percent expressed antiabortion attitudes, indicating that the nurse's attitudes about abortion were not necessarily indicative of their behavior and may be evidence of internalized abortion stigma.[4] A lack of concordance between attitudes and actions is neither new nor problematic but instead points to the importance of meeting people where they are, respecting their expertise, and working in partnership with patients to determine exactly what is best for them and their families.[5]

Moving away from binaries and polarities allows us to reimagine the language we use regarding abortion to instead focus on creating physical and social environments that support all reproductive health outcomes and decisions. Research suggests that many people who had an abortion desired to continue the pregnancy and parent the child but made a choice to have an abortion because they felt they could not adequately or ethically raise a child due to external circumstances such as lack of human, money, space, and time resources.[6] Often these circumstances could be ameliorated by enhanced social services, legal protections for pregnant people, paid parental leave, and universal childcare, to name a few. Instead of pitting the fetus against the parent, policies centered on Reproductive Justice that address the biggest threats to life and livelihood—namely poverty, barriers to health care, racism, and environmental hazards—could reduce the need for abortion *and* support those who choose to parent.[7]

Abandoning a binary framework also frees health-care providers to better care for individuals. When we lose the binary of good versus bad, right versus wrong, we make room for conversation and dialogue. When we better understand the individual's attitudes, beliefs, and priorities, we can better help them navigate health and wellness within a person-centered model of care. There is no requirement that health-care providers have the same moral frame as the patients for whom they care. In fact, a health-care provider's duty to provide care and to respect patient autonomy supersedes all other matters. Reproductive health, and abortion in particular, occurs at the intersection of health-care services and social and cultural beliefs and norms. *Opinions may abound, but the onus to provide person-centered, respectful, dignified care remains unchanged.*

To curate spaces for complexity, health-care providers and researchers must ask what pregnant people want and need. We must advocate for policies that provide financial security, high-quality health care, social support necessary for those who desire to grow their family while ensuring safe, respectful, and stigma-free abortion services that are readily accessible. Bodily autonomy, as manifested in abortion, is a human right—*and* we must improve care and services for all people who choose parenthood, especially those who have been historically marginalized. We don't need to know all the answers when it comes to talking individuals through the decision-making process. Instead, we need to listen to patients' needs and respect the multitude of beliefs that impact their choices. Furthermore, this acknowledgment of complexity and nuance must extend upstream to the policy level, so legislation and court decisions can move away from false binaries that ignore the realities of our reproductive lives.

49 Dobbs, *Democracy, and Distortion*

MELISSA MURRAY

On June 24, 2022, the Supreme Court overturned *Roe v. Wade*[1] and *Planned Parenthood v. Casey*[2]—once the twin pillars of its abortion jurisprudence—in *Dobbs v. Jackson Women's Health Organization*.[3] In so doing, Justice Samuel Alito's majority opinion noted that the right to an abortion was unmoored from constitutional text and was not "rooted in the history or traditions of this country." In such circumstances, the majority opinion insisted, democratic deliberation was the proper mechanism for resolving the competing interests at stake in the abortion debate.[4] As such, the *Dobbs* majority insisted that "it is time to heed the Constitution and return the issue of abortion to the people's elected representatives."[5]

But what does it mean to consign the recognition of women's fundamental rights and equality to the political process? It is early days to be sure, but it seems clear that leaving abortion to the people is not the noble enterprise that the *Dobbs* Court imagines. And perhaps that is because no actor has done more to distort the landscape of democratic deliberation—that is, to make it difficult for individuals to register their policy preferences at the ballot box—than the Court itself. Consider the Court's decision in *Rucho v. Common Cause,* in which it concluded that there was no workable formula for identifying impermissible partisan gerrymanders. Lacking a workable formula, the

Court declared the issue of partisan gerrymanders a nonjusticiable political question, removing the prospect of federal court oversight of state legislatures' efforts to draw lopsided districting maps.[6] In the absence of federal court oversight, it is now incumbent on state courts and governors to rein in the legislature's worst impulses.[7] Left unchecked, partisan gerrymandering allows political parties to consolidate their authority, cultivating the conditions in which more extreme laws are enacted and objecting voters have few opportunities to make their voices heard.[8]

The dangers of partisan gerrymandering in the effort to vindicate women's rights, and abortion rights particularly, can be glimpsed in state-level post-*Dobbs* developments in Kansas and Indiana. In August 2022 both states considered the question of abortion rights at the state level, albeit through meaningfully different political mechanisms. In Kansas a ballot initiative put to voters the question of whether existing abortion protections should be retained.[9] Kansans voted 58.97 percent to 41.03 percent to retain protections for abortion rights in the state constitution.[10] Just three days later, on August 5, 2022, the Indiana state legislature enacted one of the nation's most restrictive abortion laws.[11]

The difference in outcomes in these two "red" states may be attributed to the vehicle by which constituents registered their policy preferences. In Kansas voters could register their choices directly through the ballot initiative process, whereas in Indiana constituents' policy preferences were mediated through the mechanism of representative democracy.[12] One might argue that representatives' natural instincts to satisfy the preferences of constituents is heightened—and indeed, distorted—in states like Indiana, where the state legislature has been shaped by partisan gerrymandering. And importantly, the Roberts Court has allowed politicians to insulate themselves from the will of the people in other ways. In 2013's *Shelby County v. Holder* the Court invalidated the Voting Rights Act pre-clearance formula.[13] Under the pre-clearance regime states with a history of engaging in voting discrimination were required to first seek "pre-clearance" from a federal court or the Department of Justice before implementing any changes to their voting laws and rules.[14] After *Shelby County,* states were under no obligation to seek pre-clearance review, and as a consequence, many took more assertive steps to pass voting laws that might have discriminatory or suppressive effect on minority voters.[15]

The Court's 2021 ruling in *Brnovich v. Democratic National Committee*[16] likely will exacerbate the impact of suppressive voting laws.[17] There, the Court further hobbled the embattled Voting Rights Act (VRA) by concluding that a law's discriminatory effect will generally be insufficient to establish a violation under Section 2 of the VRA. The Court's decision in *Brnovich* compounds the impact of *Shelby County* by further narrowing the avenues under which discriminatory voting laws may be challenged.[18]

This is all to say that it is likely not coincidental that the Court has consigned the issue of abortion and women's rights to the democratic process at the very moment it is making American democracy *less* democratic. The Court has effectively turned the issue of abortion over to state legislators who, because of gerrymandering and voter suppression laws, "are increasingly removed from the voters' will"—and "increasingly extreme on issues of reproductive rights and women's self-determination."[19] As a result, true democratic deliberation on the abortion question will be elusive.

But perhaps such an outcome is to be expected from a Court that is itself a product of minority rule.[20] The three Trump-appointed justices who solidified the Roberts Court's 6–3 conservative supermajority were confirmed by senators who collectively represented fewer people than the senators who voted against them.[21] Moreover, those three justices were appointed by a president who received fewer total votes than the opposing Democratic candidate.

．．．

Focusing on the hollow nature of the *Dobbs* majority's commitment to democracy may reveal a more profound truth about the opinion: that the Court's "democratic deliberation" settlement is merely a waystation en route to a final destination—the abolition of legal abortion in the United States. From this perspective it is perhaps unsurprising that the Court's vision of democratic deliberation occurs in the dystopia of a distorted democracy that the Court itself has birthed. Given the limits of democratic deliberation in this climate, the *Dobbs* settlement may simply reflect an intermediate step that aims to shift political dynamics and desensitize the populace to the deprivation of access to legal abortion. For now, legal and political fights around access to abortion will be waged in state legislatures, state courts, state executive-branch offices, and through the mechanisms of popular democracy. However, it seems all but certain that, despite its broad endorsement of democratic deliberation, the Supreme Court has not spoken its final word on the abortion question.

50 *The Power of Discernment*

JUSTINA TRIM-NICHOLSON

Before I even get started, let me make some disclaimers. This essay is going to involve the usage and understanding of energy work, society-driven emotional manipulation, and the ways that mind control and trickery have been utilized to be divisive in our movement. We are at a point in history in which a portal is open. Everything is changing. World events are unfolding, politics are shapeshifting, and everything we thought we knew about our universe has been turned upside down since 2020. Living through a pandemic, being separated from our loved ones, experiencing death on a large and global scale, and hopefully learning more about ourselves and how we want to live and exist on our own but also with others has started entire revolutions.

Ahmad Arbery, Breonna Taylor, George Floyd, and Jina (Mahsa) Amini are few of many marginalized individuals who are known for their untimely and traumatizing deaths at the hands of either law enforcement or authoritarian figures since 2020. Protests have launched all across the world to bring light to their deaths and to address systemic oppression at large. As the masses become more enlightened, educated, and hungry, the games driven by those who control, maneuver, and manipulate these same systems of oppression have adapted to encompass more clever tactics. Currently some of the tactics applied include a focus on disillusionment, heightened smoke and mirrors, and increased emotional manipulation and language distortion—we can see this being actualized by governments and political parties across the world weaponizing the usage of all types of media and emotional gaslighting.

Instances in Which Discernment Is Helpful

"Discernment" is defined by *Merriam-Webster* dictionary as "the quality of being able to grasp and comprehend what is obscure; an act of perceiving something." This definition alludes to noticing when something is not what it may appear to be or seem, and also requires heeding a gut feeling. It makes sense why sometimes words, even when they seem kind or well-meaning, may not resonate or feel truthful. It also makes sense why it feels even more important to notice the slight details and nuances in our political ideologies.

However, sometimes we might conflate and assimilate our more "radical" views (whatever that means) within a greater whole or more mainstream ideology in order to get to "the same destination," but what exactly is that destination? Are we really clear on the details of how to achieve whatever form of justice we say we want? Have we collectively defined appropriate avenues to achieve said "justice"? Are we being honest about the usage of money and naming explicitly how nonprofit organizations are deeply rooted in capitalism? Are we being accountable to ourselves and our colleagues within the way we work and communicate with each other? Are we putting enough pressure on politicians? Are we truly examining money trails and the ways we have been programmed to process and measure success within the Reproductive Justice movement? Are we agreeing on language?

These are very vague and open-ended questions that allude to a bigger point. There is little unison in the way those of us who frequent Reproductive Justice movement-building spaces understand these aspects of work and life. These questions also point out that language has always been a tool, and at times it has been a tool used with malignant intent, targeting specific marginalized communities. Discernment is not only an intuitive feeling but an instrument that can be utilized to be on the offense instead of the defensive position that the Reproductive Justice movement often finds itself in.

The usage of crisis pregnancy centers (CPCs) is the classic example of language and resource manipulation referenced in the reproductive rights, health, and justice movement. CPCs are disguises, buildings, and institutions with the facade of support and help, but they are actually used to trap and trick those who are at their most vulnerable. Even the name is misleading—"crisis pregnancy center" already suggesting that a CPC is where one would go if they felt like they were in a crisis. However, CPCs are religious entities often funded by the state to spread misinformation. The number one mission and goal of CPCs is convincing people to not have an abortion, and CPC workers (who are often volunteers and are not always medically informed) will relay inaccurate information (such as how far along a person is within their pregnancy) to discourage them from making a decision that leads in favor toward abortion. Specific language and emotional manipulation is used to help shift a person's decision, and this is harmful for plenty of reasons but mostly because people who are pregnant are often in CPCs because these places advertise free services, luring in those who don't have all the resources needed for a comprehensive doctor's visit. Everyone should have access to not only accurate and medically informed care but also a doctor who can relay correct information and provide appropriate options regardless of one's income bracket.

We could say similar trickery is used in creating laws and analyzing the demographics for voting. Even after the overturn of *Roe,* and the *Dobbs* decision, white women voted more in favor of the right and the conservative political party in the 2022 midterm elections. What does this say? There has been an outpouring of white women who have taken to the streets, who have voiced their concerns, and expressed their discontent and outrage on social media and other platforms about *Roe* being overturned—and yet more white women voted in opposition than they did in the primary election of 2020 to the same rights they claim to support. The math doesn't add up here, does it?

Right—so back to discernment. These midterm election statistics elucidate that *something* is a facade, a truth is being omitted, or we don't have all the information. We can't assume what can be masked as "help" is *actually* help. The far right has used countless tactics to infiltrate and learn more about Reproductive Justice strategies. We know this because they have adopted similar language we have grown accustomed to using. Anti-choice groups and organizations such as the Family Research Council have repurposed the slogan "Black Lives Matter" to advance antiabortion sentiment by stating that "abortion is the greatest threat to Black lives in America today." The misuse and deliberate attempt to detract from the original intention of the Black Lives Matter movement is a classic case of curating disillusionment and confusion about reproductive rights discourse.

Cultivating and Amplifying Discernment

At a recent conference I sat in a room with changemakers strategizing on different priorities that the Reproductive Justice movement should focus on. In my leadership development group, representing Collective Power for Reproductive Justice, I talked about discernment being a skill that should be cultivated and amplified for young activists. The far right movement is utilizing different types of technology, similar word usage, and various algorithms as a part of their strategy to program and condition young people into thinking in a way that advances a eugenics-oriented agenda. However, not only the far right has taken this route. We can say the same for liberals, and we could certainly say the same for the Democratic Party. It is not enough to say the right things, and be connected to a certain group of people. Are politicians following through on the promises they feverishly belted out during their campaigns? What about their actions? Are these actions representative of the hopes and dreams our favorite politicians sell us?

Our new and incoming activists have to be able to pick up what is actually real and what is being used for another purpose. They have to be purposeful and intentional when making connections and collaborating with others, and especially when collaborating with institutions or corporations. They have to remember that an opportunity can be disguised as another trick for access into these spaces that are supposed to be supportive, sacred, and strategic. Discernment is not something that can only be taught intellectually, it's something that also has to be felt. This is why our society has trained us to not be fluent in understanding emotion. We have learned how to not trust ourselves, and to detach from the parts of us that drive intuitive decision-making and our overall choices. Just because someone looks the part doesn't mean they are operating in our best interest. We need to be careful of the language we are using and make sure it is more inclusive, and that we can also speak rawly to the issues and have real conversations with others who are trying to understand the work we do.

The power of discernment requires accountability. We know that we are imperfect humans; we have more than likely said the wrong thing at wrong times, and we've all had some general unlearning to do around harmful ways of thinking. Being accountable to the ways that multiple systems have us fueling capitalism, white supremacy, and patriarchal notions of thought and being is how we can continue to protect our work, reside in integrity, and consistently challenge what may not always sit or feel right internally. The clearer we can be in our thinking and envisioning, the more foundation we can build, and this process includes ensuring that we enlist tighter security as we continue the fight for Reproductive Justice.

Not everything is what it seems. Language can be manipulated. But we can identify the kinks and follow the next generation of leaders by continuing to validate their experiences when they come into spaces bringing more nuance, more critiques, more color, encouraging us on the whole to do more stretching, more expanding, more ideology-building. Encouraging young leaders to amplify their thought processes not only creates more sustainability and longevity for the movement, but it also strengthens our collective strategy and fortitude. The power of discernment is one of the many tools that will not only keep us safe, but will keep us intentional as we look ahead to the next phase of what awaits and steer how the Reproductive Justice movement adapts and responds to the current moment.

51 A Black Abortion Provider's Perspective on Post-Roe America

BRIA PEACOCK

As a Black woman raised in the South, I have seen how policies affect the ability of marginalized people to make choices about their own bodies and reproduction. Witnessing my older sister become a mother at sixteen years of age and learning that my grandmother birthed my mother at fourteen years of age, I became all too familiar with unintended pregnancies and how the complex intersectionality of racism, sexism, and classism is used to challenge the morality of abortion. Antiabortion activists often take out of context the fact that in the United States, Black women are five times as likely as white women to get an abortion, and they use this fact to push the characterization of abortion as "Black genocide." This claim contributes to the narrative feeding the impending overturning of *Roe v. Wade.*

I've always known this was a false narrative, and now as a Black gynecologist, I see how deeply it's harming our community.

Growing up, I witnessed the consequences of limited access to reproductive choice: perpetuation of poverty, intergenerational "curses," and the resentment experienced by young women who felt forced to have babies and give up their dreams. Watching Black women in my community come to terms with these situations is how I came to my pro-choice values. I wondered what life would be like if these women could decide whether, when, and how to grow their families.

Yet it wasn't until I read up on our nation's history of Black reproductive exploitation that I grew resolute in my perspective. The policing of Black bodies and reproduction dates back centuries, part and parcel of the commodification of Black bodies. The institution of slavery allowed for intrusion into nearly every realm of Black women's lives, including the birthing of babies for profit and labor. Once the importation of enslaved people from Africa was abolished, the reproduction of enslaved people in America was vital to the perpetuation of slavery as a profitable system. For capitalistic gains, white men—doctors and slaveowners alike—increased their interference into the reproductive lives of Black women by means of forced breeding and rape.

In those history books I saw the women in my community, still struggling with the same oppression generations later, and began to center my life's work around creating community and support for us. Today, facing a post-*Roe* America, I think about forced births in this population that bears the highest maternal morbidity and mortality in the country. Black women will be disproportionately affected by the lack of abortion access and overrepresented in pregnancy-related deaths. I think about our ancestors each time I support Black women as they give birth or choose not to. I think about the young women of my community whose lives are forever changed by a lack of choice. As a Black female physician, I aim to ensure that my patients can choose for themselves, knowing that I'm there to support them, not exploit them for anyone's gain.

A few weeks ago, I sat down with a patient who'd decided to terminate her pregnancy. There were many layers that connected us—from our fresh new braids to our love of southern food. I saw her, and she saw me—multidimensional Black women, unapologetically free in our choices. As I walked her to the procedure room, she asked me why I performed abortions. Caught off guard, I explained this history. I reminded her of her power. There was no need to explain her "why" to anyone; this procedure was her choice, and I supported her fully. She thanked me softly, knowing she was not alone. As I performed her abortion, I thought of that connection and that versatility, recognizing that the very fact of Black abortion providers unapologetically supporting Black women is revolutionary.

In that moment I felt an unshakeable feeling of pride and joy intertwined with Blackness and its many trials.

That's why accusations that abortion access contributes to the "genocide" of my community shake me to my core. It is not possible for genocide to look like the relief on my patients' faces as I enter the room, putting them at ease because I too know what it's like to walk through the world as a Black woman. Forced births and reproductive exploitation of Black bodies are historical facts, and history often repeats itself. When it does, marginalized people usually suffer the most. As I read those history books, I felt that truth. As I walked through life as a Black woman in the South, I felt that truth. As I think about a post-*Roe* America, I feel that truth. But those same history books, South, and future America also contain advocates who understand nonnegotiable reproductive freedoms. We know the plight of Black people who birth babies and have abortions, and we will continue to fight unapologetically for the freedom to safely do both.

52 Reproductive Justice Futurism

Trust Black Women

LORETTA J. ROSS AND ROBYNNE D. LUCAS

Amid debates on abortion politics due to the *Dobbs* decision, as Afro-futurist feminists, we are concerned about the future of reproductive politics. Incorporating the science fiction legacy of Octavia Butler, we adapt the critical queer theory of Reproductive Futurism. We describe how Black feminists can theorize about Reproductive Justice to analyze the impact of techno-utopianism and biological determinism through the embodied experiences of Black women. We update the original twentieth-century Reproductive Justice framework for the twenty-first century because we must bring discussions about assisted reproductive technologies (ARTs) beyond scientific and elite communities to center the lived experiences of society's vulnerable.

Reproductive Justice Futurism (RJF) is a blended intersection of two theoretical concepts, Afrofuturism and Reproductive Justice, that articulates an emergent Black feminist theory of reproductive science and technology. RJF examines how scientific and technological advances like ARTs may replicate the power disparities that enable persistent injustices against Black bodies. Furthermore, ARTs challenge existing ideas of heredity, identity, humanity, and kinship in pursuing profits based on assumptions of increased fertility, disease avoidance, and the alchemy of longevity.

Through RJF, we seek to develop the theory and practice of undivided justice achieved through the protection of human rights. RJF critiques neoliberalism and white supremacy, which dictate whose lives and reproductive decision-making matter. The approach must account for gender equality, individual rights, equity in opportunities and outcomes, and the cultural and sociopolitical aspects of disability. We also want to understand and cautiously monitor the potential benefits of reducing preventable causes of diseases and death.

Origins

We hope that the transformative intersectional and human rights–based lens of Reproductive Justice Futurism has the potential to examine the present and future attempts at population engineering and reproductive oppression. We define our core Reproductive Justice values in three primary ways: every person capable of being pregnant has the human right to have a child, not have a child, and parent a child in a stable and healthy environment. Reproductive Justice also disassociates sex from reproduction because healthy sexuality and pleasure are essential components of a whole and fulfilled human life.

Lee Edelman coined "Reproductive Futurism" in *No Future: Queer Theory and the Death Drive,* published in 2004. A gay critical theorist, Edelman argues that the current concept of reproductive futurism is heteronormative, child-centered, and used to delegitimize queerness as reproductive, revolutionary, and a possibility for the future. Offering a counterperspective, the late José Esteban Muñoz, in *Cruising Utopia: The Then and There of Queer Futurity,* published in 2009, pushed back against Edelman's assumption. Muñoz asserted instead that LGBTQIA2S+ people invest in family formations, whether chosen or biological: "Queerness is that thing that lets us feel that this world is not enough—the rejection of a here and now and an insistence on potentiality or the concrete possibility of another world."

"Afrofuturism," a term coined in 1994 by Mark Dery, the white author of *Black to the Future,* describes a speculative fiction genre that addresses African American concerns in the context of twentieth-century "technoculture." After further extrapolation by Black theorists, Afrofuturism explores how Black folk can reclaim our narratives and cultures while analyzing how Black bodies have historically suffered through the misuse of modern technology practiced through the prism of settler-colonialist thinking.

Preventing the Rebirth of Oppressive Systems

Reproductive Justice Futurism offers a critical perspective that questions how further technologizing human reproduction will rebirth preexisting systems of oppression based on the fiction of biological determinism—the belief that biology is destiny or that our genes determine our future—a false good genes/bad genes binary. In the 1700s scientists encouraged the creation of a racial hierarchy that entwined science with settler-colonial politics to establish rigid systems of class, racial, and gender domination. This pseudo-science was eventually called eugenics in the nineteenth century, concretizing an obsession with improving the genetic futures of white people.

Without moral guardrails, ARTs threaten to normalize biological determinism and naturalize racial, gender, and class privileges within hierarchical power structures. Proponents claim that the predictable discriminatory outcomes are objectively scientific rather than socially constructed. Some ideologues may argue ARTs are necessary for racial purity and biological or genetic integrity. RJF critiques the logic based on white supremacist imaginings that equates the social good with human futurity. Ruha Benjamin writes about how white supremacy conflates racial fictions and biological facts.

White supremacy is a biological fiction and an ideological commitment to dominate the planet. Alarmist "white replacement" fears foment rhetorical and physical violence. Carol Mason documents how "[w]hite survival for the sake of a moral order has replaced racial superiority as a battle cry" by people describing themselves as genetically favored racial innocents who face extinction.

We question the assumption that racialized science is a negligible consideration while experiencing pervasive anti-Blackness and anti-Semitism evidenced through the myth that Jews and Black people are plotting to replace white people. According to Marcia Danovsky of the Center for Genetics and Society, laboratories worldwide are rapidly adopting new gene-editing technologies. As a result, the ethical debate that divides scientific and biotech industry circles is spilling into the policy, public, and civil society mainstreams. This "genetic revolution" is an urgent human rights challenge.

Genetics in the Era of Big Thinkers

If proponents of ARTs fail to heed Afrofuturist feminists' concerns, humanity risks big thinkers making decisions that could imperil everyone's futures. Unfortunately, with so many people idolizing selfish men like Donald Trump and Elon Musk, who epitomize fragile wealth-inflated egos, society is susceptible to dangerous ideas about heredity, exclusion, and power. Musk is particularly fond of "longtermism," a neoliberal pseudo-philosophy that invests faith in the ability of technological and financial elites to use ARTs to transcend the present-day limits of human biology. This incoherent viewpoint rests not just on ARTs but on techno-utopianism, a grandiose belief that technology will create a rosy future for all if society removes any constraints on economic growth or scientific adventurism.

Longtermists generally see three key existential risks that could cause humanity to go extinct: artificial intelligence, bioengineered plagues, and an asteroid strike. However, nuclear war and runaway global warming are supposedly less calamitous because at least a few of the deservedly "fortunate" people would survive these catastrophes and could repopulate the planet. Musk is already practicing his bizarre form of cradle competition. Because of the prejudicial permanence of eugenical thinking, many people believe that biological or technological fixes exist for intractable social inequities caused by bad genes. They may surrender their freedoms and privacy to technical gurus, regardless of the pain and suffering of devalued people. They endorse the eliminationist promoters of techno-utopianism who seek to sculpt the future of the human race in their image.

Longtermism is the philosophical descendant of Ayn Rand on steroids. In their fascination with creating genetic privileges in the lives yet to be born, they are relatively indifferent to the lives already here or already destroyed. Longtermists' questionable population ethics determine which people should reproduce, which should be discouraged, and under what conditions. Human rights standards require an adequate diversity of perspectives beyond a self-referential group of scientists often funded by insular billionaires. Technological overpromises spur multimillion-dollar investments by the billionaire class, who correctly assume they'll be first in line for benefits like disease reversal if ever realized. While promising to renew humanity and make everyone young and healthy, scientists endeavor to create realistic, synthetic organs from embryos to harvest for human use. They tout the possibilities of producing young human eggs, restoring fertility to older women, and repairing immunological systems. Turning back the biological clock of time through medical rejuvenation will undoubtedly appeal to youth-worshiping consumerist societies.

The available technology doesn't match the billions of dollars invested in it. But, even then, it would still advertise dominant reproduction narratives that project white, nondisabled, and class-privileged children as the optimal outcome, like winning the genetic lottery. Moreover, women should not only bear children but bear the "right" kind of designer babies. Not racialized, disabled, queer, or low-income. CRISPR technologies that can permanently alter the human genome through gene-editing techniques may forever change humanity's DNA. Such amorally directed science is about transforming future generations, not treating, curing, or preventing present-day problems. As a result, bioenhancement technologies create the specter of "transhumans" without considering the implications for society.

In rebuking such biologically deterministic thinking, Dorothy Roberts challenges the assumption that heritable genome editing would undeniably improve the quality of human lives. She critically examines various ethical, moral, and technical limitations. In *Fatal Invention: How Science, Politics, and Big Business Re-create Race in the Twenty-First Century,* Roberts writes about how science, politics, and large corporations reconstitute a genetic definition of race. Although the Human Genome Project proved that human beings are not naturally divided by race, the emerging fields of personalized medicine, reproductive technologies, genetic genealogy, and DNA databanks reinscribe race as a biological category written in our genes. She highlights the difficulty of separating racialized science from racism. Black women don't believe that the preservation of the fiction of racialized humans is an unintended consequence.

An RJF analysis contends that all big economic and social decisions are, in effect, population policies that seek to manage human capital. The government can equalize access to ARTs or refrain from interfering in the market. Under neoliberal economics, only well-off people will access them. Either outcome is a moral statement of whose lives matter. Enthusiasts claim ethical neutrality, but that's a familiar colorblind approach that exacerbates racial and gender injustices while ignoring unjust hierarchies of power. Reproductive Justice and human rights advocates must work to ensure that biotechnologies won't usher in a world of genetic "haves" and "have-nots." Instead, a global human rights movement can redirect eugen-icist science and technology toward a just and sustainable future that preserves our collective humanity in a genetically engineered age.

Black Women Know Reprocide

We cannot consider a viable future without understanding Black women's history. Black women who have endured the monetization of life itself recognize the inherent threat among the many hyper-bolic and evangelical promises of ARTs. In the jealous protection of white patriarchal power, Black life is already regarded as dysgenic, spawning subsequent generations with inheritable and undesirable characteristics. Black women's historical and current relationships with the violence of scientific and technological advances mean that we have never had ourselves or our children deemed worthy of pro-tection. Black people endure what Achille Mbembe calls "necropoli-tics," a theory that explains indifference to Black suffering. White su-premacist logic perceives Black people as an existential threat to white futurity. Not only are we unprotected, but we are the intended victims of *reprocide*—that is, genocide achieved through reproduc-tive oppression.

Vulnerable people who are evolutionarily deselected are consid-ered unfit to reproduce for fear of passing down physically, mentally, or "morally" undesirable traits. Such practices target Black folk, Lat-inos, and Native Americans, including the poor, jobless, homeless, incarcerated, non-neurotypical, disabled, queer, and transgender people of all races. Science's tendency to manipulate people's repro-duction is a feature, not a fluke, of neo-Malthusian logic. RJF represents a way to decolonize our thinking about Black women's humanity, reproductive capacities, and sexualities. Medicine and science largely have excluded Black women except as objects of study without acknowledging our embodied theories. In our feminist and postcolonial theory of technoscience, we believe the future will be more female, queerer, and browner—an anathema to arrogant Big Thinkers.

In understanding the troubling past and present Black women have withstood, we invoke a Sankofa future where our reproductive tragedies will end. Through a "she-patriation" vision offered by Dázon Dixon Diallo, we may be the salvation of humanity. She posits that Africa and the world need Black women to reassert our place as the powerful force we are on this planet, and in doing so, we will liberate all people. We aspire for a future that is both liberatory and pleasurable. Black women must resist the false blandishments of the same kind of thinking that produced this mess in the first place. As Albert Einstein advised, "problems cannot be solved with the same consciousness that created them." Most people want to provide their children with the best future they can afford. But if they can't, it's the same quotidian reproductive injustices Black women have endured as the mothers of civilization. Black people, the blueprint of humanity and whose bodies get treated like wealth-building commodities, must ask what this techno-utopian future means to us.

We do not question Black women's ability to imagine *and* actualize a future better for humanity, but we do ask *how* and *what* that looks like. Although the transcendent struggle for justice does not solely depend on Black women, we believe we are an integral part of the eternal Chain of Freedom that stretches backward to our ancestors and toward our descendants. Our mission is to ensure the chain doesn't break at our link. Based on principle and mission, we must elevate our vision of Reproductive Justice Futurism. Like humanity's origins in Africa's past, the future begins with us. Trust Black Women!

Notes

Introduction

1. Three US Supreme Court cases are cited throughout *Fighting Mad*. The full citations are *Roe v. Wade*, 410 U.S. 113 (1973); *Planned Parenthood v. Casey*, 505 U.S. 833 (1992); and *Dobbs v. Jackson Women's Health Organization*, No. 19-1392, 597 U.S. (2022).

1. Disability, *Dobbs,* and a Black Perspective

1. Alexandra Minna Stern, *Eugenic Nation: Faults and Frontiers of Better Breeding in Modern America* (Berkeley: University of California Press, 2016).

5. Come Hell or High Water

1. "After *Roe* Fell, Abortion Laws by State," Center for Reproductive Rights, https://reproductiverights.org/maps/abortion-laws-by-state/ (accessed March 5, 2023).

2. Cisgender women have generally been the target of this criminalization, and this is the language used in the cited study; however, it is important to note that some people of all genders are able to get pregnant and may need access to abortion, miscarriage, and/or pregnancy care at some point. Hereafter I use gender-neutral language to accurately reflect this.

3. Lynn M. Paltrow and Jeanne Flavin, "Arrests of and Forced Interventions on Pregnant Women in the United States, 1973-2005: Implications for Women's

Legal Status and Public Health," *Journal of Health Politics, Policy and Law* 38, no. 2 (2013): 299–343.

4. J. D. Vance, author of the book *Hillbilly Elegy.*

5. Jessica Wilkerson, *To Live Here, You Have to Fight: How Women Led Appalachian Movements for Social Justice* (Champaign: University of Illinois Press, 2019).

6. David S. Cohen and Carole Joffe, *Obstacle Course: The Everyday Struggle to Get an Abortion in America* (Oakland: University of California Press, 2021).

6. "We Too Have Abortions"

1. Liza Fuentes, "Inequity in US Abortion Rights and Access: The End of Roe Is Deepening Existing Divides," January 2023, Guttmacher Institute, www.guttmacher.org/2023/01/inequity-us-abortion-rights-and-access-end-roe-deepening-existing-divides.

2. Chau Trinh-Shevrin, Nadia S. Islam, and Mariano Jose Rey, eds., *Asian American Communities and Health: Context, Research, Policy, and Action* (Hoboken, N.J.: John Wiley & Sons, 2009).

3. Abby Budiman and Neil G. Ruiz, "Key Facts about Asian Americans, a Diverse and Growing Population," April 29, 2021, Pew Research Center, www.pewresearch.org/fact-tank/2021/04/29/key-facts-about-asian-americans/.

4. Budiman and Ruiz, "Key Facts about Asian Americans"; H. Castañeda et al., "Immigration as a Social Determinant of Health," *Annual Review of Public Health* 36, no. 1 (2015): 375–392.

5. "NEWS: Nearly 1/3 low-income Asian women in states with limited abortion access," September 1, 2022, National Partnership for Women & Families, https://nationalpartnership.org/news-nearly-1-3-low-income-asian-women-in-states-with-limited-abortion-access/.

7. How *Dobbs* Will Deepen the Traumas of Incarcerated Pregnant People

1. Deija is a pseudonym.

2. Diana Kasdan, "Abortion Access for Incarcerated Women: Are Correctional Health Practices in Conflict with Constitutional Standards?," *Perspectives on Sexual and Reproductive Health* 41, no. 1 (2009): 59–62.

3. *Estelle v. Gamble,* www.oyez.org/cases/1976/75-929 (accessed December 23, 2022).

4. C. Sufrin, R. K. Jones, L. Beal, W. D. Mosher, and S. Bell, "Abortion Access for Incarcerated People: Incidence of Abortion and Policies at U.S. Prisons and

Jails," *Obstetrics and Gynecology* 138, no. 3 (September 1, 2021): 330–337; doi: 10.1097/AOG.0000000000004497. PMID: 34352850.

5. "Policy & Forms," Federal Bureau of Prisons, www.bop.gov/PublicInfo /execute/policysearch# (accessed December 23, 2022).

6. "Pregnancy in Prisons (PIP) Statistics Project," Advocacy and Research on Reproductive Wellness of Incarcerated People, https://arrwip.org/projects /pregnancy-in-prison-statistics-pips-project/ (accessed December 23, 2022).

7. Wanda Bertram and Wendy Sawyer, "What the End of *Roe v. Wade* Will Mean for People on Probation and Parole," Prison Policy Initiative, June 30, 2022, www.prisonpolicy.org/blog/2022/06/30/roe/.

8. "Interactive Map: U.S. Abortion Policies and Access after *Roe*," Guttmacher Institute, https://states.guttmacher.org/policies/ (accessed December 23, 2022).

9. "NCCHC Recognizes Importance of Legal Abortion for Optimizing Maternal Health Outcomes," National Commission on Correctional Health Care, August 5, 2022, www.ncchc.org/ncchc-recognizes-importance-of-legal-abortion-for-optimizing-maternal-health-outcomes/.

10. Roxanne Daniel, "Prisons Neglect Pregnant Women in Their Healthcare Policies," Prison Policy Initiative, December 5, 2019, www.prisonpolicy.org /blog/2019/12/05/pregnancy/.

11. E. Ann Carson, "Prisoners in 2020—Statistical Tables," Bureau of Justice Statistics, December 2021, https://bjs.ojp.gov/library/publications/prisoners-2020-statistical-tables.

12. Dorothy Roberts, *Torn Apart: How the Child Welfare System Destroys Black Families—and How Abolition Can Build a Safer World* (New York: Basic Books, 2022).

13. Crystal M. Hayes, Carolyn Sufrin, and Jamila Perritt, "Reproductive Justice Disrupted: Mass Incarceration as a Driver of Reproductive Oppression," *American Journal of Public Health* (January 2020), https://ajph.aphapublications .org/doi/10.2105/AJPH.2019.305407/.

14. Roberts, *Torn Apart.*

9. From College Campus to Community

1. Names in this essay have been changed to protect privacy.

10. What We Inherit

1. Diana Greene Foster, *The Turnaway Study: Ten Years, a Thousand Women, and the Consequences of Having or Being Denied an Abortion* (New York: Scribner, 2021).

2. "What Are Some Strategies for Supporting Pregnant and Parenting Teens in Foster Care?" Casey Family Programs, December 17, 2018, www.casey.org /pregnant-parenting-teens/.

3. N. Rolock and K. R. White, "Post-permanency Discontinuity: A Longitudinal Examination of Outcomes for Foster Youth after Adoption or Guardianship," *Children and Youth Services Review,* 70 (2016): 419–427, https://doi.org/10.1016/j .childyouth.2016.10.025

14. Sustaining Full-Spectrum Sexual and Reproductive Health Care after *Dobbs*

1. Lynn Paltrow, email to Jennifer Pepper, introductions from Lynn Paltrow /National Advocates for Pregnant Women, April 18, 2022.

2. N. Grayson, N. Quinones, and T. Oseguera, "A Model of True CHOICES: Learnings from a Comprehensive Sexual and Reproductive Health Clinic in Tennessee that Provides Abortions and Opened the City's First Birth Center," *Journal of Midwifery and Women's Health* 67 (2022): 689–695, https://doi.org/10.1111 /jmwh.13448.

3. Grayson, Quinones, and Oseguera, "Model of True CHOICES."

4. Sophia Tareen, "Gov. Pritzker Vows to Protect Abortion Rights in Illinois," Associated Press, September 2, 2021, https://apnews.com/article/abortion- health-us-supreme-court-illinois-f1a03ad9c1ba5dbce1293796aa72dcf8.

5. Angie Leventis Lourgos, "Nearly 10,000 Women Traveled from out of State to Have an Abortion in Illinois in 2020—a 29% Increase," *Chicago Tribune,* January 25, 2022, www.chicagotribune.com/news/breaking/ct-abortion- data-out-of-state-increase-20220125-ppqscjemmffifnvatyoqkcm6pa-story .html.

6. Pepper as quoted in Ava Sasani and Erin Schaff, "When the Abortion Clinic Came to Town," *New York Times,* November 30, 2022, www.nytimes.com/2022 /11/30/us/abortion-clinic-illinois.html.

7. "Tennessee Birth Data. 2021," National Center for Health Statistics, October 15, 2021, www.cdc.gov/nchs/pressroom/states/tennessee/tn.htm (accessed December 22, 2021). J. Martin, B. Hamilton, M. Osterman, and A. Driscoll, "Births: Final Data for 2020," National Center for Health Statistics, 2021, DOI:10.15620/cdc:112078. A. H. Blair and N. Quinones, "Internal Report on Select Birthing Parent Outcomes from the CHOICES Birth Center." Memphis, September 2022.

16. Reproductive Justice and the Fight for Queer Liberation

1. Ariella R. Tabaac et al., "Sexual and Reproductive Health Information: Disparities across Sexual Orientation Groups in Two Cohorts of U.S. Women," *Sex Research and Social Policy* 18, no. 3 (September 2021): 612–620, https://pubmed.ncbi.nlm.nih.gov/34484460/. Bianca Wilson et al., "LBGT Poverty in the United States: Trends at the Onset of COVID-19," February 2023, UCLA School of Law Williams Institute, https://williamsinstitute.law.ucla.edu/publications/lgbt-poverty-us/. Brittany Charlton et al., "Structural Stigma and Sexual Orientation-Related Reproductive Health Disparities in a Longitudinal Cohort Study of Female Adolescents," *Journal of Adolescence* 74 (July 2019): 183–187, https://pubmed.ncbi.nlm.nih.gov/31238178/. "Discrimination Prevents LGBTQ People from Accessing Health Care," *American Progress,* January 18, 2018, www.americanprogress.org/article/discrimination-prevents-lgbtq-people-accessing-health-care/.

2. Rachel Jones, Jenna Berman, and Brittany Charlton, "Sexual Orientation and Exposure to Violence among U.S. Patients Undergoing Abortion," *Obstetrics and Gynecology* 132, no. 3 (September 2018): 605–611, https://pubmed.ncbi.nlm.nih.gov/30095763/.

3. "Fact Sheet: LGBTQ+ People and *Roe v. Wade,*" Human Rights Campaign, https://hrc-prod-requests.s3-us-west-2.amazonaws.com/FACT-SHEET_-LG-BTQ-PEOPLE-ROE-V-WADE.pdf (accessed June 7, 2023).

17. Workers' Role in Defending Abortion Rights

1. Brenda Wiest, "Abortion Rights are Worker Rights," June 24, 2022, www.teamsters117.org/abortion_rights_are_worker_rights.

2. "Flight Attendants Condemn Attacks on Our Rights," AFA News Release, www.afacwa.org/attack_on_our_rights (accessed June 27, 2023).

3. "Nurses: Likely Supreme Court Ruling on Reproductive Rights Poses Major Threat To Patients' Health, Security," National Nurses United, www.nationalnursesunited.org/press/likely-supreme-court-ruling-on-reproductive-rights-poses-major-threat-to-patients-health (accessed June 27, 2023).

4. Kenneth Quinnell and Aaron Gallant, "Service + Solidarity Spotlight: Working Families Deserve Access to Unrestricted Health Care," AFL-CIO, May 4, 2022, https://aflcio.org/2022/5/4/service-solidarity-spotlight-working-families-deserve-access-unrestricted-health-care.

19. Organizing in Pennsylvania

1. R. Rebouche, "Abortion Rights Referendums Are Winning—with State-by-State Battles over Rights Replacing National Debate," *The Conversation,* November 18, 2022, https://theconversation.com/abortion-rights-referendums-are-winning-with-state-by-state-battles-over-rights-replacing-national-debate-193490.

2. G. Palosky, "Abortion Grows as a Motivator for Midterm Voters, Particularly for Democrats and in States Where It Has Become Illegal since the Supreme Court Overturned *Roe v. Wade,*" Kaiser Family Foundation, October 12, 2022, www.kff.org/womens-health-policy/press-release/abortion-grows-as-a-motivator-for-midterm-voters-particularly-for-democrats-and-in-states-where-it-has-become-illegal-since-the-supreme-court-overturned-roe-v-wade.

23. My Journey to Becoming an Abortion Doula

1. California Latinas for Reproductive Justice, https://californialatinas.org/ (accessed December 22, 2022).

2. We Testify, www.wetestify.org/ (accessed December 22, 2022); ACCESS Reproductive Justice, https://accessrj.org/ (accessed June 7, 2023).

25. Feminist Art as Feminist Activism

Thanks to the Gender, Sexuality, and Feminist Studies program and the Feminist Resource Center at Chellis House—Laurie Essig, Karin Hanta, Catharine Wright, and Marion Wells—for enabling the Public Feminism Lab. Rayn Bumstead, the lab's art mentor, and Colin Boyd, exhibit co-curator, were crucial to the exhibit's success. Thanks also to the Public Feminism Lab Fellows: Elissa Asch, Luci Bryson, Elio Farley, Isabel Perez-Martin, Emily Ribeiro, Alexis Welch, and Kamari Williams. To see an electronic version of the exhibit, check out the Center for Public Feminism website at www.publicfeminism.org/.

28. Preparing Criminal Defense Attorneys to Fight for Reproductive Justice

1. "Arrests and Prosecutions of Pregnant People, 1973–2020," Pregnancy Justice, September 18, 2021, www.pregnancyjusticeus.org/arrests-and-prosecutions-of-pregnant-women-1973–2020/.

29. What's Next for Doctors and Patients

1. "Dobbs v. Jackson Women's Health Organization," ACLU, June 27, 2022, www.aclu.org/cases/dobbs-v-jackson-womens-health-organization.

2. A.R.A. Aiken, J.E. Starling, J.G. Scott, and R. Gomperts, "Association of Texas Senate Bill 8 with Requests for Self-managed Medication Abortion," *JAMA Network Open* 5, no. 2 (2022): e221122, DOI:10.1001/jamanetworkopen.2022.1122.

3. L. Huss, F. Diaz-Tello, and G. Samari, "Self-Care, Criminalized: August 2022 Preliminary Findings," www.ifwhenhow.org (accessed June 8, 2023).

4. Radley Balko, "There's Overwhelming Evidence That the Criminal Justice System Is Racist. Here's the Proof," *Washington Post,* June 10, 2020, www .washingtonpost.com/news/opinions/wp/2018/09/18/theres-overwhelming-evidence-that-the-criminal-justice-system-is-racist-heres-the-proof/.

30. Surveilled, Criminalized, and Deportable

1. *The Matter of M,* 2 Immigration and Nationality Decisions (I&N), 721 (Board of Immigration Appeals 1946).

2. *J.D. v. Azar*, 925 F.3d 1291 (D.C. Cir. 2019).

32. Let's Talk about Money and Abortion

1. Phillip B. Levine, Amy B. Trainor, and David J. Zimmerman, "The Effect of Medicaid Abortion Funding Restrictions on Abortions, Pregnancies and Births," *Journal of Health Economics* 15, no. 5 (October 1996): 555–578. Sarah C.M. Roberts et al., "Estimating the Proportion of Medicaid-Eligible Pregnant Women in Louisiana Who Do Not Get Abortions When Medicaid Does Not Cover Abortion," *BMC Women's Health* 19, no. 1 (2019): 78.

2. To come to this calculation, I reviewed IRS tax documents for abortion funding organizations and philanthropic organizations for previous years, conducted confidential interviews with staff at funding organizations, attended virtual meetings with abortion providers trying to manage patient access changes during the COVID-19 pandemic, and used estimations of prior levels of reported external support on abortion patient surveys.

3. Sarah K. Cowan, Michael Hout, and Stuart Perrett, "Updating a Time-Series of Survey Questions: The Case of Abortion Attitudes in the General Social Survey," *Sociological Methods & Research* DOI:10.1177/00491241211043140 (2022).

33. Pre-*Dobbs* but Post-*Roe*

The author speaks strictly to the work of the client services team of the New Orleans Abortion Fund from the beginning of the COVID-19 pandemic until August 2021. Nothing the author refers to in this piece should be construed as representative of the fund formerly known as the New Orleans Abortion Fund at large nor programming provided by NOAF after that time period. The author speaks to her own experiences as coordinator of the client services team with input from comrades that she considers herself blessed to be in community with.

36. Repro Legal Defense Fund (at If/When/How)

1. L. Huss, F. Diaz-Tello, and G. Samari, "Self-Care, Criminalized: August 2022 Preliminary Findings," www.ifwhenhow.org/resources/self-care-criminalized-preliminary-findings/ (accessed January 2, 2023).

37. Employer Abortion Travel Benefits Are Important, but They Aren't Enough

1. K. Shepherd, R. Roubein, and C. Kitchener, "1 in 3 American Women Have Already Lost Abortion Access. More Restrictive Laws Are Coming," *Washington Post,* August 22, 2022, www.washingtonpost.com/nation/2022/08/22/more-trigger-bans-loom-1-3-women-lose-most-abortion-access-post-roe/.

2. E. Goldberg, "These Companies Will Cover Travel Expenses for Employee Abortions," *New York Times,* August 19, 2022, www.nytimes.com/article/abortion-companies-travel-expenses.html.

3. Goldberg, "These Companies Will Cover Travel Expenses for Employee Abortions."

4. "State Bans on Abortion Throughout Pregnancy," Guttmacher Institute, October 1–November 2, 2021, www.guttmacher.org/state-policy/explore/state-policies-later-abortions#.

5. K. Kimport, "Reducing the Burdens of Forced Abortion Travel: Referrals, Financial and Emotional Support, and Opportunities for Positive Experiences in Traveling for Third-Trimester Abortion Care," *Social Science & Medicine* 293 (2022): 114667.

6. K. Kimport and M. P. Rasidjan, "Exploring the Emotional Costs of Abortion Travel in the United States due to Legal Restriction," *Contraception* 120 (2023): 109956.

39. Jill Filipovic Interviews Rebecca Gomperts

A version of this chapter was previously published in the *New York Review*.

1. Women on Waves, www.womenonwaves.org/en/ (accessed June 8, 2023).
2. Women on Web, www.womenonweb.org/en/ (accessed June 8, 2023).
3. Aid Access, https://aidaccess.org/ (accessed June 8, 2023).
4. R. Gill, B. Ganatra, and F. Althabe, "WHO Essential Medicines for Reproductive Health," *BMJ Global Health* 4, no. 6 (2019): 4:e002150.
5. Jill Filipovic, "Should Women Perform Their Own Abortions," *Cosmopolitan*, October 3, 2016, www.cosmopolitan.com/politics/a4370287/diy-abortions-indonesia-samsara/.

40. The *Dobbs* Decision, God, and Moral Conscience

1. Judith Jarvis Thomson, "A Defense of Abortion," *Philosophy & Public Affairs* 1, no. 1 (1971): 47–66, www.jstor.org/stable/2265091.
2. Bertha Alvarez Manninen, "A Kantian Defense of Abortion Rights with Respect for Intrauterine Life," *Diametros*, no. 39 (March 2014): 70–92, https://doi.org/10.13153/diam.39.2014.565.
3. Immanuel Kant, *Grounding for the Metaphysics of Morals*, translated by James W. Ellington (Cambridge, MA: Hackett Publishing, 1993).
4. Manninen, "Kantian Defense."
5. For this history see Joshua D. Wolff, "Ministers of a Higher Law: The Story of the Clergy Consultation Service on Abortion," 1998, www.judsonclassic.org/MinistersofaHigherLaw; and Doris Andrea Dirks and Patricia A. Relf, *To Offer Compassion: A History of the Clergy Consultation Service on Abortion* (Madison: University of Wisconsin Press, 2017).

41. Open Letter from Seven Muslim American Organizations

Originally published on Muslim Girl, December 2, 2021, https://muslimgirl.com.

42. The Torah of Abortion Justice

1. Exodus 21:22–25.
2. Babylonian Talmud, Yevamot 69b.
3. Babylonian Talmud, Gittin 23b.
4. Mishnah Ohalot 7:6.

5. Rabbi Jacob Emden Responsa She'elat Ya"vetz 1:43 (1739–1759).

6. Rabbi Eliezer Waldenberg, Tzitz Eliezer 13:102 (1978).

7. Rabbi Mordechai Winkler, Levushei Mordekhai, Hoshen Mishpat 39, 1913.

8. Rabbi Aharon Lichtenstein, "Abortion: A Halakhic Perspective," *Tradition* 25, no. 4 (1991): 3–12.

9. Rabbi Yehudah ibn Ayyash of Algeirs, 'She'eilot U'tshuvot' Beit Yehudah, from Even haEzer Siman 14, 1740. Thank you to Rabbi Margo Hughes-Robinson for the text, translation, and analysis.

10. For example, "Cursed be the one who subverts the rights of the stranger, the orphan and the widow" (Deuteronomy 27:19).

11. Rabbi Becky Silverstein, "The Jewish Teaching That Supports Abortion & Trans Rights," *Hey Alma,* June 24, 2022, www.heyalma.com/the-jewish-teaching-that-supports-abortion-trans-rights/.

43. What Everyone Gets Wrong about Evangelicals and Abortion

A version of this article was previously published by the *Washington Post* as "What Everyone Gets Wrong about Evangelicals and Abortion," May 16, 2022, www .washingtonpost.com/outlook/2022/05/16/what-everyone-gets-wrong-about-evangelicals-abortion/.

1. Randall Balmer, "The Religious Right and the Abortion Myth," *Politico,* May 10, 2022, www.politico.com/news/magazine/2022/05/10/abortion-history-right-white-evangelical-1970s-00031480.

2. Neil J. Young, *We Gather Together: The Religious Right and the Problem of Interfaith Politics* (New York: Oxford University Press, 2016).

3. Billy Graham, "My Answer," *Clarion-Ledger* (Jackson, Mississippi), August 28, 1961, 8.

4. Young, *We Gather Together.*

5. Gillian Frank, "The Colour of the Unborn: Anti-Abortion and Anti-Bussing Politics in Michigan, United States, 1967–1973," *Gender & History* 26, no. 2 (2014): 351–378.

6. "Southern Baptist Convention Resolutions on Abortion," www .johnstonarchive.net/baptist/sbcabres.html (accessed March 6, 2023).

7. National Association of Evangelicals, "Abortion 1973," www.nae.org/up-dates/abortion-1973/ (accessed March 6, 2023). Young, *We Gather Together,* 160.

8. Young, *We Gather Together.* Daniel K. Williams, "The Partisan Trajectory of the American Pro-Life Movement: How a Liberal Catholic Campaign Became a Conservative Evangelical Cause," *Religions* 6, no. 2 (June 2015): 451–475.

9. Marjorie J. Spruill, *Divided We Stand: The Battle over Women's Rights and Family Values That Polarized American Politics* (New York: Bloomsbury USA, 2017).

10. Bonnie Winston, "Reproductive Justice Advocates See Link between Voting Rights, Abortion, Civil Rights," *Color Of Change* (blog), October 20, 2022, https://colorofchange.org/reproductive-justice-advocates-see-link-between-voting-rights-abortion-civil-rights/.

45. Even with Contraception, People Need and Must Have Access to Abortion

A version of this essay was previously published in the *Washington Post* as "Mississippi Is Wrong. Even with Birth Control, Abortion Access Is Necessary," December 7, 2021.

46. Building Gender Equity by Engaging Men in Reproductive Responsibility

1. "Abortion Is a Common Experience for U.S. Women, Despite Dramatic Declines in Rates," Guttmacher Institute, October 19, 2017, www.guttmacher.org/news-release/2017/abortion-common-experience-us-women-despite-dramatic-declines-rates.

2. "Birth Control Benefits," www.healthcare.gov/coverage/birth-control-benefits/ (accessed June 8, 2023).

47. Shifting Abortion Public Opinion

1. The op-ed referenced in the chapter epigraph is L. H. Harris, "I'm an Ob-Gyn in Michigan. I'm Worried about My Patients," *Detroit Free Press,* December 19, 2022, www.freep.com/story/opinion/contributors/2022/10/29/im-an-obgyn-worried-about-my-michigan-patients-opinion/69596560007/.

2. The messaging toolkit "Evidence-based messaging guidance for doctors who communicate about abortion care" is available by request from the author. It details physician messaging recommendations as well as the qualitative and quantitative research evidence for those recommendations. The email referenced here is an actual email the author received from a reader, who gave permission for his note to be used.

48. Rejecting the Abortion Debate Binary

1. Justice Marshall as quoted in James D. Robenalt, "The Unknown Supreme Court Clerk Who Single-Handedly Created the Roe v. Wade Viability Standard,"

Washington Post, November 29, 2021, www.washingtonpost.com/history/2021 /11/29/viability-standard-abortion-supreme-court-hammond/. *Roe v. Wade,* Supreme Court Case Files Collection, Box 5, Powell Papers, Lewis F. Powell Jr. Archives, Washington & Lee University School of Law, Virginia.

2. Dorothy Roberts, *Killing the Black Body: Race, Reproduction, and the Meaning of Liberty* (New York: Random House, 1998).

3. "America's Abortion Quandary," Pew Research Center, May 6, 2022, www .pewresearch.org/religion/2022/05/06/americas-abortion-quandary/.

4. Kate Coleman-Minahan et al., "Young Women's Experience Using Judicial Bypass for Abortion in Texas," *Journal of Adolescent Health* 64, no. 1 (January 2019): 20–25, www.sciencedirect.com/science/article/abs/pii/S1054139X18303070?casa_ token=c6SFSzhHciIAAAAA:eP_L7JJ94DI1x3bsQOnY6xd_d9ZrLD9BCPvKC-59SWedoE6VzeFU2gIBPPNl7kd9OjCK6hykHUQ.

5. Monica McLemore et al., "Women Know Best—Findings from a Thematic Analysis of 5,214 Surveys of Abortion Care Experience," *Women's Health Issues* 24, no. 6 (November–December 2014): 594–599, https://pubmed.ncbi.nlm.nih .gov/25442704/.

6. M. Antonia Biggs, Heather Gould, and Diana Greene Foster, "Understanding Why Women Seek Abortions in the US," *BMC Women's Health* 13 (2013), www .ncbi.nlm.nih.gov/pmc/articles/PMC3729671/.

7. "Mississippi Murder Charge against Pregnant Teen Dismissed," Pregnancy Justice, April 4, 2014, www.pregnancyjusticeus.org/mississippi-murder-charge-against-pregnant-teen-dismissed/.

49. *Dobbs,* Democracy, and Distortion

1. *Roe v. Wade,* 410 U.S. 113 (1973).

2. *Planned Parenthood v. Casey,* 505 U.S. 833 (1992).

3. *Dobbs v. Jackson Women's Health Organization,* 142 S. Ct. 2228 (2022).

4. *Dobbs v. Jackson Women's Health,* at 2277.

5. *Dobbs v. Jackson Women's Health,* at 2243. See also Editorial Board, "Kansas, Abortion, and the Supreme Court," *Wall Street Journal,* August 4, 2022, www.wsj .com/articles/kansas-and-the-supreme-court-samuel-alito-roe-v-wade-john-harris-david-von-drehle-abortion-dobbs-11659650794 ("the vote defeating a constitutional amendment to overturn a state Supreme Court ruling on abortion is a rousing vindication of Justice Alito's majority opinion overturning *Roe v. Wade*"). Joe Schroeder, "Elected Officials, Advocacy Groups React to Passage of Indiana Abortion Bill," FOX59, August 6, 2022, https://fox59.com/indiana-news

/elected-officials-advocacy-groups-react-to-passage-of-indiana-abortion-bill
/ (quoting Susan B. Anthony Pro-Life America, "After the *Dobbs* decision sent this
issue back to the people in June, the process has worked the way it is supposed to.
Elected officials made critical decisions after hearing from thousands of Hoos-
iers. The Indiana experience is illustrative for other states because it envisions
new protections for life in Indiana based on the will of the people, highlighting
that our work will continue in the future."). Howard Kurtz, "Behind the Kansas
Abortion Shocker: Why Some Red States Don't Want a Total Ban," FOX NEWS,
August 2, 2022, www.foxnews.com/media/behind-kansas-abortion-shocker-
why-some-red-states-dont-want-total-ban ("What happened in Kansas is what
the Supreme Court, and defenders of its abortion ruling, say they wanted").

6. *Rucho v. Common Cause*, 139 S. Ct. 2484, 2506–07 (2019) ("We conclude
that partisan gerrymandering claims present political questions beyond the reach
of the federal courts").

7. Critically the Court may soon limit even these narrow modes of oversight. In
the October 2022 term the Court, in *Moore v. Harper,* considered the prospect of the
independent state legislature theory, which maintains that, under the Elections
Clauses of articles I and II, state legislatures, and no other branch of state government, are authorized to regulate federal elections. If the Court credits this unortho-
dox reading of the Elections Clauses, it would allow state legislatures broad authority to enact regulations that impact federal elections with no prospect of meaningful
oversight from state courts and executives. See Eliza Sweren-Becker and Ethan He-
renstein, "*Moore v. Harper,* Explained," Brennan Center for Justice, August 4, 2022,
www.brennancenter.org/our-work/research-reports/moore-v-harper-explained.

8. See Alex Tausanovitch and Danielle Root, "How Partisan Gerrymandering
Limits Voting Rights," Center for American Progress, July 8, 2020, www
.americanprogress.org/article/partisan-gerrymandering-limits-voting-rights/.

9. John Hanna and Margaret Stafford, "Kansas Voters Resoundingly Protect
Their Access to Abortion," AP News, August 3, 2022, https://apnews.com/article
/2022-primary-elections-kansas-abortion-b6d62a852c2ce4617f2c03589fbb523e.

10. Mitch Smith and Katie Glueck, "Kansas Retains Abortion Rights in Critical Post-*Roe* Referendum," *New York Times,* August 3, 2022, A1.

11. "Indiana Legislature First to Approve Abortion Bans Post *Roe,*" *Politico,*
August 5, 2022, www.politico.com/news/2022/08/05/indiana-legislature-first-to-
approve-abortion-bans-post-roe-00050199.

12. "What Legal Implications Arise after Indiana Approves an Abortion
Ban?," NPR MORNING EDITION, August 8, 2022 (noting the differences between representative democracy and direct democracy measures).

13. *Shelby County v. Holder,* 570 U.S. 529, 556–57 (2013).

14. *Shelby County v. Holder,* at 537.

15. "The Effects of *Shelby County v. Holder* (2018)," Brennan Center for Justice, www.brennancenter.org/our-work/policy-solutions/effects-shelby-county-v-holder (noting that *Shelby County* "opened the floodgates to laws restricting voting throughout the United States" and finding that "states previously covered by the preclearance requirement have engaged in recent, significant efforts to disenfranchise voters").

16. *Brnovich v. Democratic National Committee,* 141 S. Ct. 2321 (2021).

17. See "Lawyers' Committee for Civil Rights Under the Law, Testimony of Ezra Rosenberg, Co-Director, Voting Rights Project, Before the U.S. House of Representatives, Committee on the Judiciary, Subcommittee on the Constitution, Civil Rights, and Civil Liberties Hearing on 'The Implications of *Brnovich v. Democratic National Committee* and Potential Legislative Responses,'" July 16, 2021, https://docs.house.gov/meetings/JU/JU10/20210716/113905/HHRG-117-JU10-Wstate-RosenbergE-20210716.pdf ("*Brnovich* presents new challenges [to voting rights]. Its impacts have yet to be measured, but common sense and history instruct us that those who wish to target voters of color will undoubtedly feel emboldened by a decision that can be read as making it more difficult for plaintiffs to prove a Section 2 violation giving state legislatures a 'Get Out of Jail' card to pass voter suppressive legislation, and justify it simply by claiming "voter fraud.").

18. See "Lawyers' Committee for Civil Rights Under the Law, Testimony of Ezra Rosenberg" (discussing the twin effects of *Shelby County* and *Brnovich*).

19. See Leah Litman, Melissa Murray, and Kate Shaw, "The Link between Voting Rights and the Abortion Ruling," *Washington Post,* June 28, 2022, www.washingtonpost.com/outlook/2022/06/28/dobbs-voting-rights-minority-rule/.

20. Litman, Murray, and Shaw, "Link between Voting Rights and the Abortion Ruling."

21. Litman, Murray, and Shaw, "Link between Voting Rights and the Abortion Ruling."

51. A Black Abortion Provider's Perspective on Post-*Roe* America

References

24. Krystale E. Littlejohn Interviews the Founders of Plan C

Plan C Pills
www.plancpills.org
DKT International
www.dktinternational.org/
If/When/How
www.ifwhenhow.org/
M+A Hotline
www.mahotline.org/
Hotline: 833-246-2632
Reprocare
https://abortionhotline.org/
Healthline: 833-226-7821
Repro Legal Helpline
www.reprolegalhelpline.org/
Helpline: 844-868-2812

25. Feminist Art as Feminist Activism

Bryant, Amy, Subasri Narasimhan, Katelyn Bryant-Comstock, and Erika Levi. "Crisis Pregnancy Center Websites: Information, Misinformation, and Disinformation." *Contraception* 90, no. 6 (2014): 601–605.

Chen, Alice. "Crisis Pregnancy Centers: Impeding the Right to Informed Decision Making." *Cardozo Journal of Law and Gender* 19, no. 1 (2013): 933–960.

Munson, Ziad W. *The Making of Pro-Life Activists: How Social Movement Mobiliza-tion Works.* Chicago: University of Chicago Press, 2008.

Thomsen, Carly, Zach Levitt, Christopher Gernon, and Penelope Spencer. "Anti-abortion Ideology on the Move: Mobile Crisis Pregnancy Centers as Unruly, Unmappable, Ungovernable." *Political Geography* 92 (2021): 1–10.

32. Let's Talk about Money and Abortion

Cowan, Sarah K., Michael Hout, and Stuart Perrett. "Updating a Time-Series of Survey Questions: The Case of Abortion Attitudes in the General Social Survey." *Sociological Methods & Research* 00491241211043140 (2022): 1–42.

Levine, Phillip B., Amy B. Trainor, and David J. Zimmerman. "The Effect of Medicaid Abortion Funding Restrictions on Abortions, Pregnancies and Births." *Journal of Health Economics* 15, no. 5 (October 1996): 555–578.

Roberts, Sarah C. M., Nicole E. Johns, Valerie Williams, Erin Wingo, and Ushma D. Upadhyay. "Estimating the Proportion of Medicaid-Eligible Pregnant Women in Louisiana Who Do Not Get Abortions When Medicaid Does Not Cover Abortion." *BMC Women's Health* 19, no. 1 (2019): 1–8.

37. Employer Abortion Travel Benefits Are Important, but They Aren't Enough

Kimport, K. "Reducing the Burdens of Forced Abortion Travel: Referrals, Financial and Emotional Support, and Opportunities for Positive Experi-ences in Traveling for Third-Trimester Abortion Care." *Social Science & Medicine* 293 (2022): 114667.

Kimport, K., and M. P. Rasidjan. "Exploring the Emotional Costs of Abortion Travel in the United States due to Legal Restriction." *Contraception* 120 (2023): 109956.

52. Reproductive Justice Futurism: Trust Black Women

Arditti, Rita. "Reproductive Engineering and the Social Control of Women." In *Radical America,* 9–26. Somerville, MA: Alternative Education Project, 1986.

Benjamin, Ruha. "Racial Fictions, Biological Facts: Expanding the Sociological Imagination through Speculative Methods." *Catalyst: Feminism, Theory, Technoscience* 2, no. 2 (2016): 1–28. *https://doi.org/10.28968/cftt.v2i2.28798.*

Brokowski, Carolyn, and Mazhar Adli. "CRISPR Ethics: Moral Considerations for Applications of a Powerful Tool." *Journal of Molecular Biology* 431, no. 1 (2019): 88–101. https://doi.org/10.1016/j.jmb.2018.05.044.

Conrad, Marissa. "How Much Does IVF Cost?" *Forbes Magazine*. October 19, 2022. www.forbes.com/health/family/how-much-does-ivf-cost/.

Corea, Gena. *The Mother Machine: Reproductive Technologies from Artificial Insemination to Artificial Wombs.* New York: HarperCollins, 1985.

Dery, Mark. "Black to the Future: Interviews with Samuel R. Delany, Greg Tate, and Tricia Rose." In *Flame Wars: The Discourse of Cyberculture,* 179–222. Durham, NC: Duke University Press, 1994. https://doi.org/10.1215/9780822396765-010.

Edelman, Lee. *No Future: Queer Theory and the Death Drive.* Durham, NC: Duke University Press, 2004.

Mason, Carol. "Minority Unborn." In *Fetal Subjects, Feminist Positions,* edited by Lynn M. Morgan and Meredith Wilson Michaels, 159–174. Philadelphia: University of Pennsylvania Press, 1999.

Mbembe, Achille. "Necropolitics." In *Foucault in an Age of Terror: Essays on Biopolitics and the Defence of Society,* 152–182. London: Palgrave Macmillan UK, 2008.

Muñoz, José Esteban. *Cruising Utopia: The Then and There of Queer Futurity.* New York: New York University Press, 2009.

Reineke, Sandra, and Amy Fletcher. "Reproductive and Genetic Technology Policymaking and Citizenship Rights." In *Biopolitics at 50 Years,* edited by Tony Wohlers and Amy Fletcher, no. 13, 183–196. Bingley: Emerald Publishing Limited, 2022.

Roberts, Dorothy. *Fatal Invention: How Science, Politics, and Big Business Re-create Race in the Twenty-First Century.* New York: The New Press, 2011.

Sorainen, Antu. "Remembering José Esteban Muñoz—RIP." Allegra Lab. December 2013. https://allegralaboratory.net/remembering-jose-esteban-munoz-rip/.

Smith, Zoey. "Lesbian Motherhood and Artificial Reproductive Technologies in North America: Race, Gender, Kinship, and the Reproduction of Dominant Narratives." *Pathways* 3, no. 1 (2022): 71–81. https://doi.org/10.29173/pathways29.

van Wichelen, Sonja, and Jaya Keaney. "The Reproductive Bodies of Postgenomics." *Science, Technology, & Human Values* 47, no. 6 (March 30, 2022): 1111–1130. https://doi.org/10.1177/01622439221088646.

About the Editors

KRYSTALE E. LITTLEJOHN, PhD, is associate professor of sociology at the University of Oregon, author of *Just Get on the Pill*, and a series editor for the Reproductive Justice Series at University of California Press.

MARC CAMPOS

RICKIE SOLINGER, PhD, is a historian and curator, the author or editor of a dozen books about reproductive politics and satellite issues, and the senior editor of the Reproductive Justice book series at the University of California Press.

JAMES GEISER

About the Contributors

AMY ALSPAUGH, PhD, CNM, is an assistant professor at the University of Tennessee College of Nursing.

WYNDI ANDERSON, BA, is a consultant supporting organizations and staff through organizational change, crisis, and/or expansion, using her experience in human rights and social justice work focused in the Southern and rural regions of the United States.

ASEES BHASIN, LLB-JD, is the Law & Policy Fellow at the Center for Antiracist Research at Boston University. Previously, she was a senior research fellow at the Solomon Center for Health Law and Policy at Yale Law School.

TONI M. BOND, PhD, is Associate Professor of Ethics at Methodist Theological School in Ohio and one of the twelve Black women who founded the Reproductive Justice movement in 1994.

JENNIFER L. BROWN, MA, has been involved with Democratic politics at many levels in Washington, DC, and Pennsylvania for more than two decades; she works with Melissa Shusterman.

BUILDING THE FIRE FUND is a fund whose goal is to support organizing and provide ongoing infrastructure to build Reproductive Justice in Indian Country. Their work upholds and uplifts the leadership of Indigenous women and birthing people within the larger Reproductive Justice movement. The fund is housed at and staffed by the Ms. Foundation for Women.

HOLLY CALVASINA, MA, MPA, is the development director at CHOICES. Since the 2000s, she has served as a volunteer, intern, and employee at CHOICES. She is honored to work for the patients and communities CHOICES serves.

GABRIELA CANO, BA, is an Oklahoman Reproductive Justice advocate, providing logistical support for people facing barriers in accessing abortion. They work in service of community, particularly toward a world where survivors, disabled people, and queer people of color can access safety, empowerment, and healing.

SHEILA DESAI, DrPH, MPH, is a public health researcher and abortion storyteller whose work has focused on advancing and destigmatizing access to abortion and contraception in the United States.

ERICKA AYODELE DIXON, MA, (they/them) is a disabled queer, nonbinary, Black feminist activist, writer, and facilitator dedicated to dismantling ableism, anti-Black racism, and misogyny, particularly in liberation movement spaces. They currently serve as a senior national organizer and co-lead of the Disability Project at the Transgender Law Center.

JILL FILIPOVIC, JD, is a journalist, author, and lawyer.

LINDA S. FRANCK, RN, PhD, FAAN, is a professor and the Jack and Elaine Koehn Endowed Chair in Pediatric Nursing at the University of California, San Francisco (UCSF) School of Nursing.

GILLIAN FRANK, PhD, is a historian and a visiting affiliate fellow at Princeton University's Center for Culture, Society, and Religion. He is the author of articles on the histories of sexuality, gender, and religion and coeditor of *Devotions and Desires: Histories of Sexuality and Religion in the 20th Century United States*. Frank is completing *A Sacred Choice: Liberal Religion and the Struggle for Abortion before Roe v. Wade*. His podcast *Sexing History* explores how the history of sexuality shapes the present.

ELIZABETH GELVIN (she/her) has learned and organized across abortion access, harm reduction, and climate justice movements and in oral history story collection. She serves on the steering committee of Mutual Aid Disaster Relief and is a lifelong resident of South Louisiana.

CYNTHIA GUTIERREZ (she/ella), BA, is an award-winning first-generation Nicaraguan Salvadoran Reproductive Justice organizer, full-spectrum doula, cultural strategist, writer, and public speaker. Her work looks at the intersection of Reproductive Justice, the criminal injustice system, disability justice, and environmental justice.

THE REV. DR. LAURINDA HAFNER is senior pastor at the Coral Gables United Church of Christ, in Coral Gables, Florida.

JENNA HANES, BA, is communications director in the office of Austin City Council member José "Chito" Vela.

LISA HARRIS, MD, is an obstetrician-gynecologist and cultural historian at University of Michigan. She testified in the Michigan governor's case that helped keep abortion legal in Michigan between the *Dobbs* decision and the passage in that state of Proposal 3.

COYA WHITE HAT-ARTICHOKER (she/her), BA, is a queer activist, writer, and poet raised by Native feminists resisting colonization. She has worked in movements for twenty-five years. She is on the board of SisterSong and leads Building the Fire Fund, to support Indigenous Reproductive Justice.

WARREN M. HERN, MD, MPH, PhD, is a physician and epidemiologist, the founding medical director of the first private, nonprofit abortion clinic in Colorado in 1973. He opened his private medical practice, Boulder Abortion Clinic, on January 22, 1975, and continues his work specializing in outpatient abortion services.

AZIZ Z. HUQ, JD, teaches law at the University of Chicago.

TISHAURA O. JONES, MHA, is the mayor of Saint Louis, Missouri.

ALISON KAFER, PhD, is the director of LGBTQ Studies and the Embrey Associate Professor of Women's and Gender Studies at the University of Texas at Austin.

NOMI KANE, MFA, is an editorial cartoonist, illustrator, and designer. Nomi's work has appeared in publications such as *The New Yorker, The Nib,* and *MAD Magazine.*

RAFA P. KIDVAI, JD, is Repro Legal Defense Fund Director at If/When/How. She has been a public defender at the Legal Aid Society's Brooklyn Criminal Defense Practice, a legal fellow at Court Watch NYC, and Equal Justice Works fellow in the Immigrant Justice Project at the Sylvia Rivera Law Project.

KATRINA KIMPORT, PhD, is professor in the Advancing New Standards in Reproductive Health (ANSIRH) program at the University of California, San Francisco. She is the author of *No Real Choice: How Culture and Politics Matter for Reproductive Autonomy*.

RAMEY KO, JD, is general counsel in the office of Austin City Council member José "Chito" Vela.

NIKKI LANSHAW, MPH, is the project director of the ACTIONS Program at the University of California, San Francisco (UCSF) School of Nursing.

ROBYNNE D. LUCAS (she/they), BA, is a recent graduate of Smith College with a BA in women and gender studies and a certificate in reproductive health rights and justice.

MONICA R. MCLEMORE, PhD, MPH, RN, is a professor in the Child, Family, and Population Health Nursing Department and interim director of Center for Anti-Racism in Nursing at the University of Washington.

HAYLEY V. MCMAHON, MSPH, CPH, is a PhD student at Emory Rollins School of Public Health and a doctoral fellow at the Center for Reproductive Health Research in the Southeast, where she studies structural barriers to abortion access with a focus on misinformation and criminalization.

RENEE MEHRA, PhD, is an adjunct assistant professor at the University of California, San Francisco (UCSF) School of Nursing.

AMY MERRILL, MPA, is an artist and activist who has spent the past two decades at the intersection of tech, impact, and the arts. She is president of the creative communications studio Eyes Open (eyesopendesign.com) and serves as cofounder and codirector of Plan C (plancpills.org).

MELISSA MURRAY, JD, is the Frederick I. and Grace Stokes Professor of Law at New York University. She is a leading expert in constitutional law, family law, and reproductive rights and justice.

BRIAN T. NGUYEN, MD, MSc, is an associate professor of obstetrics and gynecology and program director for the Fellowship in Complex Family Planning. He leads a research group aimed at Expanding Male Engagement in Reproductive and Gender Equity (EMERGE) and is a subinvestigator for male contraceptive clinical trials.

LAURY OAKS, PhD, is professor in the Department of Feminist Studies and an affiliated faculty member in the Departments of Sociology and Anthropology at the University of California, Santa Barbara.

ALEXIS OBINNA, BA, has been volunteering and giving back to various communities since age eight. She has two small businesses, works with nonprofits, and is a former intern at the National Foster Youth Institute.

EESHA PANDIT, MA, is cofounder of the Center for Advancing Innovative Policy, where she works with grassroots organizations and movement strategists to develop intersectional approaches to policy change. She is a member of the Crunk Feminist Collective and cofounder of South Asian Youth in Houston Unite.

BRIA PEACOCK, MD, graduated from the Medical College of Georgia at Georgia Regents University in 2021. She works in San Francisco and specializes in obstetrics and gynecology.

JENNIFER PEPPER, MBA, serves as president and CEO of CHOICES, where she has worked since 2003, as a patient educator, community outreach coordinator, deputy director, and director of finance and operations.

JAMILA PERRITT, MD, is a fellowship trained, board-certified obstetrician and gynecologist providing care at the intersection of sexual health, reproductive rights, and social justice. She has a comprehensive background in family planning and has worked more than twenty years in the reproductive health, rights, and justice spaces.

VIRGINIA RODINO is the executive director of the Coalition of Labor Union Women.

LORETTA J. ROSS (she/her), BA, is a veteran activist and nationally recognized educator, member of the MacArthur Fellow class of 2022, and author of *Calling In the Calling Out Culture*, published in 2025.

RABBI DANYA RUTTENBERG, MA, serves as Scholar in Residence at the National Council of Jewish Women (NCJW). She is the author of eight books, most recently *On Repentance and Repair: Making Amends in an Unapologetic World*.

ODILE SCHALIT, LMSW, MSC, served as founding executive director of the Brigid Alliance from 2018 to 2023. She is also a cofounder and board member of Apiary for Practical Support, a technical assistance and community building organization for practical support organizations across the country.

MELISSA SHUSTERMAN, MA, was elected state representative for Pennsylvania's 157th District in 2018 and is now serving her third term. She has authored legislation dealing with reproductive freedoms, government accountability, gun control, environmental sustainability, and animal protections.

PATTY SKUSTER, JD, MPP, is Master of Public Health teaching faculty at the University of Pennsylvania School of Medicine and a Fellow at the Center for Public Health Law Research at Temple University Beasley School of Law. Patty spent fifteen years with the global NGO Ipas, where she conducted research on abortion related to law, policy, and human rights.

JODY STEINAUER, MD, PhD, is an obstetrician-gynecologist at the University of California, San Francisco. She provides comprehensive sexual and reproductive health care, including abortions, and she loves teaching.

MEG SASSE STERN (she/her) is a queer Kentuckian with a passion for bodily autonomy and justice. Meg was on the front lines of abortion access as a clinic escort in Louisville for over twenty years (1999–2022). She cofounded one of the first Practical Support Abortion Funds (KHJN, 2012–2022) and has expertise in creating safer pathways to abortion access. Meg is a network weaver with experience in cross-movement collaboration, currently working as the Outreach and Operations Coordinator at Just the Pill, a nonprofit telehealth abortion provider offering virtual and mobile clinic visits in Colorado, Minnesota, Montana, and Wyoming. Just the Pill has seen patients from thirty-four states through virtual and mobile clinic programs.

DANIEL F. M. SUÁREZ-BAQUERO, PhD, MSN, RN, is Assistant Professor at the University of Washington School of Nursing. His research and practice concern qualitative methods, Latina/e's reproductive health experiences, community/cultural memory of ethnic minoritized women, and nursing theory.

CAROLYN SUFRIN, MD, PhD, is a medical anthropologist and ob-gyn at Johns Hopkins University. She conducts research and policy work to advance reproductive justice for incarcerated people.

DANA SUSSMAN, JD, MPH, is the acting executive director of Pregnancy Justice, the leading legal advocacy organization defending the rights of pregnant people facing criminal charges or other state action because of pregnancy or any pregnancy outcome.

DINAH SYKES, BA, was first elected to the Kansas Senate in 2016 and became the first female Senate Minority Leader in state history in 2020.

FRANCINE THOMPSON is the executive director of the Emma Goldman Clinic in Iowa City, Iowa.

CARLY THOMSEN, PhD, is associate professor of Gender, Sexuality, and Feminist Studies at Middlebury College, author of *Visibility Interrupted: Rural Queer Life and the Politics of Unbecoming*, cofounder of the Center for Public Feminism, co-creator of the Reproductive Justice Mini Golf course, and a series editor for the Reproductive Justice Series at University of California Press.

JUSTINA TRIM-NICHOLSON, MA, is a program manager at Collective Power with a particular interest in sustainable youth organizing and activism.

SUZANNE VALDEZ, JD, is the Douglas County (Kansas) district attorney. Before being elected as DA, she was a Clinical Professor of Law at the University of Kansas. She is also the co-author of *Prosecutorial Ethics* (published by West Academics).

TINA VASQUEZ is the editor-at-large at *Prism*. She covers gender justice, workers' rights, and immigration.

JOSÉ "CHITO" VELA, JD, is the Austin City Council Member for District 4. He has practiced immigration and criminal defense law and served as president of the Worker's Defense Project, a community organization for low-wage, immigrant workers in the Texas construction industry.

ROBIN WALLACE, MD, MAS, is a family physician with family planning expertise. Since 2004, she has provided and taught abortion care from California to Texas to North Carolina. Dr. Wallace joined lawsuits against the State of Texas twice as a plaintiff and once testified in federal court to challenge the state's senseless and harmful laws.

MADISON WEBB, BPS, works in fundraising and communications roles at CHOICES Center for Reproductive Health, bringing an intersectional and community-minded approach to fundraising.

TRACY A. WEITZ (she/her), PhD, MPA, is professor of sociology and director of the Center on Health, Risk, and Society at American University and a senior fellow at the Center for American Progress. Weitz cofounded Advancing New Standards in Reproductive Health at the University of California, San Francisco. She was US programs director for the Susan Thompson Buffett Foundation.

ELISA WELLS, MPH, is cofounder and codirector of Plan C. From her first job as an abortion counselor in Boston to her years of work abroad in countries with far fewer resources and rights, she brings practical solutions and passion to the fight to improve abortion access in the United States.

REBECCA WEXLER, JD, teaches law at the University of California, Berkeley.

REBECCA LOUVE YAO, MSW, is the executive director of the National Foster Youth Institute, where she draws on her unique experience in the child welfare system as a former foster youth, adoptive parent, child protection worker, therapist, and advocate.

NEIL J. YOUNG, PhD, is an independent scholar, podcaster, and historian of religion, politics, and sexuality. He is the author of *We Gather Together: The Religious Right and the Problem of Interfaith Politics* (2015). He cohosts the popular history podcast *Past Present*. He is completing a manuscript on the history of LGBTQ Republicans to be published in 2024.

Index

Abbott, Greg, 195

ableism, 18, 200

abortion access: in Appalachia, 35–37; and contraception, 292–95; in Georgia, 61; in Missouri, 117–18; and morality, 264; in North Carolina, 61–62; in Oklahoma, 223–27; in restrictive states, 59–64; as right, 106, 109, 253

abortion bans: after *Dobbs*, 1, 34, 36, 120, 245; in Appalachia, 35, 36; impact, 176, 245, 275; and medical education, 228, 229–30; in Mississippi, 268; and move to self-managed abortions, 177–78; in Tennessee, 36, 89, 90; in Texas, 63, 169

abortion clinics. *See* clinics

abortion criminalization: of healthcare providers, 190–91; legal risk, 178–79, 223; post-*Dobbs*, 5; states' laws and bills, 193–94; and surveillance, 134–35

abortion doulas, 141–43

abortion funds, 78, 196, 213, 240–41

abortion providers. *See* providers

abortions: as constitutional right, 54, 106, 120; cost and reimbursement as issues, 212–13; debate as binary, 77, 307–11; as "elective procedures," 43–44; exceptions for rape and incest, 68; harassment or intimidation, 85–86; international picture, 253–54; Jewish view, 273–74; medicalization, 177, 251–52; for medical needs, 55, 57–58; performance after *Roe*, 54–58; personal story sharing, 41, 141, 142–43; point of viability, 263; public opinion shift, 301–6; reasons for and decision-making, 304–5, 310; reporting of, 182, 190–91, 236; rights emergence, 110; as "serious medical needs," 43, 44; as stage of life for interventions with men, 299–300; as "tension of opposites," 303; textbook, 232. *See also* self-managed abortions

academic freedom, 198

access statements. *See* disability and access statements

Accreditation Council for Graduate Medical Education (ACGME), 228, 231

adoptions, 68–69, 72, 74

reprocide, 331–32; in Reproductive Justice movement, 79; support for each other, 116

boat for abortions, 249

bodily autonomy, 109, 308–9, 311

body sovereignty, 23–24

Bond, Toni, 259–60, 261–66, 289–90, 307–11

Brazil, 145, 177

Brewster, Danielle, 25–26

Briggs, Eileen, 25–26

The Brigid Alliance, 242–47

Brnovich v. Democratic National Committee, 314

Brown, Jennifer L., 119–23

Buck, Carrie, 15

Buck v. Bell, 15

Building the Fire Fund, 25–26

Bureau of Prisons (BOP), 44, 46

Butler, Octavia, 325

California, data privacy and laws, 171–72

Calvasina, Holly, 89–93

Canada, 250

Cano, Gabriela, 209, 210, 223–27

Cantrell, Katrina, 25–26

Carbondale (Illinois) abortion clinic, 90, 92–93

Carpenter v. United States, 169

Carter, Jimmy, 265

Casey case (*Planned Parenthood v. Casey*), 180, 263

Casey Family Programs, 67

Castro, Christina, 25–26

Catholics, 277–78, 279–80

cell phones data, 169

Chabria, Natasha, 79

childbirth, 252, 298

childcare, 298

"child," definition in statutes, 183–84

child poverty in the US, 66–67

children: removal from families, 3; sex trafficking and exploitation, 68

Children's Hospital (Los Angeles), 74–75

child welfare system, 65, 66–67, 70

Chism, Priscilla, 90

CHOICES: Center for Reproductive Health, 52–53, 89–93

Christian Action Council, 279, 280

Christianity and Christian exceptionalism, 262, 264–65

Christina (pregnant woman), 62–63

citizenship, and whiteness, 3, 14

Clark, Dick, 56

Clergy Consultation Service, 264

clinics (abortion clinics): closures, 178; escorts, 94, 95–96; harassment or intimidation at, 85–86. *See also* Emma Goldman Clinic

coercion, 294–95

Coeytaux, Francine, 146, 147

college campus, health care and abortion access, 59–64

colonization, 20–22, 26

Complex Family Planning fellowship, 232

condoms, 294

Confronting Pregnancy Criminalization manual, 164, 182

Congress, and evidentiary privilege, 173

Connecticut, data privacy and laws, 171–72

Constitution: Establishment Clause, 268, 274; references to right to abortion, 195

contraception: access in restrictive states, 59–64; and access to abortion, 292–95; and partners, 294–95. *See also* birth control

law enforcement: cadet-training programs, 175; deprioritization by cities, 138, 139–40; and self-managed abortions helpers, 175–79

lawyers, and evidentiary privilege, 172–73

legal defense fund, 235–37

legal issues, in US *vs.* other countries, 252

Let's Talk About Sex (LTAS) conference (August 2022), 76–80

LGBTQIA2S+ people: abortions for, 106; discrimination towards, 106–7; impact of *Dobbs*, 106, 107; rights of, 107–8

life, beginning of, 262, 268–69, 309

Littlejohn, Krystale E.: contraception and abortion, 289, 292–95; interviews by, 81–88, 144–50

locational data, from digital tools, 169

longtermism, 328–30

Lorde, Audre, 106

Lorenzo, Rachael, 25–26

Louisiana, abortion funding in pandemic, 218–22

Lozano, Stephanie, 25–26

LTAS (Let's Talk About Sex) conference (August 2022), 76–80

Luarkie, Malia, 25–26

Lucas, Robynne D., 290–91, 325–32

M + A Hotline, 149

Main, Nona, 25–26

Manninen, Bertha Alvarez, 263

marginalized people: abortion access, 63; abortion bans, 275; control by state, 13–14, 15; criminalization, 182–83, 190; and *Dobbs*, 13–14; incarceration, 47; motherhood stereotypes, 74; newborns surrender in safe havens, 75;

pregnancy-related criminalization, 182–83; reprocide, 331–32; reproductive health care in Iowa, 83–84; and *Roe*, 11, 24, 144, 242; self-determination, 13, 16–17

marriage, protection of, 108

Marshall, Thurgood, 308

Mason, Carol, 328

Mastriano, Doug, 122

The Matter of M, 193

Mbembe, Achille, 331

McClinton, Joanna, 121

McGuire, Kimberly Inez, 78, 79

McLemore, Monica R., 289–90, 307–11

McMahon, Hayley V., 12, 34–37

media, 77, 184

Medicaid, 44, 212–13

medical data and records, as potential problem, 168–69, 172

medical education, 228–33

medical information and services, 167, 254–55

medical students, impact of *Dobbs*, 60

Medical Students for Choice, 232

medication abortion: discovery, 177; information and advice about, 255, 256; legal status, 5; online provision, 167; supervision, 255. *See also* mifepristone and misoprostol

Mehra, Renee, 289–90, 307–11

Memphis (Tennessee), abortion restrictions, 90, 91, 93

men and male partners: in *Dobbs* protests, 296–97; stages of life for sensitization, 298–300

Merrill, Amy, interview of, 103, 144–50

messaging recommendations and toolkit for doctors, 302, 343

Mexico, 197

zation laws and bills, 193–94; defense against statutes, 183–84; digital traces and privacy, 168, 169–72; faculty in hostile states, 198–200; gerrymandering, 313; pre-clearance reviews, 314; pro-choice responses to digital threat, 171–73; response to *Dobbs*, 120; self-managed abortions as crime, 189. *See also* restrictive states; specific states

Steinauer, Jody, 210, 228–33

sterilization: involuntary sterilization, 3, 14, 15–16; as stage of life for interventions with men, 298–99

Stern, Meg Sasse, 53, 94–97

Stewart, Scott G., 292–93

structural racism, 178

Suárez-Baquero, Daniel F. M., 289–90, 307–11

Sufrin, Carolyn, 12, 42–48

Summer of Mercy (Wichita), 124

Supreme Court: amicus curiae brief, 268–69; on data from phones, 169; and democratic deliberation, 312–13, 314–15; *Dobbs* as decision, 1; on gerrymandering, 312–13; medication abortion, 5; as minority rule, 314; and religion, 259; *Roe* arguments, 54; on sterilization, 15; and "viability," 308; Voting Rights Act decisions, 313–14

Supreme Court justices: and adoptions, 69; appointments, 1, 57; and human dignity, 261; impact on democracy, 262–63; and other precedents, 195. *See also* individual justices

surrendered babies in US, 73–74

Sussman, Dana, 164, 180–84

Sykes, Dinah, 102, 124–29

Talmud, 273

techno-utopianism, 328–29

telemedicine or telehealth, 167

Tennessee: abortion ban, 36, 89, 90; abortion provision, 90; abortion restrictions, 91–92; full-spectrum model of care from CHOICES, 89–93

Texas: abortion ban, 63, 169; abortion protection, 136–40; abortion restrictions, 60, 63; abortion training for doctors, 231; arrest for self-induced abortion, 234, 236; authority of cities, 137–38; consequences of *Dobbs* (examples), 57–58; contraception, 60; disability and access statements for students (example), 200, 201–5; GRACE Act in Austin, 138, 139–40; immigrants, 195; Reproductive Justice initiatives, 78; safe haven relinquishments, 74; SB8, 231, 244; trigger law, 76, 137; universities and faculty, 198–200

textbook for abortions, 232

Thomas, Clarence, 195

Thompson, Francine, interview of, 52, 81–88

Thomsen, Carly, 103–4, 151–59

Thomson, Judith Jarvis, 263

Thurmond, Strom, 56

Tiller, George, 124

Title IX, 202

Torah, and abortion, 271–75

transgender youth and adults, 108

travel benefits from employers, 238–41

travel for abortions: after the first trimester, 242–47; and Brigid Alliance, 242–43; and pandemic changes, 219–20; research study, 239–40

Founded in 1893,
UNIVERSITY OF CALIFORNIA PRESS
publishes bold, progressive books and journals
on topics in the arts, humanities, social sciences,
and natural sciences—with a focus on social
justice issues—that inspire thought and action
among readers worldwide.

The UC PRESS FOUNDATION
raises funds to uphold the press's vital role
as an independent, nonprofit publisher, and
receives philanthropic support from a wide
range of individuals and institutions—and from
committed readers like you. To learn more, visit
ucpress.edu/supportus.